VISUAL COMMUNICATION DESIGN

BLOOMSBURY VISUAL ARTS
Bloomsbury Publishing Plc
50 Bedford Square, London, WC1B 3DP, UK
1385 Broadway, New York, NY 10018, USA
29 Earlsfort Terrace, Dublin 2, Ireland

BLOOMSBURY, BLOOMSBURY VISUAL ARTS and the Diana logo are
trademarks of Bloomsbury Publishing Plc

First published in Great Britain 2017
Reprinted 2019 (twice), 2020, 2021 (twice)

Cover design: Louise Dugdale and Meredith Davis
Cover image: Iona Inglesby

The cover image was created by **Dot One** (dotone.io) from the DNA profile
of author Meredith Davis. The pattern is the result of converting the genetic
values of her DNA profile into set colors and represents information from
the 0.1% of our DNA which makes each person unique. It contains enough
genetic information to identify one individual from the other 7.4 billion people
on earth.

A catalogue record for this book is available from the British Library.

Library of Congress Cataloging-in-Publication Data
Names: Davis, Meredith, author. | Hunt, Jamer, author.
Title: Visual Communication Design: An introduction to design concepts in
everyday experience / Meredith Davis and Jamer Hunt.
Description: New York : Bloomsbury Visual Arts, 2017. | Series: Required
reading range
Identifiers: LCCN 2016048837 | ISBN 9781474221573 (paperback) |
ISBN 9781350031838 (epub)
Subjects: LCSH: Design--Textbooks. | Visual communication--Textbooks. |
BISAC: DESIGN / General. | DESIGN / Graphic Arts / General.
Classification: LCC NK1510 .D29 2017 | DDC 745.4--dc23 LC record available
at https://lccn.loc.gov/2016048837

ISBN: PB: 978-1-4742-2157-3
      ePDF: 978-1-4742-2159-7
      eBook: 978-1-3500-3183-8

Series: Required Reading Range

Typeset by Struktur Design
Printed and bound in India

To find out more about our authors and books visit www.bloomsbury.com
and sign up for our newsletters.

VISUAL COMMUNICATION DESIGN

An introduction to design concepts
in everyday experience

Meredith Davis and Jamer Hunt

BLOOMSBURY VISUAL ARTS
LONDON • NEW YORK • OXFORD • NEW DELHI • SYDNEY

Preface

Introduction:
an evolving context
for design

The form and content of visual messages work together to create meanings that are heavily influenced by the cultural contexts in which we interpret them. If someone yells "fire in a crowded theater, our immediate response is to head for the exits. If that same person yells the same word at a shooting range, we understand the command quite differently. It is difficult to assign gravitas to text set in the typeface Comic Sans, regardless of its content or arrangement on a page; we know from experience that this style of lettering is associated with comic strips.

The twentieth-century practice of design rejected ornament and other references to culture or history, instead foregrounding fundamental principles for the aesthetic arrangement of visual form that were presumed to be universal, common to human experience. Many schools today acknowledge these principles as the foundation of undergraduate design education by making them the content of first-year study. The curricular legacy of the Bauhaus Preliminary Course (Vorkurs) organized investigations of these concepts in a series of assignments using abstract forms, which are often repeated in contemporary classrooms with few references to their origins in perception and culture. And because first-year courses typically serve a variety of visual disciplines, rarely do early explanations of visual phenomena address the specific demands of communication design for combining image with text (language) and the challenges presented by particular contexts or formats of use (in posters versus time-based media, for example).

While matters of context and content are frequently deferred until later stages of the curriculum under this modernist model of education, it is in relation to surrounding conditions and intended meaning that fundamental principles make the most sense to beginning students. It is impossible to ignore the influence of context on what we think things mean or to ignore the forces exerted on interpretation by our experiences of living in a physical and social world.

Any interpretations of visual communication, therefore, are necessarily contextual. Even when referring to abstract shapes, perceptual experiences shape our impressions of what things mean. A large black square "feels" heavier than a smaller one because we've learned to associate weight with mass. We assign expression and reading order to the size and placement of typographic elements, because a word set in all capital letters feels more like yelling than lowercase letters and, in most cases, we read English from the upper left to lower right of compositional space. These are not rules—they are expectations established by accumulated physical and cultural experience. Some visual messages succeed by delivering on these expectations, some fail, and others deliberately subvert the very things we anticipate. That is, we construct meaning by attention to forms that meet our expectations in specific contexts, but we also respond positively to messages that creatively undermine and play with our learned experience.

This book traces the origins of visual phenomena and principles for the arrangement of form by providing examples we encounter in going about our daily lives. It also suggests that the interpretive and behavioral effects we share in responding to these phenomena and principles—that is, what we are likely to think and do in everyday interactions with the world around us—can inform the design of communication. If they are truly shared by people in the same culture, then they can be useful in constructing visual messages.

Underlying this premise is the notion that a goal of design is to create supportive conditions for someone's experience; that the application of visual phenomena and principles of form are driven by the designer's intent to narrow the range of possible interpretations and to satisfy the audience or users by making communication useful, usable, and compelling. To that end, concepts in this book are clustered according to a role they play in the interpretive experience: getting people's attention; orienting them to the use of the artifact; shaping their interpretation of meaning; and retaining and extending the significance of messages. The structure of the text is not focused on the steps a designer takes in constructing messages, the design process. Instead, the book describes the audience's interpretive process as insight for how to design. The influences of various phenomena and principles are not restricted to one aspect of the interpretive experience, but they are described under a specific outcome where they are especially significant.

Entries in the following chapters represent the "stuff" of design; the formal elements and general strategies for their combination that shape a communication experience. Introductions to chapters describe the overarching aspects of the interpretive process that unite entries in the chapter. Each entry begins with a definition of the phenomenon or principle and provides an example from everyday life that links the concept to personal experience. Diagrams in some entries isolate the concept in a visual explanation and examples from professional practice show the concept in application. Form and content matter, of course, but the book demonstrates that they cannot do their work unless the designer is equally attuned to the context of their reception.

INTRODUCTION:
AN EVOLVING CONTEXT FOR DESIGN

What do we mean by "design"? Ask any two designers and you'll probably get slightly different answers. For some, design is making well-crafted objects that enrich people's lives and that surpass the ordinary as contributions to visual culture. For others, it is a process of open-ended thinking through which designers imagine a preferred set of conditions that don't yet exist. For still others, it is a practice that meets people's needs and solves problems by envisioning environments, products, and communication that are useful, usable, and desirable. All of these definitions are true but they fall slightly short in telling us how the work of communication design in the twenty-first century is different from previous times.

Architect Christopher Alexander described design as the goodness of fit between form and context (Alexander, 1964). Form is anything designers can shape; the physical qualities of environments, objects, and messages and the character of plans, stories, services, and conversations. Context, in this sense, is made up of the physical, social, cultural, technological, and economic forces in the surrounding environment, as well as the characteristic thinking and behavior of the people who engage with the products of designers' work. Designers and clients have no control over the nature of context, but they do decide how much of it to address in decisions about form.

Context is always in state of flux. It is a moving target made up of a number of interdependent forces, but there are general trends that have long-term influences on design practice. These forces shape how designers frame contemporary design challenges, the methods they use to understand them, and their views of the people who benefit from their work. And they guide how form is interpreted within and across diverse settings.

From artifacts to experiences

Traditionally, designers produce artifacts—that is, they craft and refine the physical characteristics of messages, objects, and environments on behalf of clients to make things look and work better for audiences and consumers. The history of design is filled with beautiful objects that are contributions to the visual culture of their times. Most of us can name a book we bought entirely for its cover, a car we'd love to drive regardless of its miles-per-gallon efficiency, or a building that is a "must see" when visiting an unfamiliar city. And we can identify "that 80s vibe" in everything from fashion to furniture. Design history honors signature works by well-known designers and associates them with particular philosophies or approaches to form at different times in history.

Over the last two decades, new design approaches, technology, and software changed the role of communication design in society and how designers think about the people who benefit from their work. Participatory design, user-centered design, and ergonomics brought designers' attention to the experiences, good or bad, that design prompts in users—to the effects of design on what people think and do rather than the design of an object or message as an end in itself.

Expert software systems now make it possible for anyone to create and publish visual communication. Today's computer users choose fonts, retouch photographs, and output finished-looking work without any design training or programming expertise. While they probably don't make objects that compete well aesthetically with the artifacts of accomplished design professionals, many people are satisfied with DIY solutions to problems of limited consequence and use experts only for the most important projects or when the quality of form is a high priority. This change in who can create and publish messages means that many designers now create the tools and systems through which others design communication, building into software principles of good form.

The rapid development of technology has also changed where people go for information. Digital technology is a common portal to our relationships with people, places, and ideas and its qualities shape our expectations of communication. Technology defines much of our social experience. In 2013, 95 percent of teenagers used Facebook and each averaged 425 "friends" (Pew Research Center, 2013). We can question how many of those "friends" will still be around years from now, but the number indicates that many teens are comfortable communicating in ways absent of the visual cues we once found important in face-to-face encounters. We also want information anywhere on demand and engagement with messages that deliver meaningful experiences. In 2016, 30 million Americans got their news via the internet each day, but digital systems filter the form and content of what we see, based on preferences in our search histories. These tools influence our understanding of any issue. The accelerating demand for connectedness means that the goal of design is to shape the qualities of interaction and human behavior and to craft the conditions for satisfying experiences.

The concerns of today's designers, therefore, are the relationships and conversations that design makes possible; that is, the stories, tools, and platforms for content production, services, and communities of interest that are significant to people in their everyday lives. This perspective on design doesn't mean that beautiful artifacts go away under new types of practice. Apple Computer succeeds to a great extent because it has cool-looking devices, exciting store environments, and clever advertising. But more importantly, the company builds brand loyalty through user-centered tools and systems, a strong service ecology, and a technological platform that allows others to build applications that live on Apple devices. Artifacts, in this sense, perform as components of a larger effort to establish long-term relationships with people as their needs change and evolve. Artifacts communicate something about the character of a company, but more importantly, they express concern for the qualities of interaction with people over time. In other words, today's design is all about experience.

Today's design problems are increasingly complex
Complexity, in this case, is not a description of the way things look. It is a network of important connections among settings, people, and activities and the long-term consequences of design action. For example, a designer can frame a communication task as the design of a new logo or as the design of how a company tells its story to consumers. The former addresses the range of visual possibilities and formats for identifying the company in a simple graphic mark. The latter concerns all aspects of people's experiences with the company—including the company's position in the larger culture, the role its products play in supporting people's motives for purchasing them, and the services through which the company establishes face-to-face or online relationships with customers over time. Certainly, a logo makes some contribution to identifying things associated with the business. But alone and by definition, it ignores too much of the relevant context to carry the full burden of public perception; it is only one element of a much larger experience people have with the company. No matter how effective the design of a logo, a bad service experience makes people question the good impressions generated by the graphic mark.

Today, we recognize that changes in the design of a single component ripple throughout a system and that systems interact with each other in increasingly complex ways. Apple changed the music industry by nesting a device (iPod) within a music distribution system (iTunes). Facebook and Twitter changed the ways in which we interact with people, standards of written language, the speed with which news travels, and our sense of privacy. Entirely new behaviors (tapping, pinching, swiping, and so forth) now comprise meaningful gestures for interacting with technology and information. Some of us are restless if not chatting or texting constantly with friends. And for better or worse, there is a look to smartphone applications that stands for technology in general, a vocabulary of form that characterizes much of our everyday communication.

This growing complexity in the nature of contemporary problems means that today's designers cannot think of their work as merely crafting beautiful things. Every environment, object, or message needs to be informed by an understanding of the systems of which it is a part and by anticipation of the conditions for the experiences it is likely to create.

Individual or single disciplines rarely solve complex problems

In today's design practice, teams of experts tackle challenges from different perspectives, knowledge, values, and modes of inquiry. Design was once at the cosmetic end of a decision-making food chain; the goal was to make things look and work better, not to decide what to make in the first place. The scope of work included giving appropriate form to management's vision for products and communication and shepherding them through production. By contrast, today's designers often sit at the table with management, acknowledging that how designers think and strategically work through problems have something to do with the overall innovation potential of the organization and its long-term relationships with people.

Form plays two roles in the interdisciplinary work of new practices. First, it is a vehicle through which diverse experts reach consensus about what things mean and negotiate the contributions of their various disciplines to the larger project. Concept maps, for example, overcome the limitations of language in describing how elements or phases of a project relate to each other. Engineers and designers, for instance, have very different meanings for the term "usability." A diagram that shows all the expectations a user has for how an object must perform to meet his or her needs transcends vocabulary and resolves misunderstanding. Quick prototypes and simulations help a diverse team predict the implications of choosing one solution over another.

Second, form is an expression of social values, attitudes, and patterns of behavior. Anthropologists help designers understand the cultural settings in which objects and communication must function. Instructions for purchasing a fare card by a harried commuter or unfamiliar tourist need to be very different in form from a manual for using a software program. Technologists provide detail about how systems work so that design can express them accurately in user interfaces. A spinning beach ball lets us know our computer is working behind the scenes so we don't repeat a command. And psychologists identify how form is or is not a good fit with the thinking and actions of particular users. In addressing today's complex challenges, the invention of form is often a team effort.

People as producers

Among those now contributing to the form of communication are the very people who use the tools and systems created by designers. Throughout the twentieth century, the relationship between designers and audiences was one in which designers made expert judgments about what people wanted and needed. People were consumers of the products and messages made by designers (Sanders, 2006). In some cases, marketing studies and focus groups informed expert opinion. At other times, designers' intuition and taste determined what was made and particular kinds of form. The designer was clearly in control. Alastair Parvin, founder of WikiHouse (an open-source housing system that allows users to construct dwellings from modular components), describes this perspective as one in which design is something done to people.

Under technology that is increasingly participatory, however, some designers think of the people for whom they design as users whose behavior can be observed in ways not possible in a print-based world. Human factors—a field that integrates psychology, engineering, and design—emerged in the middle of the twentieth century as a discipline for the study of the interactions among people, information, and machines. In many cases, human factors studies are done within laboratory settings and result in guidelines that describe the optimal qualities of form best suited to the average user. For example, studies of people's eye movements when reading web pages suggest that the left and top of pages receive the most attention and should contain the information most crucial to navigation and interpretation (Nielsen, 2006).

But human factors is not especially concerned with why people come to networked communication in the first place, what they expect to accomplish through its use, and the role it plays in their lives outside of the lab. As the volume of messages and capabilities of devices expand, designers recognize that people are not only users of technology but also producers of content and form. Some designers now see audiences as co-creators, as participants in determining the subject matter and shape of communication (Sanders, 2006). This means a shift in control from designing for people to designing with and by people and greater emphasis on the qualities of experience made possible through design objects and messages.

Design methods, therefore, now include people in the design process. Participatory culture widens the scope of design concerns regarding the role of design in shaping experience. The design of a child's interaction with an online math tutorial, for example, should probably acknowledge that girls and boys tend to view the study of mathematics differently. The system may need to accommodate a parent who does homework with the child and wants to be a "math hero." The methods for finding out about these things engage people in the design process so that decisions about content and form are authentic and truly address people's wants and needs.

Greater involvement of people in the development and customization of design shifts the work of designers, in some instances, from creating discrete artifacts or displays of information to inventing tools and systems through which others create their own experiences. The design task is no longer one of designing the appearance of interaction (buttons, rollovers, menus, and so forth), but one of designing the behaviors that support people's reasons for engaging with information and technology (searching, authoring, curating, and so forth). Form, in this case, is not arbitrary. It underpins experiences that satisfy the user's needs in very specific ways.

The rapid evolution of technology changes its influence in our lives

Media theorist Marshall McLuhan, in his famous phrase, "The medium is the message," asserted that the importance of any technology is its effect on everything else, not the content of any individual message it makes possible (McLuhan, 1994). The invention of movable type and the printing press in the fifteenth century, for example, spread literacy beyond the clergy and nobility by making books cheaper and more easily reproducible. Email changed the urgency of communication and the extent to which history is no longer documented in letter writing.

Digital media not only transformed how designers practice but also the role of communication in everyone's lives. New technologies of the late twentieth century reshaped the cultural landscape and shifted the scale at which we exchange information. The design challenge today is to go beyond simple interactions with technology and information, and to use new tools and media to shape the conversations that bring people together.

For example, National Geographic asked designer Hugh Dubberly to imagine its future. The organization began in 1888 as a group of members interested in geographic expeditions, documented in a scientific journal. In 1905, a contributor missed a deadline and the journal

editors substituted photographs of Tibet, launching the publication's reputation for photographic essays. If the goal for the organization's future were only about producing a more interactive journal, an online version of the publication would satisfy the design brief. Clickable stories, pop-up maps, videos, and dynamic diagrams would make use of sound and motion not available in the printed version. But Dubberly expected more for the organization and returned to its roots in which members engaged in conversation around topics of mutual interest and in which fieldwork played an important role. He suggested that using citizen scientists from around the world to collect and upload information; following photographers in the field as they develop stories; using the organization's resources in the classroom; and making connections through members' data profiles are possible under today's technology. Rather than just adding new types of interactive content and form to a traditional publication or website, Dubberly's vision for the redesign of National Geographic as an organization was to use it as a platform for building relationships among people within a community of interest. So while interaction designers create tools, systems, and simulations, new forms of design practice focus on designing conversations, services, and communities, as well as the new technologies necessary to support these activities.

How design establishes the conditions for interpretive experiences in the contemporary context for communication comprises the content of this book. Overall, chapters move from a focus on perceptual experiences that are grounded in visual phenomena to investigations of the ways in which the design of visual messages gets our attention, orients us, creates meaningful experiences, and then endures as retrievable, significant memories. Chapter 1 describes the nature of experience and how we make sense of the things we see and hear. Chapter 2 describes the elements of communication through which designers craft messages that contribute to interpretation. Chapters 3–6 deconstruct experience into aspects of attention, orientation, interpretation, and memory and extension. Chapter 3 offers ways in which the properties of form separate messages from an environment of information overload. Chapter 4 describes the means by which design orients readers/viewers to the task of interpretation. Chapter 5 suggests the qualities of form that make interaction compelling and provides a bit of theory regarding the interpretation of visual and verbal messages. And Chapter 6 addresses issues of memorability and the extended life of messages in culture. Each chapter presents a range of phenomena and examples, as well as constructed illustrations that encourage readers to move from insight to action.

Designing for experience

Imagine you are walking down the sidewalk on a busy urban street, looking for a quiet place in which to collect your thoughts before a job interview in the same neighborhood. The street is typical of any large city: a riot of signs, bright colors, images, and activity, all competing for your attention. A simple black awning with white letters indicating "espresso" stands out and promises a break from the chaos of the city. You step through the shop door into a room with waist-high railings that direct your movement to the end of a counter and a menu of options. You interact with a pleasant clerk who efficiently signals your selection to a barista, collect your drink at the opposite end of the counter, and sit in a comfortable chair in a quiet corner. You tell yourself that if you get the job, this is a place to spend more time.

Your interaction with the coffee shop is an experience shaped by design; the physical characteristics of the shop and the training of the staff produce outcomes that match your goals. The experience is made up of a sequence of interpretive episodes that get your attention, orient you to the appropriate behavior, and support compelling interactions that are both satisfying and, hopefully, memorable.

Now imagine assembling a piece of furniture using printed instructions, selecting a concert to attend from a poster on a bulletin board, or buying a book through an online book store. Although varied in the number and duration of episodes, each of these tasks requires distinct interpretations of visual cues in a specific order. In assembling the furniture, you need to isolate the components and location for a particular step from the overall assembly instructions. In selecting a concert from the advertised schedule, you must orient yourself to the display of possible dates and times. And to purchase a book online, you need confirmation that the actions you have taken to complete the purchase were successful and repeatable when you return for your next order. In other words, your interpretive engagement with visual messages is no less about sequenced experiences than are your interactions in the coffee shop. They just happen faster. And unless something goes wrong, you are less aware of the boundaries between them than you are when moving through a clearly coded physical space like the coffee shop.

Design influences the efficiency, effectiveness, and character of communication experiences. If the furniture instructions show only photographs of the fully assembled object, you are unlikely to know where to start and which hardware and tools to use for each step of the assembly process. If the concert schedule includes dozens of performances, making a decision from a matrix that crosses dates and times in a grid is probably easier than from a list. And if the steps in the online ordering process provide feedback along the way—perhaps a green check mark that pops up to confirm completion of each step—you find your buying experience more satisfying than discovering at the very end of the process that you've missed critical information.

The design of visual communication, therefore, creates conditions for experience. The designer's task is to match form to the external forces in the users' context that shape the qualities of his or her interaction with information. The influence the designer has over context resides in deciding how many factors to consider in making judgments about form. Keep in mind that any context is more than just the physical, built environment; it includes all social and cultural values as well as the interpretive predispositions and behaviors of stakeholders (clients, designers, users, and the culture at large). As users or audiences we can evaluate design by the formal qualities of objects and communication. Were the materials stylish or bland? Was the interaction smooth or awkward? Or was the typography clever and made us smile? But we also judge design by the contribution form makes to satisfying our goals for engaging with the communication in the first place.

In order to demonstrate more fully the connection between the forms designers use and how their choices reflect and shape our interactions with context, this book traces visual phenomena to their origins in perceptual and cultural experience. Repeated, everyday encounters with these phenomena in many different settings build a kind of visual intelligence that influences the meanings we assign to our interactions with environments, objects, and messages. To illustrate how designers and their audiences make sense of sensory stimuli—in seeing wholes among parts, heartbeats as rhythm, and sound as pattern, for example— discussions in this book explore the inseparable link between perception and interpretation.

As a structure for understanding this relationship between visual form and context, the book breaks down the user's interpretive experience into phases that order explanations of phenomena in a logical sequence of time and purpose: getting attention, orienting behavior, facilitating interpretation, and extending experience through memory. Framing design in this way moves the focus from the physical artifacts of design (the letterforms, the page, the book, and so on) and shifts attention to the behaviors and experiences their forms make possible.

Making sense of experience

What is an *experience*? Aren't we immersed in experience during every waking hour? And what does communication design have to do with making sense of experience? Experience is a term that creates confusion because of its multiple meanings. There are *sensory experiences* and *cultural experiences* that we all accumulate through living in a physical and social world. Then there are experiences that result from specific conditions created by design professionals that are intended to satisfy our motives for interacting with environments, objects, and messages. This book focuses on designers' contributions to human experience; that is, on the ways in which designers use the sensory and symbolic qualities of form in the things they design to create the conditions for unordinary, meaningful, and ultimately memorable audience experiences.

Philosopher John Dewey (1859–1952) made a useful distinction between *experience* and *having an experience*. Dewey described ordinary *experience* as being continuous but often characterized by distraction and even conflict between expectations and actual outcomes. Throughout everyday life there are times when what we observe and what we think don't match, when what we expect and what we get are at odds (Dewey, 1934). By contrast, *an experience* is when our interactions with people and our surroundings reach a conclusion that is satisfying. Things don't simply end, they end in ways that are noticeably fulfilling. This type of experience has an emotional quality that we can identify and that separates it from the ordinary—that exciting first date, that scary thunderstorm, that exceptional meal. In other words, we know when an experience begins and ends and we recognize how it is different from the ordinary interactions of daily life.

Dewey also described *an experience* as having pattern and structure (Dewey, 1934). It is composed of distinct episodes that flow from one to the next. One part leads to another but without interruption. And unlike everyday experiences, there is a balance between the physical and mental aspects of an experience; between doing and thinking or feeling. Dewey warns that an excess of doing or an excess of thinking stands in the way of the successful completion of an experience. For example, a novice software user probably spends more time deliberating and needing confirmation that she has taken the right action than feeling the flow of a well-executed task. For an expert software user, on the other hand, the dialogue boxes that ask questions about the simplest operations are annoying and interrupt the progress of work. In a perfect world, software would learn about a user's growing expertise and adapt its behavior to her needs.

These kinds of imbalances between doing and thinking also occur in our experiences with printed communication. Imagine you are hiking in a national park and want to identify various species of plant life on your journey. If the printed guide to plants organizes information alphabetically in textual descriptions of native species, then you do a lot of extra reading to identify that little yellow flower in front of you. On the other hand, if the guide allows you to search plant species by color or leaf shape through groupings of photographs, then you find the structure of information better matched to the task of learning about something in the field. There is a better balance between doing and thinking and your experience of using the guide on the trail is more likely to be emotionally satisfying.

The human mind imposes structure on experience, even when no structure is inherent in the stimuli themselves. We naturally seek order from chaos in determining what things mean. The concept of keeping time, for example, is a human invention. In agrarian societies, farmers determined the sequence of activities during a day by observing changes in the position of the sun, not by clocks. The complexity of work in the industrial age and the resulting development of modern timekeeping devices (punching a clock!) broke the day into smaller, hourly segments that we now think of as natural. Digital devices focus our attention on even more precise units of measurement and there are fewer references to the cyclical passage of time once found in the rotating hands of analog clocks. Nature didn't change, but our reasons for imposing a different order did.

Through our interactions with the world, we build an inventory of mental structures for organizing experiences. These structures are shortcuts for processing information; we don't approach every new experience from scratch. We learn, for example, that eating out at any restaurant requires a set of similar actions and that menus contain roughly the same information for placing an order. We know that desks facing a blackboard or projection screen usually signify a classroom, even when we haven't been in that particular room before. We are not surprised that dictionaries and encyclopedias order entries alphabetically rather than by concepts; that search engines list results by popularity; or that major roads on maps look different from side streets. These are familiar structures, organized by event, place, alphabet, continuum, and category, respectively. We recognize them through lived, cultural experiences, and they carry expectations of appropriate interpretations and actions. We spend very little time rethinking *how* they mean and engage with them as long as *what* they mean is useful, usable, and desirable in meeting our needs.

Few things, however, reveal how culturally specific (or even arbitrary) these conventions are more than travel in a foreign country. For instance, the act of eating out at a restaurant can take on surprising twists: the vast numbers of unordered side dishes (*banchan*) that accompany any order at a Korean restaurant; or the large, shared flatbread (*injera*) that all members of a dining party tear off, share, and use as a scoop for eating stews at an Ethiopian restaurant. The mental and physical structures that order our world can vary dramatically from culture to culture, or even within a culture. Therefore, design must respond to the specific characteristics of audiences and contexts.

Experience and time

A story is a sequential structure organized by time; an unfolding of events ordered in anticipation of reaching a conclusion or goal. Stories are situated in settings that influence the actions of characters or the participation of readers, and they have clearly identified beginnings, middles, and ends. Unlike other conceptual structures, stories are goal-oriented; each episode moves us one step closer to an outcome (Mandler, 1984).

Think of the weather report. It describes high and low temperatures, the likelihood of snow, and the speed of wind during the upcoming twenty-four hours. But what the weather report means to our preparation for the day is much clearer if we know that the morning and afternoon will be sunny and warm, and that an approaching cold front will bring flurries in the evening, long after we have returned home from work or school. The hour-by-hour *story* of how the day will unfold is much more informative and memorable than a compilation of statistics, even though both reports include the same information in all other ways. Stories, therefore, are efficient, information-rich structures that help us connect conceptually and emotionally to experiences. And when we invest mentally in their outcomes, they are memorable and contribute to achieving our goals.

Effective communication strategies engage people in stories. It is much easier to learn software, for example, from a manual that describes a sequence of steps in executing a task we care about than from one that randomly inventories tools and their general functions. The story of the task reveals the logic of the program we are likely to encounter in other functions, and our end goal provides a context for executing and evaluating the process.

The visual and verbal components of good branding contribute to the story of a company or organization and the relationships it hopes to establish with people over time. Symbols and typefaces are not the brand, however. The value of design resides in the story that brand elements describe and deliver as actual experience. The brand is the narrative that people construct through their interactions with the organization's communication, products, environments, and services (all of which are designed) as experiences across time.

As an example of the difference between the story *told* and the story *delivered*, the swastika has all the characteristics and purposes we associate with symbols of its kind. It is visually compact, easily reproduced, instantly recognizable, and has an early history of positive associations with good fortune, security, and a variety of religious deities. But since its adoption as a symbol of German nationalism by the Nazis, its story is that of the Third Reich, and more recently, of neo-Nazi supremacist groups. It is impossible for the symbol, regardless of its form, to overcome its negative narrative. Nothing about the visual properties of the artifact changed over time, but the experience of its story did. The story of a brand told through design elements, therefore, needs to be consistent with people's experiences, not just with the organization's aspirations expressed in visual form.

Not all stories are intentionally persuasive, morally instructive, or designed to incite people to action. Many simply put information in a narrative form that is more easily understood than other structures. For example, off the eastern coast of the United States there are thousands of tiny sensors recording the speed and direction of moving water at various depths and distances from the shore. Scientists can view the record of sensor data as numbers in a spreadsheet or as many fluttering flags in a three-dimensional animation of water currents. It is difficult to detect pattern in the numerical chart—that is,

to link data points one after another as a representation of movement—but the depth and direction of currents at different times of the day are immediately apparent as one fluttering flag follows another in the animation. In other words, the choice to connect data in a time-based animation and to represent current direction by the orientation of flags tells a story of ocean movement not evident in the numerical chart. We can imagine linking that story to consequences for ocean life, coastal erosion, maritime navigation, and weather.

People differ in their understanding of stories. While marketing tends to segment audiences by demographics (for example, by age, gender, class, or ethnicity), designers should go deeper to determine the readiness of people for dealing with ideas from various perspectives. Imagine a city wants people to conserve water during a long drought. Some people don't know or believe there is a drought; they turn on the tap in the kitchen and water comes out, so what's the problem? Others know water is scarce but have no opinion regarding their personal obligation to conserve. And still others know there is a drought and understand their social responsibility to save water, but don't know what actions will produce meaningful results unless provided with instructions. These three audiences are not well served by the same story; people won't feel compelled to stop watering the lawn if they don't first believe there is a shortage or understand the long-term implications of continued, individual water use. The goal of communication, therefore, is to convert ignorance to understanding; understanding to the acceptance of a challenge; and acceptance to action. To do so may mean building the story for the same audience over time (through a campaign) or tailoring the story for audiences at different levels of understanding. It is very difficult for people to act on things about which they have little or no knowledge or opinion and even more difficult for single messages to accomplish all of those communication tasks for all audiences at one time.

Experience and media

The effectiveness of various media through which stories are told (print, television, websites, etc.) depends on the readiness of audiences to hear the message and the affordances of the medium. For example, if the communication goal is to persuade people to conserve water, broadcast television may not be the most economical choice. It is difficult to predict who is watching—perhaps many who don't yet understand the water shortage problem—and to tell a complete story for all audiences in expensive, thirty-second sound bites. On the other hand, printed messages in residential water bills allow city officials to tailor different conservation messages for high- and low-volume water users and to praise conservation efforts with follow-up messages when the customer's subsequent bills show reduced use.

People differ in their preferences for particular media or forms of communication and the behaviors associated with them. According to Nielsen ratings (a service in the United States that measures the size and composition of audiences for various media), the average American teenager in 2010 sent more than 3,000 text messages per month, with girls sending nearly twice as many as boys (Nielsen, 2010). In this age group, there is a decline in voice communication. Such behavior tells us something about the media culture of teenagers and about their perceptions of intimacy in the absence of face-to-face communication.

The Pew Research Center reports that 62 percent of adults get their news from social media (Gottfried & Shearer, 2016). Because news aggregators, such as Facebook and the Huffington Post, deliver articles that match users' previous search histories, the sites ensure that news stories are consistent with individuals' current interests and values. Internet activist Eli Pariser refers to this personal customization of the news as a *filter bubble* and questions its effect on critical thinking and decision-making in a democracy (Pariser, 2011). If we never see opposing opinions, how critical can we be about the positions we hold? In other words, there are social implications in the way people encounter and use media stories—in their cultural experiences—and these patterns shape expectations for new designed experiences.

The affordances of media constrain and enable particular kinds of interpretive experiences. Time-based media are especially well suited to the structure of storytelling. Film and video control the release of information over time and everyone watching sees the same message components in the exact order as designed. Websites, on the other hand, yield greater control to users who may not see aspects of a story in any particular sequence, but unlike television audiences, have the opportunity for immediate feedback in response to content. Sequential print media, such as books and magazines, control the ordering of information but lack movement and sound as variables that enhance readers' understanding. A still image of the fluttering flags in the previous water example contributes little to our understanding of the speed of water currents.

We also make judgments on the importance, relevance, or credibility of messages, partially through the medium of delivery. An invitation that arrives in an envelope with a first-class stamp feels more special than a postcard sent by bulk mail. We are more likely to save a museum catalog printed on thick glossy paper than a weekly newspaper review of the same exhibition because we interpret the commitment to high production values as signifying curatorial importance and lasting relevance. And because we understand the editorial checks and balances associated with serious journalism, we are likely to view the evening news on a major television network as more credible than stories in a newsprint tabloid at the supermarket checkout line.

Changes in technology redefine our experience with information. Think about watching a movie on a computer rather than in a movie theater; corresponding through email rather than handwritten letters; and searching for information on Google rather than through books in the library. In all cases, the information is essentially the same, but the experience is not. In the early stages of transition to a new technology, technologists transfer the functions and characteristics of older media to the new one, making some aspects of the experience familiar as people develop new skills. Internet communication began with many of the typographic behaviors and limitations of a typewriter; the only way to yell was by typing in all caps. But as new technologies develop, new opportunities emerge. Emoticons and emojis are just two instances of newer forms of expression that users created to supplement or even replace text-based messages with emotional content. Media theorist Henry Jenkins described the most inventive period in any technology as the time immediately after its introduction when designers and users figure out what the technology is good for and how to get around its perceived limitations (Thorburn & Jenkins, 2003).

The importance of any technological change is its impact on the experiences associated with it (McLuhan, 1994). You may choose to watch a movie on your computer, but that is a different experience from laughing or crying alongside a crowd of moviegoers in a darkened room. Being able to follow a photojournalist online as she builds a story provides insights not available by flipping print magazine pages in your doctor's waiting room. But not all contexts call for rich, dynamic content. A brief, witty text message can sometimes diffuse an argument faster than a lengthy email or telephone call. It is the job of designers to anticipate these cultural experiences in the design of tools and systems—that is, to include concerns for how the medium shapes or supports experience, over and above the content of any individual message.

Denotation and connotation

We interpret meaning in visual messages at two levels. First, we interpret the literal content of words and images. Then we expand that meaning through a field of related associations that arise from the qualities of form and the use of words and images in various contexts. *Denotation* is the explicit dictionary definition of something, exclusive of the feelings and extended ideas that it suggests. Denotatively, a smartphone is a telephonic device through which people access the internet, send text messages, upload music, and take pictures and videos. *Connotation* is the implied meaning, a secondary feeling or association that expands or repositions the denotative meaning. Connotatively, a smartphone stands for people's anytime-anywhere connection to information; decline in the correctness of spelling and grammar in personal communication (LOL); and changes in etiquette and patterns of social interaction. A director recently described his preference for flip phones in his music videos because any smartphone calls attention to itself and raises too many connotations beyond making a phone call (Zeitchik, 2015).

Some contexts demand highly denotative messages. We expect airport signage to get us to the appropriate departure gate by requiring as little mental processing as possible. Until we arrive at our destination, we don't want to be distracted by thinking about the adventure of flight or the culture of the city in which the airport is located. If we are using instructions to understand the operation of a power tool, renewing our driver's license,

or seeking the nutritional content in a particular brand of breakfast cereal, we want a straightforward message with no ambiguity of meaning. Emotions and associations play little part in these activities and we value the objectivity of literal messages.

Because connotation operates in the open-ended realm of cultural associations, it presents expanded opportunities for meaning-making through design. A single word or image can signify a variety of concepts and emotions relevant to the communication task. For example, if communication is to persuade people to volunteer for an important cause, they need to be inspired beyond the literal description of job requirements. The nobility and selflessness of volunteering and their contribution to a significant goal need to be apparent. Consider the subtle difference between the words "volunteer" and "serve." The former is a literal reference to the action asked for in the communication. The latter, on the other hand, connotes a much more humble relationship between volunteers and the beneficiaries of their efforts. It calls forth notions of self-sacrifice and social responsibility, not just the unpaid status of participants.

Images are equally open to connotative meanings. Imagine that the organization looking for volunteers is an animal shelter. There are connotative differences in using a pit bull versus a beagle in advertising. Both breeds may be victims of animal abuse who need good homes, but the reputation of pit bulls as aggressive and resistant to rehabilitation (accurate nor not) may give some people second thoughts about volunteering. Pit bulls make the news, beagles do not.

Because connotations develop through social and cultural experiences, they vary from audience to audience and from context to context. For example, it is unlikely that your grandmother understands the concept and construction of an internet meme. Similarly, slogans from the anti-war movements of the 1960s probably mean little to today's teenagers. These connotative variations mean that designers cannot rely on their own experiences as typical. They must investigate possible interpretations by specific audiences and anticipate connotations that arise from the cultural and physical contexts in which people encounter messages.

It is important to study both what people *say* and *do* in understanding the meanings they assign to words and images. Fred Dust of the design firm IDEO described talking with a woman about the concept of "luxury" in his research for a client. The woman was firm in saying that she led a very simple life and luxury was not important to her. After a week of observation, however, the researcher noticed her scheduling weekly manicure appointments. When asked about this, the woman said, "Well, that's not a luxury, that's a necessity." In other words, her connotations of "luxury" were not those of the designer.

The extended meanings we give to images and words also change over time. We often miss the symbolism in historical works of art, design, and literature because the connotations they depended upon are no longer part of our culture. And when designers pull visual references from the past, they reposition their older meanings under new purposes and contexts. The many, often humorous, commercial uses of Da Vinci's *Mona Lisa* or Grant Wood's *American Gothic* make it difficult for today's audiences to understand the paintings only as expressions of their own times. Similarly, changes in the surrounding context can recast the field of associations we hold in memory. For most Americans of a certain age, for example, the twin towers of the World Trade Center in New York City now stand for something entirely different from their pre-2001 meaning as collaboration between government agencies and corporations in international trade. Media exposure reinforces new interpretations at an ever-accelerating pace. This constant churning of meanings tells designers that visual language is always in a process of renewal, never entirely stable.

It is under these multifaceted notions of experience and context that designers do their work. It is convenient to talk about form and meaning as though they are two distinct concepts. But form is meaning, inseparable in experience. And what we think form means in any communication depends both on our accumulated experiences in a physical and cultural world and the specific conditions of the context in which we encounter messages.

SUMMARY

The shift in professional practice from designing objects to designing the conditions for experience argues for exploring what makes encounters with people, places, and things fulfilling and memorable. Philosopher John Dewey described *an experience* as a continuous unfolding of episodes that involves a relationship between doing and thinking. How satisfying the experience is depends on that relationship. Communication design organizes experience in a variety of structures. A story is structured by time and has a beginning, middle, and end; we understand and remember things easily through this recurring structure. The effectiveness of various media through which stories are told depends on the readiness of the audience to accept messages and to take action. Denotation and connotation are two levels of meaning we assign to messages. The first is the literal interpretation of content, while the second depends on associations we build by living in a physical and social world. The next chapter discusses how the vocabulary of messages contributes to these conditions.

The vocabulary of visual messages

All visual messages share a similar inventory of components through which designers shape the conditions for interpretive experiences. They are made up of *elements* arranged in *compositions*, which audiences interpret through visual *codes* or a grammar of form appropriate to the surrounding culture. Particular qualities in the rendering of elements, structure of compositions, and adherence or non-adherence to cultural codes constitute *style*, which we often associate with particular time periods, contexts, or philosophies.

Elements

Elements are the physical signs and symbols (for example, images, words, colors, and graphic devices such as lines and shapes) used to communicate the subject matter of a message. The meaning of an element varies with its visual characteristics and surrounding context.

A drawing of a tool, for example, communicates differently from a photograph of the same object. We understand that in rendering the illustration, the designer chooses to include some features and to eliminate others. The quality of the rendering says something about the communication goal of the designer. A technical drawing executed on the computer evokes a different meaning (cool, clinical, precise) from a gestural marker drawing of the object in action (imperfect, human, expressive). In other words, most audiences assume some subjective intent in the choice to hand render an object through drawing rather than through other media.

In contrast—and because the camera includes in the image everything within its frame as a complete and literal representation of the subject (captured by an unbiased machine)—many viewers interpret a photograph as objective. This is why many consider photography to be a journalistic medium, impartial and accurate. But photographs can be just as subjective and connotative as drawings. Lighting, focus, cropping, depth of field, and pose or point of view can manipulate the meaning of the image, despite the mechanical means of its production (Barthes, 1977). And with today's software, photographers and image editors can digitally alter images, creating new meanings altogether. How elements are made and reproduced, therefore, carries connotative meanings over and above the subject matter of the elements themselves.

Words communicate differently from images. In some cases, they are more open to a range of possible interpretations. Consider the word "home." The meaning of the word alone depends on our personal experiences with the places where we have lived and our history of interactions with family, roommates, or neighbors in those places. A photograph of a particular home or the resident family, on the other hand, closes down the meaning to a much narrower definition (Figure 2.1). We make specific inferences about time, place, and people in ways not required by the word alone. While viewers may compare their judgments about the image to their own experiences, it is clear by the picture that the message is not about all homes in general. By contrast, the word "home" leaves these issues unresolved. In some communication, specific meanings are important. In other cases, a wider range of connotations encourages readers to "fill in" with details of personal experiences as part of the interpretive process.

Context also matters in determining what elements mean. A message that announces "Demonstration here!" means one thing at a science fair and another at the site of a campus protest. The words are the same in both contexts, but the surrounding environments lead to different conclusions about likely activities. Similarly, the individual meanings of any two elements may be very different from that of the same two elements in combination. An image of an apple means different things when combined with a book (teacher or education); a serpent (Adam and Eve, temptation); a computer (Apple Computer, Inc.); or a banana (fruit). Nothing about the image of the apple needs to change across the various compositions, but the presence of a second image shifts meaning in each case. Further, the range of potential meanings can vary even further when the audience doesn't share a particular cultural background.

Figure 2.1
The word "home" evokes many different meanings, each influenced by the specific experiences of the interpreter. On the other hand, a photograph of a particular home focuses the interpretation. While the viewer makes personal judgments of the time and place in the image, the range of possible interpretations narrows by ruling out meanings that do not fit the image.

Typographic form also depends on its juxtaposition with other typographic elements for its connotations. Designer Sibylle Hagmann developed a family of typefaces called "Triple Strip" (Figure 2.2). Individually, any one of the three typefaces is formally complete and has visual characteristics distinct from the other two typefaces. When used together, however, the three typefaces reflect the vibe of a city street; the energy of colliding styles and messages we find in urban environments. This intentional lack of visual harmony among the three typefaces is in contrast to the design of many other type families in which there are strong similarities among the weight and proportional variations within the family. The meaning implied by Hagmann's design, over and above the literal meaning of words set in the typefaces, depends entirely on the three typefaces appearing together.

Type/image relationships present additional opportunities for the construction of meaning. Under the simplest relationships, words "label" images and images "illustrate" words. In these instances, the individual meaning of the two elements are roughly the same and largely redundant. They reinforce each other or tell us what to think about the other in case the single element doesn't do the job. An advertisement that shows a sport utility vehicle splashing through a mountain stream bolsters the emotional content of the image with the words "rugged," "sporty," and "fit for adventure." The words label what the designer intends

us to feel about the image. In other cases, an image can illustrate and narrow the possible interpretations of a word. The word "women" on a lacey pink background reinforces traditional ideas of femininity, shutting down alternative representations of women that might come to mind from the word alone. For better or worse, the image directs the audience to the specific meaning the designer intends by means of illustration.

More interesting, however, is when an element expands the interpretation or raises questions about the meaning of the other. Lacey pink typography that says "women" sitting next to a photograph of a woman in a hard hat with a sledgehammer says something about the diversity of women and their roles. The two views of women, one captured in typographic form and the other in photographic form, are in a dialogue that undermines conventional perceptions and expands meaning.

In another example, "Billions and billions sold" is an advertising slogan that describes the number of hamburgers served by a popular American fast food chain. When coupled with images of overweight children, however, the text/image combination serves as critical commentary on the causes of obesity—a "third meaning" not present in either of the two messages alone. And the text/image message is stronger than single images of overweight children and hamburgers because the

Figure 2.2
TripleStrip typeface
Sibylle Hagmann,
Kontour
Hagmann's design of the type family Triple Strip combines seemingly dissonant typeface designs. While any single typeface is formally complete, its true character is defined by its contrast to other members of the family. Used together, these three typefaces mimic the eclectic qualities of an urban street.

КЛИНОМ КРАСНЫМ БЕЙ БЕЛЫХ

ΛΛ.   N 19   Литиздат Политуправления Запфронта   Уновис

Figure 2.3
Beat the Whites with the Red Wedge, 1919–1920
Lazar Markovich Lissitzky, 1890–1941
El Lissitzky's abstract composition refers to factions in the Russian Civil War immediately following the 1917 revolution. Even without knowing the history behind the work, the aggression of the red wedge is apparent. Its relationship to the white circle is a metaphor for violent conflict.

company sees the slogan as something to brag about. Many remember the phrase emboldened on the sign outside the restaurant. In this way, the combination of typographic and photographic elements expands meaning beyond that of the elements alone and invites conversation by the questions it raises.

Abstract shapes also take on different meanings in combination. The red triangle in El Lissitzky's "Beat the Whites with the Red Wedge" is more threatening when combined with a circular shape than when seen alone (Figure 2.3). We need not know the title of the work or its reference to the violent history of the Russian Civil War to understand the aggression of the red wedge. In this case, abstract form is metaphorical. The association of the triangular element with the physical attributes of

weapons and military action (for example, bayonets and the forward movement of an attack) versus a softer, more vulnerable object in a static position is consistent with the message content.

Elements also have cultural significance and mean different things to different people. A raised thumb online tells others how many people "like" the content of a website or comment, but the same gesture is offensive on the streets of Greece. Red is used as a sign for danger in many countries but means "good luck" in China. And 0/1 is familiar to digital natives but probably less so to a technologically challenged grandparent (Davis, 2012). The choice of elements, therefore, has varying content significance for different audiences.

Composition

Designers arrange elements to form *compositions*. The meaning of a message depends not only on the choice of particular elements, but also on their organization within a visual field (or in a sequence of visual frames, as in a film, book, or website). Composition determines which elements the audience encounters first and last; the perception of relationships among particular elements and not others; the affiliation of elements with specific areas of the surrounding visual field (for example, top/bottom, foreground/background, or presence/absence within the frame); and the construction of meaning through the integration of all aspects of the composition.

Contrasting size, color, shape, location, direction, and/or movement can draw attention to one element over others, to a hierarchy of importance among units of information. Designers influence our perceptual judgments of the importance or "behavior" of elements in terms of their appearance of weight or size in relation to other elements, balance with other elements, and distance from the viewer, even though all elements are simply marks or pixels on a flat, two-dimensional picture plane. Bold type appears to weigh more than light type. Two small squares on the right appear to balance one large circle on the left. A very large hat at the bottom of the visual field appears closer to us than a tiny horse at the top because we know the real sizes of the two objects and understand the illusion of depth achieved through size and position. The wiggling letterform on the screen seems poised for action or movement, while static text appears at rest. In other words, we assign meaningful behaviors to designer's choices about the formal qualities of elements in two-dimensional compositions on the basis of our real experiences with objects in a physical world. Contrast with the surrounding field and novelty within a group of elements can direct attention to a single word over the entire sentence; the edge of the visual field over things in the more obvious center; or the smallest element in a field of really big shapes.

Figure 2.4
Céline Condorelli:
Support Structures,
2009
Sternberg Press
Designer:
James Langdon
The topic of Céline Condorelli's installation, *Support Structures*, is what bears, sustains, props, and holds up. Langdon's design for the catalog reflects the diverse nature of the subject through images that bear little obvious relationship to each other. Compositionally, within spreads and from spread to spread, Langdon establishes relationships through color, shape, and alignments that govern how viewers group elements.

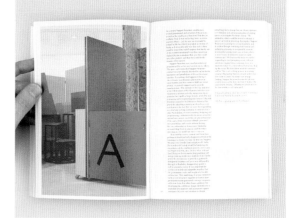

Visual similarity among elements, alignments in their placement within the visual field, or ordering by some principle (such as a gradation in size or color) signal the viewer that certain elements share some particular relationship not shared with others in the composition (Figure 2.4). A reader distinguishes the chapter titles of a book from subtitles and footnotes by their visual treatment and placement—chapter titles are usually set consistently in larger type, surrounded by white space, and at the top of a page. If the numbers representing high and low temperatures in a weather report are typographically alike but different from other numbers (such as wind speed or dew point) readers interpret them as related, indicating how extreme temperature variations during the day will be. And photographs that share similar proportions or typographic elements with aligning edges may be seen as categorically alike but different from other elements in the visual field (for example, as representing a sequence of steps in a process). The compositional strategies that designers use not only create hierarchies of relative importance among visual elements, but they also identify groupings of elements that are similar in their contribution to meaning. These strategies direct attention to relationships that are informative, beyond the literal subject matter or visual character of the elements alone.

Compositional strategies can create narrative relationships among elements as well, implying unfolding actions or suggesting stories through interacting elements. We interpret a stack of shapes as "tipsy" and likely to topple if there is sufficient empty space into which the shapes could "fall." If there are eight people in a photograph but only two are looking at each other, we intuit some significant relationship between the two by virtue of the line formed by their gaze. A vertical financial bar chart tells a story of gain and loss in ways not as obvious in a horizontal chart of the same data. And when the sequence of pages in a book, frames in a film, or screens in a website exhibit deliberate pacing (from quiet arrangements to chaos and back again to quiet, for example) we read significance from one visual experience to the next (Figure 2.5).

Figure 2.5
El Taller de Gráfica Popular (The Workshop for Popular Graphics), 2015
Designer: Roy Brooks's Courtesy of the Georgia Museum of Art
The spreads in Brooks' book design are as diverse as the graphic works and artists in the collection. There are layouts that match the bold straightforwardness of the art and others that encourage scholarly reflection. Together, they represent a compositional strategy that produces a specific experience for the reader.

Figure 2.6
Fashion advertising often crops images to highlight a single perfect feature. In doing so, it robs the image of any story about the person, focusing instead on the model as an object.

Cropping, or the selective framing of image content, can dramatically change the meaning of an image. When designers tightly crop images, they intentionally reduce the narrative possibilities. There is less potential for interaction among elements, and meaning depends entirely on the content and qualities of the emphasized element. Advertising product or fashion photography, for example, often isolates specific attributes of a subject to highlight an attractive feature, avoid qualities that are less than perfect, or distract the audience from focusing on elements that are less relevant to creating the desired emotional response (Figure 2.6). In doing so, cropping eliminates the action or interaction among elements necessary for storytelling. Our attention is drawn to the sleek lines of the computer or the dewy eyes of the model, but we struggle to assign a story to these compositions.

Likewise, symmetrical compositions frequently stabilize all elements, shutting down the possibility of action communicated more typically through asymmetrical compositions. Symmetrical compositions align all elements along a central axis. This alignment is usually stronger than the effect of other visual variables that could signify specific relationships among some elements and not others. Such compositions often rely on top-to-bottom or center-outward hierarchies and the individual characteristics of elements (size or color, for example), reinforce the order of reading but rarely tell a story (Figure 2.7).

Compositional strategies also zone areas of the visual field, dedicating specific locations within the picture plane to certain types of information. For example, newspaper design frequently discriminates between content that appears "above and below the fold," favoring the uppermost area of the paper for high-appeal headlines and images. Maps often cluster legend information in the corner of the printed page. And websites typically place navigational information at the top of the screen.

In other cases, clusters of like elements in particular locations can reinforce meaning. For example, isolating two contrasting political opinions in the left and right halves of the visual field support the interpretation of contrasting liberal and conservative positions on an issue. Locating general ideas at the top of a concept map with increasing specificity as the nodes cascade down the page helps viewers understand the hierarchy among elements better than a randomly distributed network of nodes. In these instances, placement adds to or strengthens the meaning of elements.

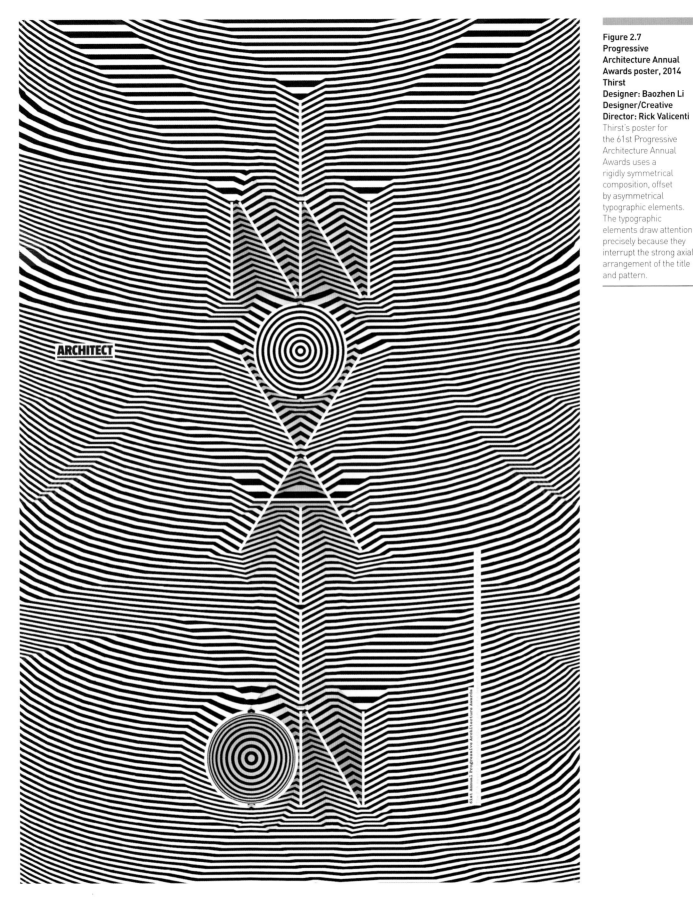

Figure 2.7
Progressive
Architecture Annual
Awards poster, 2014
Thirst
Designer: Baozhen Li
Designer/Creative
Director: Rick Valicenti
Thirst's poster for
the 61st Progressive
Architecture Annual
Awards uses a
rigidly symmetrical
composition, offset
by asymmetrical
typographic elements.
The typographic
elements draw attention
precisely because they
interrupt the strong axial
arrangement of the title
and pattern.

Code

Just as the physical characteristics of architecture establish a visual and spatial grammar that orders the activity expected of us in different spaces—where to enter, where to linger, and where to keep moving, for example—there is a code to visual communication that shapes our interpretive experience. Culture determines these conventions for reading visual form. For instance, for those of us who read in English, there is a top/down, left/right code for working our way through text on a printed page. Not so in Mandarin Chinese. In Western cultures, it is typical for parallel lines in a composition—such as the two sides of a railroad track—to diminish in width and converge as they go into the distance. This system of artificial perspective is understood as a Western convention for creating the illusion of depth in a two-dimensional composition. Historically, Chinese and Japanese compositions communicated depth or distance by lines that converged in the foreground, grew wider in the background, and avoided any shadows that undermined the flatness of the picture plane. In other words, the meaning-making practices of a culture determine these grammatical codes for the arrangement of form, whether through repeated use by producers of visual artifacts or as extensions of attitudes, habits, dispositions, or belief systems built up by the culture over time. While seeming permanent, they are, in fact, frequently in flux and often evolve with the times.

Conformity with cultural codes reduces the audience effort required to interpret the meaning of a message; we rely on past experience to recognize repeating structures. For example, we are used to seeing a monthly calendar arranged in a grid with Sunday at the front of each week and Saturday at the end. There are other ways to organize thirty consecutive days—we find many in contemporary day planners—but scheduling under these alternatives requires more thought to orient ourselves to the structure before doing the actual scheduling.

Designers can subvert codes for expressive reasons through careful decisions about elements and compositions. For example, if the upper right and lower left corners of visual compositions tend not to attract attention under the typical reading order in English, then placing a visually dominant element (by size, color, or shape) in the fallow corners pulls the viewer out of the normal reading pattern and slows down the mental processing of the composition. If the goal of the design is contemplation, then subverting the typical reading order may add some value to the interpretive experience. It could be an asset in the design of a thought-provoking poster, but not useful in the layout of a novel where maintaining the rhythm of reading from page to page is important (Figure 2.8)

Figure 2.8
Dead Man's Float **book cover, 2006**
Véhicule Press
David Drummond
Drummond uses the conventional visual code for the typeset design of a book chapter with descending sizes of type as the text moves from the upper left to the lower right. He then undermines this code, turning the text into water by overlaying an illustration and annotating the cover with handwriting in the upper right corner. In doing so, he calls attention to the visual grammar of books while at the same time inserting elements that carry a story.

a novel

Nicholas Maes

Dead Man's Float

Is this how it ends?

I'm in my bedroom, or was a moment ago. My dressing gown is around my ~~shoulders and~~ my underwear is halfway on. The ~~stove, as is the bureau~~ with the Meissen fi~~gur~~es. The window is shimmering: the elm outside and the street with its houses appear to be resting at the bottom of a river. And, *Gottverdomme!* My legs, my arms, my head, my... my boundaries! They're water, water, everything is water! I can't... I have no... everywhere, yes everywhere...!

My mother, dressed in yellow, swings me in circles.... My father, Dad, he's reading in his armchair.... My uncle's request that I hear his last confession, the pang of thirst when I found out they'd been killed, my meeting with Pete inside the Hotel Manhattan, the derelict my wife almost crushed with our Buick, Netti's cry of exultation, his suicide by gas dear God, and floating at the center, gloating at the center, his face, his, when he met his rock 'n' roll maker....

Memories. I'm floating in my memories, each so fresh

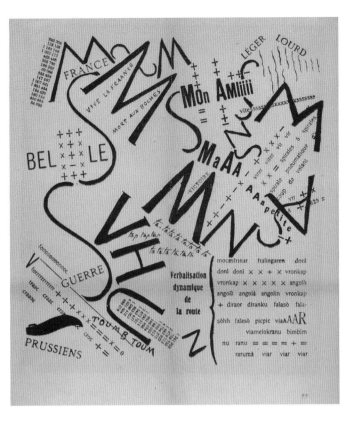

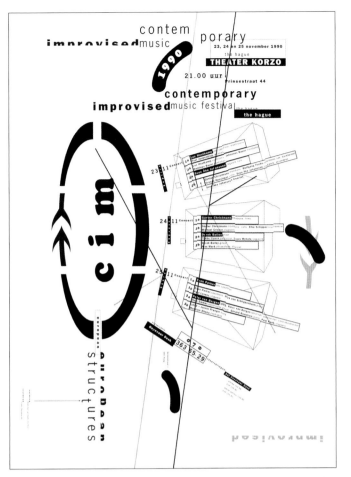

Breaking the rules or undermining the accepted code is a typical strategy for design movements that challenge the status quo. In the early part of the twentieth century, the Futurists experimented with fragmenting the linear reading order or *syntax* of text. By breaking apart the logical sequencing of words in sentences and paragraphs—instead arranging typography in compositions with random letterforms of different sizes and fragments of sentences—designers sought to "wake up" readers for more critical interpretations of the social and political discussions of the time (Davis, 2012) (Figure 2.9).

At the end of the twentieth century, communication designers turned their backs on modernist compositional codes that favored clear typographic hierarchies thought to communicate the singular meaning of an author's text. Believing that meaning is inherently unstable and ultimately constructed by the reader—that we think differently about a text each time we read it and on the basis of our cultural position—designers explored compositions in which every element had multiple relationships with other elements on the page. No single element overshadowed another, and therefore, many meanings were possible. The shifting relationship could never be seen as producing a single interpretation because elements were always in struggle for dominance with others in the composition (Figure 2.10).

In both historical examples, designers challenged conventional Western reading codes to express new ideas and to produce specific experiences for readers. Such challenges usually arise from shifts in theories about how meaning is made and associate the disruption of visual conventions with particular philosophical movements or time periods in design history.

Figure 2.9, top left
After the Marne, Joffre Visited the Front by Car, 1915
Filippo Tomasso Marinetti (1876–1944)
The avant-garde Futurists used the disruption of syntax—the visual ordering of words and images—to challenge the traditional visual codes of printed communication with the intent to "wake up" a complacent reader.

Figure 2.10, top right
CIM Poster, 1990
Allen Hori
Like the avant-garde work in the first part of the twentieth century, postmodern designers of the 1990s explored the role of syntax in visual messages. Forgoing an obvious hierarchy among elements, these compositions challenged a singular reading of the text.

Style

Although *aesthetics*, *taste*, and *style* are concepts often used interchangeably, they have slightly different definitions. *Aesthetics* is a set of principles concerned with the nature and appreciation of beauty, as well as a branch of philosophy that grapples with these notions. Philosophers debate the role of sensory and emotional experiences on our judgments of what is and is not beautiful and what is and is not art. While there are different perspectives across history and across cultures regarding what constitutes beauty, philosophies of aesthetics deal with a general class of concepts that are thought to transcend time and place.

Taste is an individual's pattern of preferences for certain qualities of form over others. Social and cultural experiences influence taste, so our preferences for form may change over time as we are exposed to education, advertising, popular culture, or new experiences. The distinctions between "good" and "poor" taste are often aligned with class, age, or ethnic differences and taste can be used as a means to discriminate against those whose likes and dislikes are different from our own. For example, a fundamental idea underpinning modern design movements of the early twentieth century was that by surrounding ordinary people with "well-designed" objects and environments they would overcome the limitations of their social class and economic status. Not everyone agrees that qualities such as detail, imperfection, or traditionalism are real limits to social mobility, so there is rarely a cultural consensus regarding issues of taste. *Kitsch* is a term used to describe objects thought to be in poor taste because they are garish, cheaply made, or nostalgic but appreciated in an ironic way or from a critical position on culture. These objects are often read in different ways by different social classes or subcultures.

Style is a distinctive form or way of presenting something that is characteristic of a time, place, or philosophy. While we often refer to individual artists and designers as having *personal styles*, the more common use of "style" in design refers to the collective approach of many designers to the rendering of elements, composition, and conformity or non-conformity with the visual codes of their times. Toward the end of the nineteenth century, commercial manufacturers produced poorly made goods in styles that imitated artifacts from the distant past. Stamped and cast metal replicated forms once carved in wood and stone, and industrial printing presses churned out thousands of reproductions an hour with little concern for the fine art of bookmaking. The efficiency of these processes allowed average consumers to purchase the illusion of higher social status by owning stylistic facsimiles of objects previously available only to the wealthy. The Arts and Crafts movement in Europe was a reaction to the shoddy quality of these faux objects and to public nostalgia for styles of the past. Members of the movement advocated handcrafted work by trained artisans, "truth to materials," and forms found in nature as a means for bringing good design to every home. This approach was economically unsustainable as a business strategy, yet the visual vocabulary of the movement survived in a popular turn of the century style called, *Art Nouveau*. The style used colors and intricate ornament inspired by botanical forms (curling vines, leaves and petals) and can be found in objects as diverse as subway gates, furniture, and books.

Later periods of design history viewed style as something superficial that distracts the viewer from the direct experience of message content, as the opposite of substance. Mid-century modern movements such as De Stijl, the Bauhaus, and the International Typographic Style (sometimes called Swiss Design) developed new visual forms that celebrated the inherent characteristics of modern materials and machine production. Communication designers of this period favored geometric form, asymmetrical arrangements of elements on a grid, sans serif typefaces, and a color palette limited to primary hues, black, and white. Of course, this was no less a style than previous approaches but its origins were in function, not in cultural symbols of the past. More recent philosophies, however, view style as something that extends meaning beyond that of function and subject matter alone. Style evokes connotations built through our previous experiences of form or represents a deliberate break with the past. We associate typefaces, color, and the treatment of images with particular periods of history or contexts of use—as in the Vienna Secessionist, Constructivist, Art Deco, and Postmodern styles, for instance.

There is a difference between *imitating* style and *referencing* style to evoke and repurpose the connotations we associate with the original use. Paula Scher's hand-drawn maps, for instance, refer to well-known cartographic styles: the airline flight paths in onboard magazines; nodal diagrams in contemporary subway maps; and typography that follows landscape contours and political boundaries

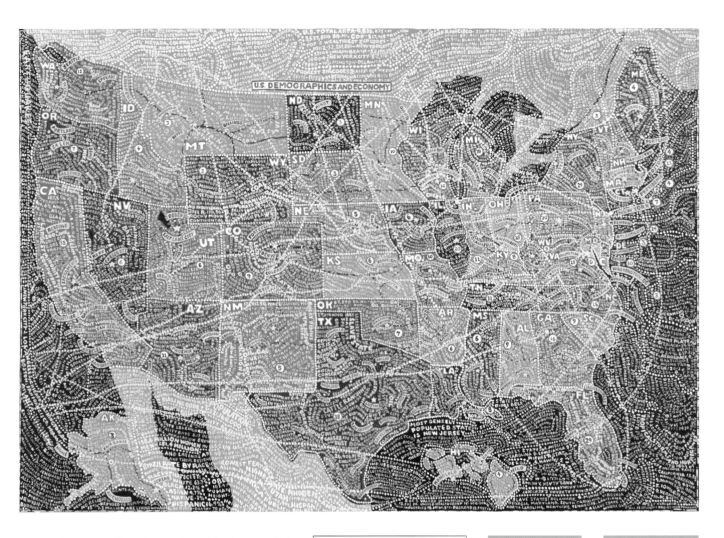

on historical maps. The colors and graphic elements feel familiar, yet Scher's versions are fresh reminders of other maps without being literal reproductions of existing styles (Figure 2.11).

We classify typefaces by their styles, often noting references to the tools that originally contributed to the form of their stylistic predecessors. Old Style typefaces, for example, were originally created between the fifteenth and sixteenth centuries. The thicks and thins in their strokes and left-leaning stress—an imaginary line connecting the thinnest parts of the letterform—originally resulted from the use of a calligrapher's flat-nosed pen (Figure 2.12). Although fonts are no longer drawn with pens, contemporary versions of Old Style typefaces still carry these connotations. These typefaces recall the elegance of hand-drawn form and the singular importance of the formal documents of the time.

Figure 2.11, above
***U.S. Demographics and Economy*, 2015**
Paula Scher
Scher's painted maps refer to the style of topographic and airplane flight maps. They do not literally replicate these familiar artifacts or attempt to display accurate data, but instead use cartographic form to recall readers' experiences with graphic representations of geography.

Figure 2.12, left
Goudy Old Style typeface, 1915
Frederic W. Goudy (1865–1947)
For American Type Founders
Goudy's type design exhibits the characteristics of Old Style typefaces (thick and thin strokes, oblique stress, and cupped, angled serifs). Many of these characteristics result from the tools used to draw the letterforms. The flat nib of a pen makes a thick stroke in one direction, a thin stroke in another. Contemporary typefaces that exhibit these characteristics may also be classified as Old Style and reflect the historic associations of the category.

Figure 2.13
The 9/11 Report:
A Graphic Adaptation,
2006
Ernie Colón and
Sid Jacobson
Comic artists Colón and
Jacobson condensed
the report of the 9/11
Commission, which
published the findings of
events leading up to the
2001 attack on the World
Trade Center in New
York. The original report
involved interviews with
1200 people and a review
of 12.5 million pages of
documents. The artists
made an important
report understandable
to the average American
by using a style that is
both accessible and
expressive.

We also relate style with particular contexts of use. There are styles we associate with first-person shooter games, cellphone interfaces, international travel signage, and tabloid newspapers. When designers use these styles, they borrow the meanings associated with their use. In 2006, comic book artists Ernie Colón and Sid Jacobson released a graphic adaptation of the 580-page report of the *9/11 Commission*, which investigated the 2001 attack on the World Trade Center in New York (Figure 2.13). The intent was to provide a more accessible explanation of the event in a style that the average American might actually want to read. Although some critics felt the graphic approach to the publication diminished the account of personal tragedy and government shortfalls, most reviewers praised the artists for making an important report comprehensible.

The interplay of message content, elements, composition, code, and style are the stuff of visual communication design. They shape people's use of information, influence their interactions with the world, and contribute to their histories of meaning-making. The chapters that follow describe principles and concepts through which designers construct the conditions for meaningful experiences. Discussions connect the visual vocabulary of messages with the sensemaking we apply to interpreting content. How does the treatment of elements, for example, draw attention to some elements over others? What are compositional cues that tell us where to begin reading? How do cultural conventions for the arrangement of form reinforce the meaning of texts and the hierarchy of information? What qualities of visual signs make them compelling and memorable? The explanations that follow connect our everyday experiences of perceptual phenomena with the tasks of visual communication designers and interpretations by their audiences. While there are no rules for the invention of form, it is possible to ground design decisions in experiences that are fundamentally human.

SUMMARY

All messages include elements—words, images, and/or symbols—that contribute to the construction of meaning. How these elements are generated and the contexts in which we see them shape our interpretations. We make different assumptions about a photograph versus a drawing and respond according to expectations built through prior experience with representations and their contexts.

The arrangement of elements within a visual field or across time also influences what we think messages mean. Composition communicates a hierarchy of importance among elements and provides information about relevant interactions among particular components of a message. The ordering of elements can be narrative, communicating a story of evolving actions or relationships. Cropping robs images of their narrative potential, focusing our attention instead on image features rather than interactions that contribute to a story.

Visual codes constitute a grammar or set of rules for reading visual form. They are culturally defined and shared by people with common experiences and language. For example, readers of English interpret text from the upper left to lower right of a page unless the visual properties of particular elements pull attention to fallow areas of the composition.

Style is distinct from aesthetics and taste. It is often associated with specific periods of time, cultures, or philosophies. Style connotatively expands the literal meaning of messages, and when repurposed in a new context or time, brings forward content associated with its original use. A successful repurposing of style refers to these meanings without being direct imitations of the original.

Getting attention

Attention is the process of selectively focusing on one aspect of the sensory environment while ignoring other things that seem less important or less worthy of consideration. It is a means for concentrating the mind on a single object, element, or thought with the goal of narrowing the number of stimuli in a complex perceptual field.

Attention is important to our species' survival—we pay the most attention to things that are biologically significant or driven by our emotions, such as predators and babies for example. It is human nature to focus on things that could threaten our lives or well-being and to be drawn to things that are unusual or distinct from other things in our field of vision.

Contemporary times, however, bombard us with too many demands on our limited capacity to focus. We simply cannot give equal attention to everything. Writer Alvin Toffler in his 1970 book, *Future Shock*, coined the term "information overload" to describe the glut of information reaching the senses in modern society. Toffler wrote, "When the individual is plunged into fast and irregularly changing situations, or a novelty-loaded context...his predictive accuracy plummets. He can no longer make the reasonably correct assessments on which rational behavior is dependent" (Toffler, 1971, p. 35). It is impossible to think critically about every message we encounter, so we either ignore those that seem unimportant or skim information for first impressions that are rarely accurate or complete. As a result, our relationship with much of the content we encounter is superficial and temporary.

Electronic media now circulate messages at lightning speed in a race for our attention. The Union of Concerned Scientists estimates that the average American is exposed to as many as 3,000 advertising messages a day and spends roughly 4.5 hours watching television and even more time on computers and smartphones. Clearly, there is no shortfall of digital information and it is impossible to reflect rationally on this much content. Rhetoric professor Richard Lanham says that if we define an economy by things that are scarce (typically, money or goods), then we currently live in an "attention economy," rather than an "information economy" (Lanham, 2006). There is no deficit of content in today's technological world but we lack the human capacity to allocate attention to all of it (Lanham, 2006).

Under this attention shortfall, what we choose to process has as much to do with its form as its substance. For many centuries, the aim of printed typography was to disappear so readers could get to the content of the text without thinking about its physical form. The "best" design was one in which readers didn't think about how things looked and became completely absorbed in the story or message (Lanham, 2006). Think about reading a good novel; we notice typography only if it gets in our way of reading. But today, says Lanham, there is significance in the surface qualities of the message, in style (Lanham, 2006). Typefaces and motion in screen-based communication are carriers of content that may not be present in the literal meaning of words. In some cases, this visual content corresponds with the subject matter; in other cases it does not and causes us to question the meaning of the text.

Designer Richard Saul Wurman warned us in his 1989 book, *Information Anxiety*, that our current condition is characterized by an "ever-widening gap between what we understand and what we think we should understand. It is the black hole between data and knowledge, and what happens when information doesn't tell us what we want or need to know" (Wurman, 1989, p. 34). In other words, we have a lot more information than in earlier times, but not necessarily more understanding. In campaigns, for example, politicians utilize complex statistics in support of ideological positions. For the most part, however, such statistics do little to explain complicated issues. In social networking sites there is no shortfall of opinion, but few ways to judge the credibility of contributors. Grabbing attention, therefore, is not the only thing communication design aims to do. Attention is only the first step toward informing, explaining, orienting, persuading, or supporting people in taking action. Design has to follow through on the promise of attention, to deliver on first impressions.

So how things look matters. If form fails to attract our attention or to make us feel that our attention is well deserved, there are plenty of other important stimuli fighting for our consideration. The first task for the communication designer, therefore, is to configure how things look, sound, or move in ways that compete effectively for human attention in an environment of information overload and that are consistent with the essential nature or goal of the communication. Unless designers are successful in this task, the content and value of the message will be lost.

But what kinds of form are likely to be effective in gaining attention and on what basis can designers make decisions among the many options for how things might look? What are the origins of assumptions about the attention-getting aspects of form and are they rooted solely in biology or also the product of culture and context?

Perceptual and cultural experience

The concepts discussed in this chapter straddle perceptual and cultural experience; that is, some are phenomena that are thought to be universally human regardless of people's experience of living in a specific place and time. Others are learned through living in a particular social world. For instance, we can argue that human response to figure-ground relationships (for example, recognizing a bear as separate from the field in which he stands) will be similar from person to person. Our brains are wired to distinguish objects from their backgrounds, especially when the object moves or exhibits extreme visual contrast with its surroundings. Does this mean, therefore, that the ability to determine *any* figure-ground relationship is a trait shared by all of humankind? Here, things become trickier.

If we take objects out of their normal context and consider them under various representational strategies, such as drawn or graphic form, is the interpretation so clear? In the case of the famous Rubin vase, our ability to identify the object depends on having seen Grecian vases and having been trained visually to read their abstracted form—that is, as a rendering of a three-dimensional object as a flat silhouette (Figure 3.1). Some people have little or no cultural experience with such objects or are limited in their exposure to Western visual frameworks. They are, therefore, unable to switch between seeing a vase and seeing two facing human profiles.

Science has attempted to describe the nature of attention and interpretation throughout modern history. At the beginning of the twentieth century, a branch of experimental science called *Gestalt psychology* tried to sort out what and how we perceive. Working in Germany in the years around the First World War, practitioners of the Gestalt movement proposed a set of principles through which we mentally construct *wholes from parts*. Proximity, constancy, similarity, and figure-ground, for example, describe general concepts that apply to our perceptions of visual elements, as well as motion and sound.

Max Wertheimer, a leading figure in the Gestalt movement, posed the question in relation to music: "Is it really true that when I hear a melody I have a sum of individual tones [parts] which constitute the primary foundation of my experience? Is not perhaps the reverse of this true… Instead, what takes place in each single part already depends upon what the whole is" (Wertheimer, 1924, p. 5). Wertheimer referred to our ability to interpret music as a cohesive melody rather than a series of distinct notes in a row. Similarly we experience a group of abstract marks—a circle, two dots, and a curved line—as a smiling face. We build complete and often more memorable wholes from isolated parts through the process of the perceptual association of elements.

But while the Gestalt psychologists were helpful in describing distinct perceptual phenomena, they were not as clear in explaining how such phenomena help us make sense of the world and construct meaning. In particular, they did not tell us much about how these principles interact or how context intervenes in our interpretations. For example, the Gestalt principle of similarity states that things that are similar are more likely to be perceived as related than things that are dissimilar. The principle of proximity suggests that objects close to one another tend to form groups. But which of these principles dominates when in combination, or when the structure of language and histories of meaning intervene?

Figure 3.1
Rubin vase
Edgar Rubin
(1886–1951)
This drawing is based on a set prepared in 1915 by Rubin, a Danish psychologist, to illustrate the ambiguity of figure-ground relationships. The drawing presents two possible interpretations (a vase or two faces in profile) but the viewer can only maintain one reading at any given time because the black and white shapes share a bounding contour.

For example, the Gestalt principle of proximity allows us to perceive a square within a square at the top of Figure 3.2. The closeness of the grouped elements in the inner square tells us they have a relationship that is different from their relationship with the elements in the outer square, even though all elements are equal in size. Further, we do not perceive the circle elements as a separate whole from the square elements; obvious groupings are established by distance alone, not by similarity. In the square on the bottom, however, rectangular and circular typographic elements (now the letters H and O) are spaced in the same way as elements in the original composition at the top. The red type and our cultural knowledge of Santa's "Ho, Ho, Ho!" override the effects of proximity with regard to our attention. Color choices further reinforce the Christmas association. Our attention, therefore, is drawn to a message defined by similarity (in color), the structure of language, and our past cultural experience, despite the proximity characteristics of the composition. We move through the composition on the bottom differently from our path through the composition at the top and we assign meaning to that path.

The concepts described in Chapter 3, therefore, connect abstract perceptual phenomena and principles to the attention-getting task of communication design and distinguish how their effects relate to the surrounding context. The discussions are organized around several issues, although they clearly overlap in application. The first group of phenomena describes the role *contrast* plays in the attention-getting properties of design. The second group addresses how we make judgments about *size* and the differences between actual measurements and our perceptions of size. The third group focuses on the role *space* plays in assigning importance to elements in the visual field. And the last group concerns *movement* and holding attention across *space and time*. All contribute to form that attracts attention in an environment of information overload, but they do it in different ways.

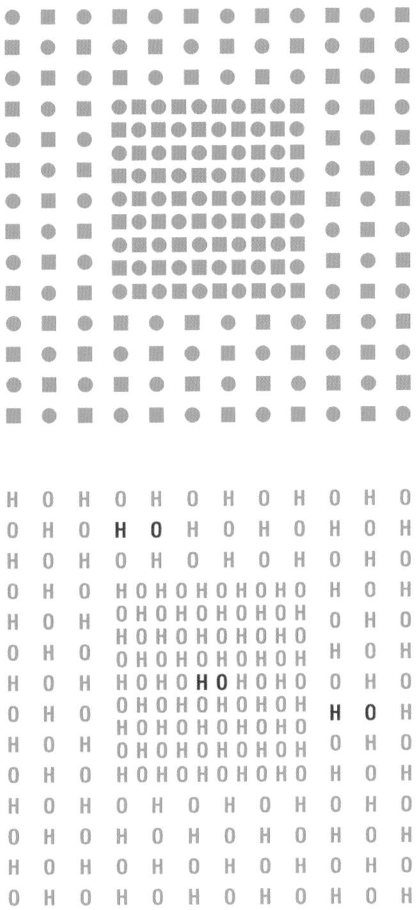

Figure 3.2
Interaction among Gestalt principles
The Gestalt principle of proximity creates the perception of two squares in each composition, solely on the basis of the distances among elements. In the image on the bottom, the principle of similarity dominates proximity relationships in getting viewers' attention. The red letters are read as a "whole," despite groupings based on distance. The cultural associations of color and phrase with the holidays reinforce the dominance of HO!HO!HO!

CONTRAST

Contrast is established by difference; there is no contrast unless there are at least two things to compare, even if one of those things is simply the background on which the other sits. Contrast intensifies the individual properties of the things being compared: black versus white, big versus small, rough versus smooth, moving versus stationary. It influences the order in which we see things and the importance we assign to them.

Through contrast, we allocate attention to some things over others; the degree of visual difference heightens or lessens our ability to distinguish between a message and its environment and between message elements and other objects in the visual field. What grabs our attention depends on how much difference there is between something and its surrounding context, not just whether something is big or small. When everyone screams, it is the quiet person who is noticed.

We are naturally wired to detect contrast. Our survival depends on recognizing those things that are unexpected in an otherwise undifferentiated environment. Something that moves in the forest is to be feared or seen as prey. We hide by "blending into the background," by not distinguishing ourselves by visual features or behaviors that contrast with our surroundings.

Our attention is also drawn to things that do not seem to fit conceptually with other elements in the scene. Studies of eye movement, for example, show that the greatest number of fixations (places where our eyes stop moving around a picture and rest on something in particular) occur in the areas of the picture that are least predictable (Spoehr & Lehmkuhle, 1982). A tiger in a barnyard of farm animals,

for example, draws more attention than other animals, not just because it is fierce but because it contrasts with the animals we expect to see on a farm (Davis, 2012). We view such conceptually different elements as informative because we seek a reason for them being present with more predictable elements of the message. We perceive the contrast as meaningful.

In gaining audience attention, designers must first separate messages from an environment of information overload. With too many things competing for our attention, important messages must be distinct from the visual or sound qualities of the surrounding conditions. Do you have trouble locating your favorite breakfast cereal on the supermarket shelves? Think about the visual qualities necessary for packaging to stand out in this visually cluttered aisle. Bright colors, big type, and a frantic layout certainly won't be enough (Figure 3.3). On the other hand, a bright and dynamic arrangement of big type can draw our attention to an otherwise unexceptional building in an industrial section of town (Figure 3.4). Getting attention does not depend on the visual properties of the message alone, but instead, on the contrast between the properties of the message and its perceptual context.

**Figure 3.3, below
Contrast**
Standing out has less to do with the visual properties of the element or object than with its relation to everything around it. Getting attention depends on contrast with the surrounding visual field. Contrast among too many elements and nothing stands out.

**Figure 3.4, right
MoMA QNS, 2002
Michael Maltzan
Architecture
Photography:
Christian Richters**
The oversized signage identifies the Museum of Modern Art in industrial Queens, New York.

face-width	extended	roman	oblique	condensed	oblique condensed	ultra condensed
light		Univers 45	Univers 46	Univers 47	Univers 48	Univers 49
regular	Univers 53	Univers 55	Univers 56	Univers 57	Univers 58	Univers 59
bold	Univers 63	Univers 65	Univers 66	Univers 67	Univers 68	
weight black	Univers 73	Univers 75	Univers 76			

Figure 3.5
Univers type family, 1957 release
Adrian Frutiger (1928–2015)
Frutiger's systematic design of the Univers type family includes forty-four different variations that allow designers to achieve both subtle and dramatic contrasts among information units. The first digit in the typeface number indicates weight and the second digit refers to face-width. The completeness of the system makes it possible to establish a clear hierarchy among elements without sacrificing the harmony gained by using a single type family.

Figure 3.6
Exocet typeface, 1991
Jonathan Barnbrook
For Emigre Foundry
Unlike other typefaces that create harmony through similarity among the twenty-six characters of the alphabet, Barnbrook's design maximizes the contrast in certain letterforms. When set in paragraphs, the typeface creates random patterns of emphasis.

Designers also use contrast to direct audience attention to certain elements *within* messages to emphasize specific content or to signal where in the composition to begin the interpretive task. Used sparingly, contrast establishes hierarchy. It tells us where to look first, second, and third. In a word-processing application, for instance, we are able to use simple but effective differences in type weight (bold or light), posture (italic or Roman), or even underlining to draw the reader's attention or emphasize particular words.

Variations within type families (in weight, proportion, or posture) and changes in type size allow designers to differentiate groupings of content. The goal of late modernist typography, for example, was to communicate with maximum clarity the author's hierarchy among units of information. A quote was to look different from a headline. Annotations in the margin were to be different from and less important than the primary text. Modernist type families designed in the middle of the twentieth century assisted designers in this task through carefully articulated levels of contrast among the typeface variations in the family. Bold type attracted the eyes to keywords in an otherwise light block of text. Italics identified captions or subheads by distinguishing them from other kinds of text by contrasting posture.

Adrian Frutiger's 1957 systematic design of the Univers type family, for example, ensured that contrast within typeset text could be achieved through an array of variations without sacrificing overall unity among typographic elements. Unlike many other type families, the height of lowercase letters (called x-height) set in Univers is the same across all typeface variations in the family. This standardization achieves harmony when members of the family are used together and emphasizes contrasting changes in weight or proportion by keeping height constant. And by designing many Univers typeface variations, Frutiger gave designers maximum flexibility in ways to create emphasis. While we might not detect the subtle difference between bold and regular in the same body of text, we will see contrast between bold and light (Figure 3.5).

Contrast is also important in establishing the visual characteristics of a single typeface across twenty-six letters. Typefaces are composed of very particular relationships between strokes and open spaces, thicks and thins, straight lines and curves. The degree of contrast among these parts of letterforms determines the texture of typeset text. Some typefaces maximize contrast (they sparkle), while others even out the distribution of black strokes and white spaces across the alphabet. *Bodoni*, for example, uses extreme contrast between thick and thin strokes to establish its visual character, while *Futura* has more uniform stroke widths and a consistent distribution of white space. Jonathan Barnbrook's *Exocet*, on the other hand, draws attention to very specific characters of the alphabet, using extreme contrast among individual letterforms to create random patterns within typeset text. The degree of contrast within typeset paragraphs influences how much of our attention those letters or paragraphs command in a composition (Figure 3.6).

EXOCET IS DESIGNED BY BRITISH DESIGNER, JONATHAN BARNBROOK

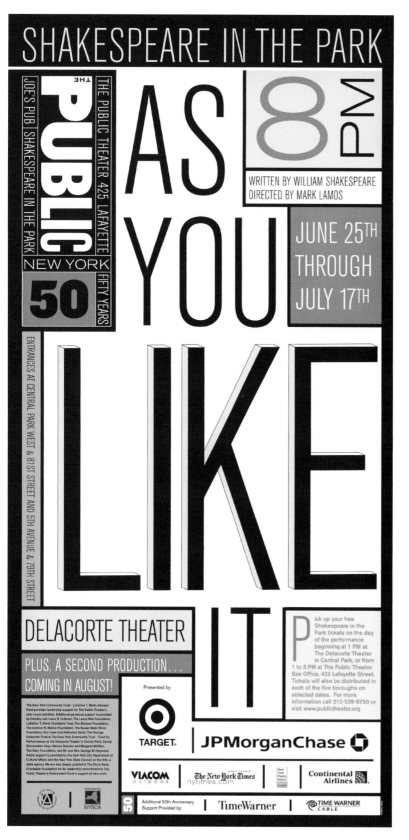

Under different philosophies, some designers use contrast to feature certain compositional elements over others in a clear hierarchy of importance, while other designers challenge whether design should suggest a single interpretation of the text. Paula Scher's poster for the Shakespeare in the Park Festival blows up type to cartoonish size to draw the viewer's attention to the simplicity of the phrase, "As you like it" and its importance as the title of a play (Figure 3.7). Katherine McCoy's poster advertising a college design program, on the other hand, treats all typography equally, reinforcing the contradictory nature of words in the text. The lack of contrast in McCoy's work produces no obvious visual hierarchy among elements, consistent with a theory of design that no single interpretation is possible (Figure 3.8).

Figure 3.7
Public Theater /
Shakespeare in the Park
/ As You Like It, 2012
Paula Scher
Contrasting size, color, and orientation in the typography control what readers see first and interpret as most important.

Figure 3.8, opposite
Cranbrook Academy
of Art Design poster,
1989
Katherine McCoy
Postmodern work of the 1980s and 1990s rejected the notion of a clear visual hierarchy that leads to a single interpretation. Typography and images struggled for dominance, consistent with the theory that there are many possible meanings and that the reader "writes" the text.

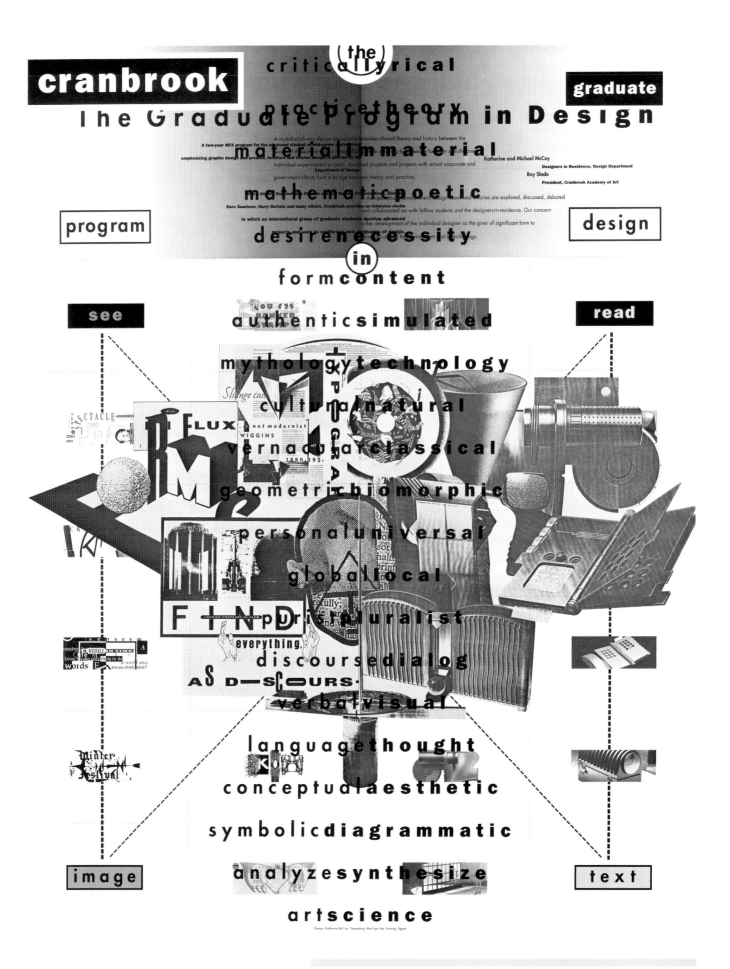

Contrast is important in determining emphasis among and within images as well as text. In a mostly black-and-white composition, color draws our attention. We notice organic forms when surrounded by geometry, typographic forms when surrounded by photography (Figure 3.9). In a line drawing of an object, contrast in line weight tells us what features are most important or serve a similar function (Figure 3.10).

Contrast, therefore, is an important attribute in gaining attention. It is a means through which designers emphasize what is important in a composition and how the meanings among various elements differ.

Figure 3.10
Line weight variations
Contrasting line weights
in a drawing assign
emphasis to particular
features of the drawing.
It is important to be
consistent in the use of
lines so that random
changes in weight don't
appear meaningless.

FIGURE-GROUND

Figure-ground refers to our ability to separate elements, based on contrast, into an object and a background. A figure can be any object, person, shape, or sound. Ground is the limitless background or field on which figures sit. Our visual system interprets objects primarily in terms of their contours. Figure-ground reversal occurs when two shapes share the same edge and we switch our attention from one shape to the other, trying to separate the figure from the ground.

Figure 3.11, below
Figure-ground
Humans are perceptually wired to detect the difference between an object and its background.

Figure 3.12, below right
Figure-ground orientation
When shapes share a horizontal contour boundary, there is less trouble in distinguishing figure from ground than in compositions where the shared contour boundary is vertical.

When we look at a painting on the white wall of a museum gallery, we have no difficulty focusing our attention on the painting. The artwork is the *figure* and the wall is the *ground*. This ability to separate the object of our attention from its surrounding environment develops very early in life—separating our mother's face from other stimuli, for example—and may have its origins in survival strategies, in our desire to be a hunter rather than prey. Whether distinguishing a lurking tiger from its lair in savannah grasses or identifying a mother's voice in the babble of a crowded subway, our perceptual system is built on a foundation of figure-ground distinctions.

In the photograph in Figure 3.11, the ground appears to extend beyond the edge of our vision—that is, beyond the frame of the image. There is content in the ground but we have little difficulty assigning it a role secondary to the figure (the ladybug) in the image. So although the photograph frames a discrete section of a much larger visual field, it is still possible to separate the figure from the ground. This perception is supported by studies showing that figures have more definite shapes and grounds are usually shapeless (Koffka, 1935). Figures are also perceived as being smaller and closer to the viewer in space than grounds (Koffka, 1935). And recent studies indicate that areas or shapes appearing in the lower portions of a composition are more likely to be perceived as figures than those appearing in other areas of the composition (Vecera, Vogel & Woodman, 2002) (Figure 3.12).

Motion also determines figure-ground relationships. Consider camouflage in the animal kingdom. As long as the animal remains stationary, its protective patterning and color allow it to merge with its environment; it is part of the ground. As soon as the animal moves and we detect its motion, it becomes a figure. This concept is useful in motion graphics and interaction design. Designers can direct users' attention through motion to particular locations in otherwise complex compositions, indicating the order in which to read information. It is also typical for interaction designers to use motion—for example, a flashing button—to tell users when the computer is waiting for an action.

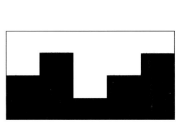

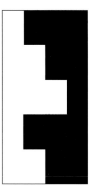

Visual compositions, therefore, often contain an object that appears to be complete—or nearly complete—and a background that is perceived to be around and behind the figure. When the object sits on an empty visual field, we often refer to the figure as *positive* and the ground as *negative space*. Communication designers sometimes refer to the ground in typography as *white space*, no doubt a reference to the white printing paper that sits beneath printed shapes (Figure 3.13).

Figure-ground relationships are fundamental to the design of logos, which must appear on a variety of complex surfaces in the application of corporate identity systems (Figure 3.14). Because it is easier to apply contained shapes than soft-edged or textured forms in many different formats at many different sizes, designers often reverse simple elements out of solid geometric or typographic shapes. The surface on which the logo sits frequently shows through as the negative space, unifying the form with its background. This strategy also economizes on the number of colors required to reproduce the identity and allows logos to be interpreted quickly.

Figure 3.13, above
Driekoningenavond,
De Theatercompagnie
poster, 2006
Experimental Jetset
Photography: Johannes
Schwartz
Figure-ground
relationships create
ambiguity about what
is object and what is
"white space."

Figure 3.14, right
National Aquarium in
Baltimore logo, 1980
Tom Geismar,
Chermayeff & Geismar
& Haviv
Logos make frequent
use of figure-ground
relationships to integrate
these simple shapes
with their backgrounds
and other elements.
Geismar's logo for the
aquarium refers to
water and sea creatures
through shapes that shift
from figure to ground.

ABCDEFGHIJKLMNO
PQRSTUVWXYZ
1234567890

H H H H H

E E E E

WALKER
WALKER-ITALIC

WALKER-UNDER
WALKER-BOTH
WALKER-OVER

Figure 3.15
***Kama Sutra* book cover,
sketch**
Malika Favre
Seeing the figures in
this image for a book
cover on the Kama
Sutra depends entirely
on shared contours and
figure-ground reversals.

Under certain circumstances the relationship of figure to ground can be unstable. This phenomenon occurs when the amount of space occupied by each is roughly the same and cropping makes the outer contour of the figure incomplete or shared equally with the ground. As a result, the viewer's attention shifts back and forth from one to the other. This unstable figure-ground relationship is called *aspect shifting*. Malika Favre's sketch for the cover of a book on the Kama Sutra depends on aspect shifting. Pairs of black and white figures emerge in the illustration through shared edges. Reading them as embracing couples requires shifting back and forth between the male and female figures (Figure 3.15).

Figure-ground relationships can be crucial to the readability and visual character of type design. Type designer Matthew Carter designs the whole space, the negative territory that surrounds the letterform as well as its positive strokes (Blauvelt, 2005). Carter's typeface for the Walker Art Center has been described as strokes interrupting the ground, an approach that is repeated in how the institution uses abstract pattern in combination with the typeface (Figure 3.16). Serifs, in Carter's type design, are often used to shape and expand the space between letterforms.

Therefore, an understanding of figure-ground is essential in directing audience attention. The relationship either draws our attention to appropriate content for audience consideration or creates a dynamic interplay between objects and their surroundings, which compels us to resolve conflicting visual interpretations.

WALKER

ABCDEFGHIJKLMNOP
QRSTUVWXYZ

ROMAN
REGULAR
OVER
UNDER
BOTH

ITALIC
REGULAR
OVER
UNDER
BOTH

1234567890$¢%
.,:;!?'"''()[]{}\|×+-—#^~*@⟨→⟩

*"I THINK OF THEM RATHER LIKE STORE WINDOW MANNEQUINS
WITH GOOD BONE STRUCTURE ON WHICH TO HANG MANY
DIFFERENT KINDS OF CLOTHING."*

Figure 3.16
Walker typeface, 1994
Matthew Carter
Carter's typeface for
the Walker Art Center
offers a number of
variations. It uses
"snap-on" serifs that
attach to the bold sans
serif at the designer's
discretion, creating new
shapes in the negative
spaces. In a 1995 article
in *Eye Magazine* titled,
"The Space between
Letters," Walker design
director Andrew Blauvelt
described the font as "a
revision of modernist
typography insofar as it
focuses attention on the
space between letters,
words, and lines of text."

COLOR

Color is the quality of an object perceived when wavelengths within the visible spectrum of light interact with receptors in the human eye. It is defined by three main attributes: hue, value, and saturation. Hue is the dominant wavelength in the color—for example, red, blue, green, yellow, etc. Value refers to how light or dark the color is. Saturation describes how intense the color is, ranging from the pure hue to gray.

Color is a primary means through which designers establish contrast and character in design. It often distinguishes elements among those that have many other attributes in common (Figure 3.17). In doing so, it can direct attention to specific elements within larger structures, thus establishing relationships that would not be apparent were all elements the same hue, value, or saturation.

Part science, part alchemy, and part emotion, color has been described in many ways. We process it physiologically, cognitively, psychologically, and culturally, forming our interpretations through unpredictable applications of these various perspectives. We perceive red and green of similar value and saturation, for example, as vibrating when used in equal amounts, but they are also culturally linked to Christmas. Many people feel serene in cool-colored rooms, while warm-colored interiors are cheery and thought

to stimulate conversation. Red signifies danger in one culture and good fortune in another. To complicate matters, context influences color. We perceive color as the color *of something*, in a setting, and never in its pure state. We might be comfortable wearing a pink shirt but not driving a pink car. And flowers look one way in a sunlit field and another in a vase in the shade.

Despite these complexities, there are some facts about which we agree. In one sense, things in the world do not really have color; what we perceive are differences in light, either reflected off the surface of objects (such as a printed poster) or emitted from a light source itself (such as a computer monitor). Software systems express color in three ways: CMYK, RGB, and PMS (Figures 3.18–3.20). Reflected or *subtractive color*, as produced in offset or inkjet printing, results from CMYK (standing for cyan, magenta, yellow, and black, the process pigments

Figure 3.17
The Fifty State Strategy. **Poster for Barack Obama's 2008 Presidential campaign Michael Bierut/ Pentagram Design**
Bierut's poster separates tightly spaced names by color. Because the colors are equal in value and saturation, no single state dominates another in the alphabetical listing.

The Fifty State Strategy, 2008.

through which other colors are made by overlapping printed screens of the four colors at various percentages). Projected or *additive color*, as displayed in computer monitors or through LCD projectors, results from RGB (standing for red, green, and blue, the primary color wavelengths that produce white light). A third system, *Pantone Matching System* (PMS), mixes pigments or inks other than the CMYK process colors used in printing reflected color. There are hundreds of PMS colors, each with an individual color formula.

Hue is the named color in its purest state (red, blue, yellow, green, etc.) and depends on its dominant wavelength. The purest hue is produced by only one wavelength. *Value* is the lightness or darkness of a color. Variations in value are sometimes called *tints* (light) and *shades* (dark) of the hue. When mixing colors in pigment, value is controlled by adding white or black to the pure hue. In printing, changes in value can be achieved by using different ink colors (PMS), by screening the color to reveal the white paper beneath the ink, or by overlaying the color with a dot screen of black. In digital screen-based work, value depends on the level of illumination and is expressed in percentages.

Saturation is the brightness or dullness of a color along a continuum from the pure hue to gray. It is sometimes called *intensity* and depends on the presence of another color in the hue. In pigments, we control saturation by adding the opposite of the hue on the color wheel. Blue added to orange or red added to green, for example, dulls or grays the intensity of the original hue. Four-color (CMYK) printing simulates these pigment mixtures by overlapping dot screens of the primary colors of cyan, magenta, and yellow. We "mix" these colors through our eyes and brain. In digital screen-based work, saturation depends on how much of the light is distributed across different wavelengths.

Artists and designers manipulate hue, saturation, and value to produce different perceptual effects. As a result, color is *relational*. Our perception of any single color and its attention-getting qualities are influenced by its properties in juxtaposition with the other colors surrounding it. Bauhaus artist Josef Albers demonstrated the relational qualities of color in a series of experiments summarized in his book, *Interaction of Color*. In one famous example, Albers illustrated that one color can appear as two, depending on its background (Figure 3.21).

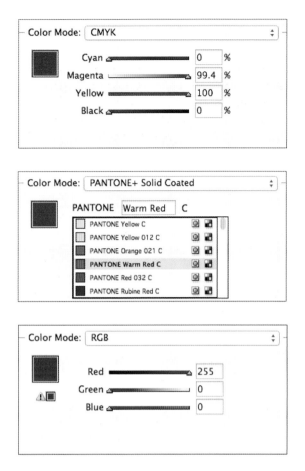

Figure 3.18
CMYK process color
In offset printing, color is achieved through four-color process inks: cyan, magenta, yellow, and black (CMYK). Color photographs are separated into varying percentages of these colors and printed in a rosette pattern of dots. Non-photographic areas of color are also built from CMYK screens.

Figure 3.19
Pantone Matching System (PMS) color
In offset printing, individual ink colors mixed according to specific formulas are an alternative to CMYK process colors. There are hundreds of PMS colors and they can be printed in solids and tints. PMS color may be simulated in CMYK, but it is not used to produce natural looking color in photographs. Laser output converts PMS colors to CMYK for printing.

Figure 3.20
RGB color
In light, the primary colors are red, green, and blue. When combined in equal amounts, they produce white light. RGB color is used for screen-based or projected light.

Figure 3.21, left
Interaction of Color
Based on studies by Josef Albers
Albers's Bauhaus color studies are memorialized in a book titled *Interaction of Color*. The orange squares are identical but appear different, depending on the background color. Differences are less apparent in the thin strokes of typography, with the orange type also vibrating on its blue complement.

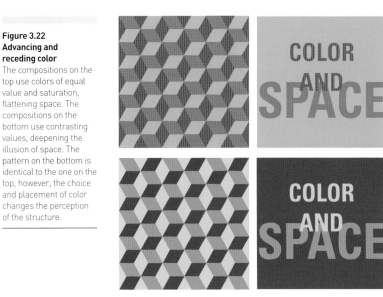

Figure 3.22
Advancing and receding color
The compositions on the top use colors of equal value and saturation, flattening space. The compositions on the bottom use contrasting values, deepening the illusion of space. The pattern on the bottom is identical to the one on the top, however, the choice and placement of color changes the perception of the structure.

Color effects make some elements appear to advance and others to recede (Figure 3.22), determining what messages grab our attention in a given context and the order in which we see or assign importance to certain elements within the message. A bulletin board announcement printed on colored paper is most likely to earn our attention if all of the others are printed on white bond. In a composition of mostly neutral colors (grays, black, and white) our attention typically goes to the colored element, over and above the attention-getting properties of other elements (for example, size or complexity). Like the previous example of the breakfast cereal aisle in the supermarket, however, complex color schemes—with too many colors of similar value or saturation—often reduce our perception of hierarchy among the elements.

Design professor Dennis Puhalla studied the role of color in readers' assignment of importance among groupings of textual information in PowerPoint presentations. Controlling the effect of other variables—such as the size and location of type and the content of the message— Puhalla found that hue had little or no influence on what readers thought was the most important information in the display (Puhalla, 2005). The only exception was the color red, which carried strong cultural connotations— such as "danger" and "emergency"—that interfered with purely perceptual decisions. Instead, contrast in value and saturation (between the element and its background and between the element and other elements) determined which information readers assigned the most importance.

Colors with little contrast appear to reside at the same depth in space. Brighter or lighter colors on dull or dark backgrounds appear closer, regardless of other spatial cues, such as overlapping forms or high versus low placement in the visual field (Figure 3.23). When shapes

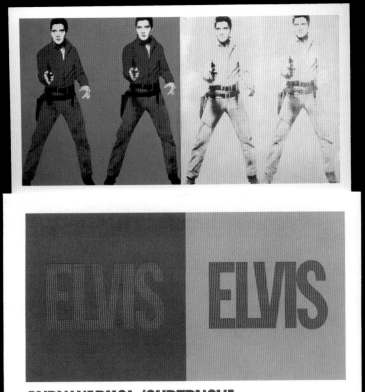

Figure 3.23, left and opposite
Andy Warhol/ Supernova: Stars, Death, and Disaster 1962–1964
Walker Art Center Studio, Scott Ponik
This catalog for an exhibition of work by Andy Warhol has six different variations that reflect the colors of the artist's multiple silk-screen prints. The complementary color combinations vibrate because they are equal in saturation.

share boundaries and are similar in their saturation they compete for attention, exhibiting some of the aspect shifting mentioned in the discussion of figure-ground. Obvious differences between the values or saturation of the two colors reduce this instability. In the art direction of photography, for example, choices about surrounding color can emphasize qualities of the objects being photographed (Figure 3.24).

Color can also signify some meaningful relationship among elements. Wayfinding systems identify buildings or rooms in vastly different locations through signs of the same color, thus marking them as belonging to the same organization. We navigate by looking for the identifying color as a contrast to other kinds of signs. It is generally understood, however, that people have little memory for complex color-coding systems—for example, that yellow signs in an art museum lead to contemporary British works, while blue signs direct visitors to objects from the ancient world—and that signage should reinforce color designations with language.

Figure 3.24
Heston Blumenthal at Home, 2011
Art Direction and Design: Graphic Thought Facility
Photography: Angela Moore
Color is important in the art direction of photography. The color in the background of these cookbook photographs provides a strong contrast to the food. The color of the cookware complements the natural ingredients that are the subject of photography.

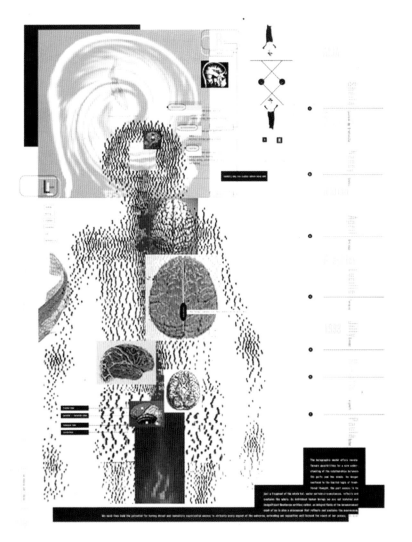

Figure 3.25
**AIGA communication
graphics poster, 1993
April Greiman**
Greiman's poster uses
color to designate the
gender of speakers
(in the column on the
right). In general, male
designers dominated
in professional design
presentations and
conferences of the time,
despite the large number
of women in the field.
Greiman foregrounds
the presence of women
as speakers.

Likewise, we presume that elements of the same color in a single message have some relationship not shared with other elements in the composition. In April Greiman's poster for AIGA, all but one of the speakers listed on the right are women (Figure 3.25). Contrasting color (pink and blue) groups women and men, and foregrounds gender participation at a time when women were a small minority of the organization's membership. Had Greiman printed the names of all speakers in the same color, the issue of gender would have been absent from the message.

Typography presents particular challenges for the use of color and contrast. Swatches of color read differently from the alternating strokes and spaces of type. Because the background surrounds thin lines of type, the color is less assertive than in broader areas of color (Figure 3.21). Dark colored text type, for example, tends to appear even darker on a white background than in a swatch. Contrast is maintained, but with a less distinct color presence than if shown in a more expansive shape. Accordingly, the color in light type weights will be less noticeable than color in bold type weights, which have more surface area exposed. Type in a color complementary to its background color (for example, red on green) tends to vibrate unless the levels of contrast in value and saturation are carefully controlled. Type that exhibits extreme contrast with its background tends to advance, while low contrast type recedes, often even in the presence of contradictory spatial cues such as overlapping form. These qualities determine which among various typographic elements command our attention.

Iona Inglesby is interested in the intersection between design and science. Her Dot One project takes DNA profiling out of the lab and into the world of design. An algorithm translates an individual's unique genetic DNA into one-of-a-kind color patterns, which Inglesby applies to a variety of formats (Figure 3.26). The author's DNA generated the color pattern on the cover of this book. Inglesby's application of technology is consistent with current interest in data-driven form in both art and science.

Adobe maintains an internet application called *Adobe Color*, formerly called *Kuler*, through which participants name and share favorite color schemes. Each color scheme is composed of five colors and many show examples in application. The system allows users to manipulate values and saturation to see effects (see http://kuler. adobe.com). Regardless of the software, exploring the same composition in different color combinations—with different results for the hierarchy among elements—is a useful strategy when developing ideas.

Color is often one of the most powerful attention-getting attributes of visual communication. It can define the location of elements in space, signal the importance of some elements over others, and express emotion.

Figure 3.26
DNA personalized prints
DNA personalized scarf
Dot One, 2015
An algorithm converts
the 0.1 percent of human
DNA that is unique
to individuals to color
patterns that are then
applied to textiles and
other surfaces (including
the cover of this book).
Dot One provides DNA
kits and returns printed
items to customers.
This strategy reflects
increasing interest in
the generation of visual
form from data.

SIZE CONSTANCY

Size constancy is our mental ability to make sense of the approximate size and scale of objects, even when visual evidence suggests alternate interpretations. Constancy requires that a number of visual cues be present in order to accurately interpret what we see. In the case of a human figure walking toward us in the distance, the consistency between the figure and the diminished size of other objects surrounding the figure allow us to calibrate our perceptual assumptions against that body of evidence; we do not perceive the figure to be a tiny human.

A small visual trick: look at your face in a mirror within arm's reach (Figure 3.27). Without moving your position, reach out and trace with a marker on the mirror's surface the outline of your face. Then measure and compare the dimensions of the outline you traced to those of your face. Despite the fact that you have lived your entire life assuming that the mirror image is identical in size to your own face, it is in fact, substantially smaller. The Gestalt principle of size constancy allows you to adjust your perceptual estimation of size in the mirror to conform to your understanding of real dimensions.

In the fifteenth century, Renaissance artists and engineers devised a revolutionary system of geometrical relationships and vanishing points, called *linear perspective*, for rendering objects and landscapes with optical consistency. This logical but artificial system is in contrast to other ways of communicating depth—for example, by simply overlapping objects or assigning vertical locations to objects within the picture plane, strategies we find in many traditional art forms. Because the system is consistent with both our perceptual and cultural experience—that things diminish proportionally in size as they approach the horizon line—we accept such representations of diminishing size in pictorial form as *natural*.

Without the intermediary evidence of surrounding objects or distorted scale relationships, however, the scene is potentially more confusing and the relationships among the elements in the picture plane are more dramatic (Figure 3.28). In other words, inconsistency with the typical perceptual experience attracts more attention. In his poster for the Swiss Automobile Club, designer Josef Müller-Brockmann heightened the viewer's sense of

Figure 3.27
Image in the mirror
The Gestalt principle of size constancy allows viewers to perceive an image in the mirror as actual size rather than smaller than reality.

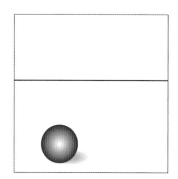

Figure 3.28
Size constancy
The ability to maintain an understanding of the size of an object across distances depends on making comparisons to known objects. There is no reference in the image on the top against which to estimate the size of a rolling red ball. In the image on the bottom, general knowledge of the dog makes possible judgment about the size of the ball, even when moving and changing its size within the picture frame.

protégez l'enfant !

disorientation through an interruption of size constancy (Figure 3.29). Is this a giant motorcycle or a really tiny child? Is there enough space between the two for the motorcycle to stop? Without other objects or additional information regarding the content of the background (does it represent the road or the horizon line of the landscape?) we lack the spatial context necessary to make judgments about distance. The designer, therefore, gives us the momentary perspective of the bystander, who worries whether the cyclist can adjust his speed before closing the gap between the bike and the child.

Communication designers, therefore, use size constancy to reinforce seemingly natural juxtapositions among elements of a composition or to eliminate contextual cues, thus gaining attention by destabilizing normal judgments about scale.

Figure 3.29
"Protect the Child"
Swiss Automobile Club
poster, 1953
Josef Müller-
Brockmann (1914–1996)
© DACS 2016
In this poster, the absence of information in the landscape creates anxiety regarding the distance between the motorcycle and the child. The bystander (the viewer) cannot judge at first whether there is sufficient distance to reduce speed and avoid an accident.

SCALE

Scale is a proportional relationship between the size of something and the sizes of other things. We often make sense of the world around us, both consciously and unconsciously, by testing how things size up to human form.

While size constancy involves an adjustment we make in our perception of things—a mental judgment of the size of something despite conflicting visual evidence—scale is a means for comparing measurements. We determine that the size of a model is one quarter the size of the actual object it represents or that the vertical proportions of a building can be expressed in increments that correspond to the height of the average man.

Unexpected scale relationships are effective in gaining attention for environmental applications. In 1996, Doyle Partners commemorated the seventy-fifth anniversary of the passing of the nineteenth amendment by applying the text of the law in eight-foot letters (9,276 point type) on the marble floor of the waiting room in Grand Central Station in New York City (Figure 3.30). Passersby read the one-sentence amendment, granting women the right to vote, as they walked to and from the station on their way to work each day.

Similarly, Bruce Mau's 2006 exhibition at the Museum of Contemporary Art in Chicago, titled *Massive Change*, challenged audiences to think about sustainable design through typography and image collections that exceeded the usual discrete labeling and display techniques of

Figure 3.30
Nineteenth amendment, Grand Central Station, New York, 1994
© Doyle Partners
In commemorating the seventy-fifth anniversary of the nineteenth amendment to the United States Constitution, which gave American women the right to vote, Doyle Partners applied the text of the amendment in 9,276 point type to the floor of Grand Central Station. The terminal has forty-four train platforms, more than any other station in the world.

art museums (Figure 3.31). Audiences confronted the excess of modern living through the sheer number of images and entered and left the galleries through a big, overarching question (literally) about the future. Rather than a few enlarged photographs that occupied the space, audiences saw a plethora of photo-album sized images that dominated by their sheer number; the scale of the images was small but together they made a big impression.

Figure 3.31
Massive Change
exhibition, Museum of Contemporary Art, Chicago, 2005
Bruce Mau Design
Mau's exhibition, and the companion book, explored how design methods could be used to solve problems at the level of social, political, environmental, and economic systems. The exhibition not only inhabited large gallery spaces, but the sheer number of average-sized photographs expressed the value of working at a variety of scales on issues of sustainability.

April Greiman's 8,200 square foot media installation on buildings in Koreatown, Los Angeles uses the enormous scale of a hand and rice bowl to contrast with the street-level distraction of Wilshire Boulevard. In this case, unnatural scale relationships attract attention and communicate the cultural content of the area (Figure 3.32). The over-scaled photography in the landscape is reminiscent of photomontages in early twentieth-century work.

James Langdon faced a scale challenge in his design for an exhibition of Tony Arefin's graphic design work (Figure 3.33). Graphic design objects are typically small and can be overwhelmed by gallery walls. Langdon grouped publications on color-blocked horizontal surfaces, creating a bigger impression than would have been possible by simply hanging objects on white walls, but also maintaining the intimacy of printed books. A large typographic panel anchors the space.

Figure 3.32, above
Koreatown technology wall, 2007
April Greiman
Located at the intersection of Wilshire and Vermont in Los Angeles, Greiman's technology wall on the building by Arquitectonica frames the entrance to the subway station in Koreatown. At 8,200 square feet, the image of the rice bowl was photographed in the area and overshadows the typical chaos of the urban street. The resulting streetscape becomes a photomontage of images at different scales.

Figure 3.33
The Graphic Design of Tony Arefin, 2012
Ikon Gallery, Birmingham, England
Curator: James Langdon
Photography: Stuart Whipps
Langdon's exhibition of Tony Arefin's work clustered small publications on color-blocked tables, massing form for a bigger impression. Langdon used typography on the walls to attract attention and provide a shift in scale.

The relative scale of elements to the overall size of the composition (as defined by its perimeter) influences how we interpret something. In Figure 3.34, the size of the hand tells us how large the spider is; the size of something we know (the hand) is compared to something that could be many different sizes (the spider). So in this case, scale tells us it is a very big spider. But because the top image enlarges the two objects to exceed the limits of the page, the spider is even more threatening, although the scale relationship between the spider and the hand is the same as in the bottom image. What has changed is not the scale relationship between the two objects, but the scale relationship between the objects and the visual field.

One important aspect of scale is that as the sizes of elements change, so do the internal relationships among their parts. This effect is called *scaling fallacy*; as elements scale up or down, not all relationships remain the same. For example, type can be reduced in size photographically. But doing so alters how strokes meet and the perception of stroke weight at these intersections. Similarly, the spacing between characters may not be optically even or readable when scaled up or down. Digital typefaces generally accommodate for this scaling problem in programming by *tracking* (adjusting the letterspacing overall) or by *kerning* (adjusting the spacing between selected letter combinations).

British type designer Matthew Carter created Bell Centennial as a typeface for the telephone book (Figure 3.35). Knowing that it would be printed at six points on highly absorbent paper, Carter drew letterforms that anticipated the spread of printer's ink. He notched the intersections of strokes (a technique called *ink traps*), increased the openness of counterspaces, and widened the gaps on tightly closed forms to make the letterforms legible at very small sizes.

Figure 3.34, top
Scale and the visual field
While the scale of one element to another is important in determining relative size, the scale of the element to the surrounding visual field is equally expressive. The spider in this illustration is more menacing when it fills the visual space. The relationship between the spider and the hand is the same in both illustrations but zooming in on the spider so it expands beyond the frame of the image makes it scarier. A similar effect can be seen in the typographic compositions.

Figure 3.35
Bell Centennial typeface, 1976
Matthew Carter
The internal relationships of strokes and counterspaces change as type is scaled to different sizes. Similarly, in printing on different surfaces the stroke width and spaces can change as ink bleeds into paper. Carter's design of Bell Centennial marked the 100th anniversary of AT&T and was designed to be legible at extremely small sizes, as in the telephone directory. Ink traps—notches cut into the intersections of strokes—accommodate ink bleed when printed.

At the other end of the size continuum, environmental graphics like those in New York's Times Square must account for reading at extreme distances and in competition with a very cluttered visual field. In environments such as this, bigger is better, and without enormous scale the elements would be lost in a cacophony of messages. Josh Goldstein's billboard for discount store Target functions at two scales (Figure 3.36). From a distance it reads as the company's corporate logo, dominating other messages in the city. Closer viewing shows the image is assembled from smaller signs found in New York's bodegas (corner stores).

It is such surprising scale juxtapositions (very small to very large) that attract viewers' attention. Scale is always a comparative relationship, not just among differently sized objects, but also in relation to our own size and position. Perception of scale, therefore, is an embodied experience.

Figure 3.36
Target in Times Square, 2009
Josh Goldstein
The scale of buildings and the chaos of the urban landscape easily overshadow signage and any individual message. Goldstein's Times Square installation for discount store Target displayed the company's familiar bullseye logo, constructed of hundreds of smaller signs from New York's bodegas—small stores selling a variety of items. An estimated 330,000 people pass through the intersection every day.

PROPORTION

As a noun, *proportion* refers to a consistent relationship among parts of a whole, regardless of its size. As an adjective, *proportional* or *in proportion* describes the quality of something that is harmoniously sized in relation to something else. And as a verb, *to proportion* something means to change its size without changing its *aspect ratio*, maintaining its height-to-width relationship without cropping it.

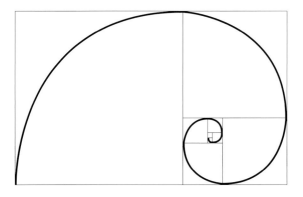

Proportional systems answer the question, "What size should I make this element?" At their most basic, proportional systems establish a set of parts-to-whole relationships that can be applied logically in making decisions about the sizes of elements and their associations with other elements in the composition. The goal is harmony, which is achieved when an element *does not stand out* by dimensions that are inconsistent with the aspect ratios of other elements. Instead, the dimensions of elements are not random or unique but are based on proportional relationships.

Proportional systems have been around for centuries and were used by various cultures as expressions of ideal beauty. Early measurement systems were based on the human body (hands, feet, and the length of a stride or arm reach). Natural forms also inspired proportional systems. The golden ratio or "divine proportion"—a shape based on the proportion of 1:1.618—can be found in

naturally occurring forms, such as the spirals of a nautilus shell (Figure 3.37). When a square is removed from the golden rectangle (a shape based on the 1:1.618 ratio), the remaining shape is another golden rectangle. In various ways throughout Western history, designers utilized this proportion to configure relationships among elements in fields as diverse as architecture and book design.

Social practice, too, can influence proportional design strategies. The floor plans of traditional Japanese houses are based on the tatami mat as a unit of measurement (Figure 3.38). One mat sleeps one person and multiple mats combine to form social groupings. The size of the mat dictates the distance between columns supporting the base of the house. In colonial American homes, builders determined the standard size of bricks by the average length of logs cut for fireplaces. Other materials follow suit; 4' × 8' sheets of plywood, for example, correspond in size to a row of adjacent bricks.

Figure 3.37, above
Golden Section
The Golden Section or Golden Rectangle is a form in which the ratio of the shorter side to the longer side is 1:1.618. Throughout the history of art and architecture, this proportional relationship has been seen as the most aesthetically pleasing.

Figure 3.38
Japanese tatami mats
Tatami is a type of mat used for flooring in traditional Japanese houses, originating as seating in aristocratic homes of the Heian period (794–1185). Although the size of the mat varies by region, the proportions of a room in a house are often determined by the mat as a unit of measurement.

Designers use proportional grid systems to organize typography and images within layouts. Grids describe columns, margins, and horizontal divisions of space that guide decisions about the size and placement of elements on the page. Grid modules are used singly or in combination, thus achieving harmony through common units of measurement and the visual alignment of elements (Figure 3.39).

Overly simple grids offer few alternatives for the diversification of form within the layout; a two-column grid, for example, presents designers with only two possible line lengths for text type, one of which is probably too long for readability at small point sizes (Figure 3.40). By contrast, a twelve-column grid suggests more possible line lengths and offers other typographic and graphic opportunities that add interest to the layout, such as a one-column indent at the start of paragraphs or alignments among figures in a complex financial chart. Combinations of equally sized columns achieve visual harmony among elements. Swiss designer Karl Gerstner memorialized the aesthetic merits of proportional grid systems in his book, *Designing Programmes*, in which he argued that the more elaborate the system, the greater the artistic freedom, but that all elements must be accountable to the same mathematical logic (Gerstner, 1964).

By defining formal possibilities through a system of proportionally related sizes, the grid also allows designers to code different types of information visually. The line length in a caption is different from the text of the major feature article. The space between baselines of type in a paragraph are half that of lines in a raised quote. Through such decisions, the proportional grid supports a hierarchy among elements on the page, directing attention to the most important elements first, while maintaining their ability to live harmoniously with other elements on the same page (Figure 3.41).

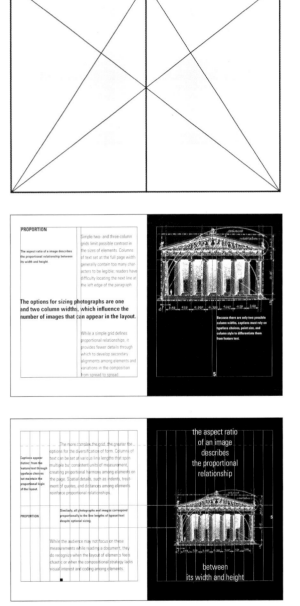

Figure 3.39
Layout grid for Penguin Books, 1940s
Jan Tschichold
(1902–1974)
German typographer Tschichold discussed the importance of proportion in *The Form of the Book*, referring to the relationship of text to margins in medieval manuscripts. The text area of the layout used the proportions of the Golden Rectangle.

Figure 3.40
Complex grids
Complex grids offer more opportunities for sizing photographs, text blocks, and graphic elements than do two- and three-column grids. This complexity allows designers to "code" elements by size or line length and to establish relationships through shared alignments. The grid maintains proportional unity through multiples of the same units of measurement.

Figure 3.41
Dwell Magazine, 2008
Design: ETC (Everything
Type Company)
Designers:
Brendan Callahan,
Suzanna LaGasa,
Ryan Gerald Nelson

The layouts of
contemporary magazines
are based on grids that
govern the size and
placement of typography
and images on the
page. Spreads in *Dwell
Magazine* vary in their
content from page to
page but maintain visual
continuity by recurring
proportional relationships
and typography.

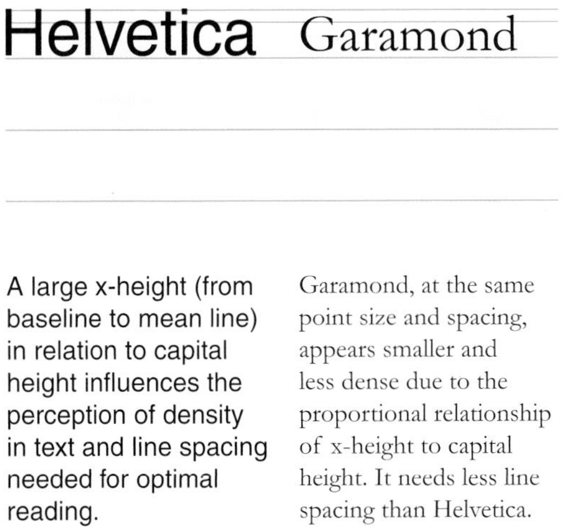

Helvetica Garamond

A large x-height (from baseline to mean line) in relation to capital height influences the perception of density in text and line spacing needed for optimal reading.

Garamond, at the same point size and spacing, appears smaller and less dense due to the proportional relationship of x-height to capital height. It needs less line spacing than Helvetica.

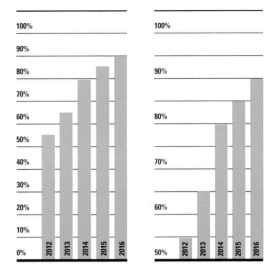

Figure 3.42
Type proportion
The proportional relationships in the design of a typeface determine its visual properties and legibility when set in blocks of text.

Figure 3.43
Proportional charts
These two charts are mathematically accurate equivalents, but they create very different perceptions of growth. The chart on the left plots gains from 0–100 percent, while the chart on the right uses 50 percent as the starting point. As a result of these proportional differences and despite the similar overall size of the two charts, gains appear more dramatic in the chart on the right.

The character of typeface design also relies on proportional relationships. The regular version of a typeface has a particular relationship of the lowercase letters (x-height) to uppercase letters and of strokes to counterspaces. These relationships distinguish one typeface from another. Helvetica looks larger than Garamond of the same point size because its lowercase letters are larger in proportion to its capital letters than in Garamond (Figure 3.42). Variations within a type family also offer differently proportioned versions. Condensed and expanded variations, for example, adjust the size of counterspaces (the open spaces enclosed by the strokes of the letterform) in order to alter the overall width of letterforms without changing the weight of the typeface. These variations are carefully calculated to allow designers to achieve recognizable contrast among different typographic characters but to maintain the proportional logic across the twenty-six letters of the alphabet.

Distorting these relationships has implications for interpretation. Software functions that allow designers to stretch typography or to manipulate the aspect ratio of photographs alter the aesthetic intent of the type designer and the veracity of the original image. They reconfigure the parts-to-whole relationships disproportionately to the original design.

Proportional distortions can also mislead. It has been reported that in the 1950s—at a time when owning a big automobile carried status—car manufacturers made the keyholes on automobile doors elliptical rather than round. Doing so made it possible for photographic lenses to optically stretch the length of the automobile. The resulting shape of the keyhole was round and the consumer was none the wiser that the photograph "enhanced" the actual length of the car. Similarly, some annual reports, through which stockholders make decisions to buy stock in particular companies, use financial bar charts that start at 50 percent rather than 0 percent. In this way, they exaggerate the differences among percentages or amounts in ways that favor the company. Both charts in Figure 3.43 are accurate in the relation of one bar to another, yet they create very different impressions of the company's ability to increase profits.

Sensitivity to the proportional relationships among elements is one of the ways in which professionally designed work differs from the work of amateurs. When elements respond to a proportional logic, they live comfortably with each other on the page or screen.

PROXIMITY

The Gestalt principle of proximity states that objects or elements that are close to one another appear to form groups, even when they are dissimilar in other ways. If elements overlap or touch, we assume they share something in common or have some conceptual affinity. If one element encloses another, we read this as a dependent or hierarchical relationship.

Composition is never neutral. We assign meaning to the order or position of objects within a visual field, even when they are abstract and lack literal content. We are likely to read elements that are close to each other in space or that share common distances among them as a group or constellation, and separate from other elements on the page (Figure 3.44). In this way, we assume some relationship that is important to our understanding of the message. Sussman/Prejza's logo design for the Museum of the African Diaspora uses proximity to represent the dispersal of people from Africa through slavery (Figure 3.45). Designer Abbott Miller's Swarm logo imitates the proximity behavior of bees (Figure 3.46).

The principle of proximity is particularly important in typographic compositions as it can either determine or undermine the traditional reading order of text. We expect words that are part of the same thought to be close to each other. When there is physical separation of words from other text in the composition, it draws our attention, provides emphasis, or distinguishes its subject from other content in the message.

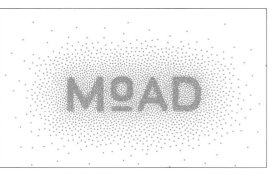

Figure 3.44, above
Proximity
The distances among people sitting on the steps of this building hint at the strength of relationships. Familiarity determines social proximity; strangers are kept at a distance while friends and family often enter personal space.

Figure 3.45, above right
Museum of the African Diaspora logo, 2005
Sussman/Prejza
The graphic identity for the Museum of the African Diaspora uses visual proximity to signify the migration of people from Africa to communities all over the world.

Figure 3.46
Swarm Logo
Imagery courtesy of Abbott Miller, Pentagram
Exhibition logo for Fabric Workshop and Museum, Philadelphia, Pennsylvania (2005)
This logo is autological; the word looks like what it means. The proximity of tiny figures that create letterforms is consistent with the closeness of insects in a swarm.

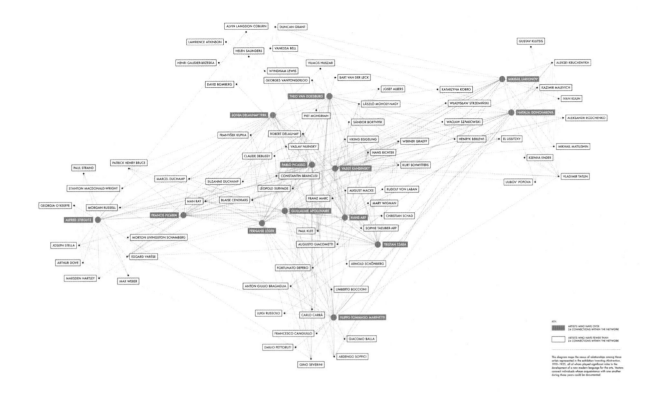

Proximity is equally important in representing the relative strength of relationships among elements. The distances we feel are comfortable between ourselves and family members are much smaller than with social acquaintances and strangers. Web-like diagrams use space to indicate the strength of the relationships among nodes (Figure 3.47). In the Museum of Modern Art website, *Inventing Abstraction*, artists and designers who were part of the Avant-Garde from 1901 to 1925 are connected in a web according to their personal relationships and shared philosophies.

The space between things, therefore, is meaningful. It defines and draws our attention to relationships over and above the meaning of elements themselves. We see significance in spatial patterns and make judgments about where to look on that basis.

Figure 3.47
***Inventing Abstraction*
website
Museum of Modern Art**
Image: The Museum of Modern Art website for its 2012–2013 exhibition *Inventing Abstraction*, 1910–1925, designed by Second Story. Pictured: Artist Network Diagram. The diagram was a collaboration between the exhibition's curatorial and design team and Paul Ingram, Kravis Professor of Business, and Mitali Banerjee, doctoral candidate, Columbia Business School. Contributors at MoMA were Allegra Burnette, Masha Chlenova, Hsien-yin Ingrid Chou, Leah Dickerman, Sabine Dowek, Jasmine Helm, Nina Léger, Jodi Roberts, and Catherine Wheeler. © 2016 The Museum of Modern Art, New York

The MoMA website, *Inventing Abstraction*, identifies connections among modern artists and designers. The proximate distance between nodes in the site tells users about the strength of the relationship between any two individuals.

FOCUS

Focus is the process of selectively concentrating on one aspect or central point of the visual environment while ignoring others. Our eyes focus by squeezing or stretching the lenses. We are physically capable of depth perception from birth, but the ability to interpret depth-related information changes over time.

Look through any screen door (Figure 3.48). You can see beyond the grid of lines to the outside or you can examine the mesh closely and objects in the scene outside become less distinct. Suppose a spider is moving across the screen. You concentrate on the spider and the screen behind it dissolves—it loses sharpness and detail. This instant spatial analysis of objects in the field of vision, close and far, is instinctual and happens so fast that it is almost unconscious. The change in focus accomplishes two important functions: it is one way in which people locate themselves in space and it actively narrows or selects the most significant elements from the general field of vision. In design, focus refers both to a property of the image (areas that have clearly defined edges) and to the viewer's selection of a particular view on content.

The eyes are like a zoom lens in their ability to rapidly change the field of focus. Focus helps us to distinguish a figure from its ground. Human eyes are also stereoscopic; we capture two images simultaneously through two lenses and what we "see" is the convergence of the two images. Our spatial awareness results from a rapid collection of many glances, which incorporate various angles and viewpoints. It is the relentless double-lens search across a scene for more views and information that separates our perception of reality from the conventions of photography.

The camera functions differently from the human eye. A photographic image is produced from a single lens, calibrated for a particular level of detail from a single viewpoint. It can focus near or far but not show detail equally well at all distances at the same time. While we experience the world through our eyes as constantly changing images from many points of view, our ability to detect detail at distances (if we have 20/20 vision) has less to do with focus than with the size of objects and atmospheric interference. On a clear day, our perception of the contour edge of the Rocky Mountains is sharp, even if we cannot see individual trees and rocks.

Filmmakers use focus to highlight objects, characters and their emotions, and actions that are important in moving the narrative forward. We anticipate an action that has yet to come. The camera focuses on the phone that will ring, the poison that will be consumed, the doorknob that will turn. In photography and film, the relationship between what is in focus and what is not is called *depth of field*. It tells us roughly where the viewer is positioned with respect to the overall setting. Are we close to the items in focus or viewing everything from a distance? Are we a participant in the scene or a spectator taking things in from afar? In dynamic media, objects may go in and out of focus as they create the illusion of moving forward or backward on the Z-axis of the screen. Focus in this sense is visual but it also tells us what to pay attention to in the image at particular times and what is important in interpreting the message (Figure 3.49).

Photographers, filmmakers, and illustrators make decisions about which areas of a scene's depth are sharp and which are less distinct, but not all communication involves single scenes and we have shifting needs met by one view of information over another. Presenting simultaneous views in the same layout overcomes the zooming limitations of print media. Much like the spider on the window screen, an inset map provides details not evident when looking at the larger map. At the same time, the inset allows us to locate the detailed view in its wider context. The inset may also better meet the needs of a pedestrian, while a driver finds the broader view more useful (Figure 3.50). Our understanding of other kinds of content benefits from more than one view. To understand the human circulatory system, we may need to see the

Figure 3.48
Focus
Focus is the center of interest. Viewers can focus on the spider or on the screen but not on both. Depth of field in photography is the distance between the nearest and furthest objects that are in focus.

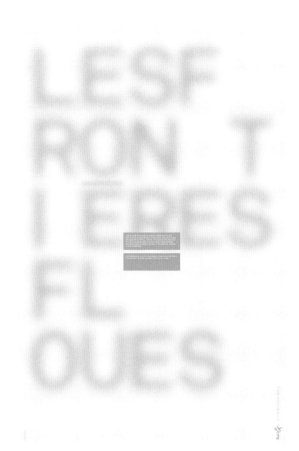

anatomy of the heart, but also its location in the body and its relationship to other organs. Shifting back and forth between multiple views in the same composition reveals connections not apparent in a single view.

In interactive media, the user zooms between views. We select the spatial viewpoint that best serves a particular purpose for narrowing the focus of attention. For example, we can locate a destination through satellite imagery of the neighborhood in *Google Maps*. But if we have never been to the site, zooming in to the street view assists us in finding the location by also showing the appearance of the building. An interactive information graphic by Catalogtree for *Popular Science* shows the increase in calculation processing speeds over time (Figure 3.51). The visualization allows users to toggle between two views of the same data and to filter the data according to various computing devices. The linear view shows development over time but the scatter diagram uses proximity to illustrate overlapping devices and accelerating development of processing speed.

Focus, therefore is not just an optical property of images but a conceptual shift on our part that places us in another spatial relationship with the subject of attention. Our attention zooms in and out of visual content as the interpretive task demands.

Figure 3.49
Les Frontières Floues (Blurring the Boundaries), 2007
Paprika
This exhibition poster uses depth of field in referring to the less obvious division between art and design.

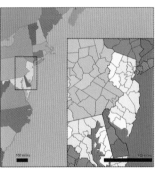

Figure 3.50
Map insets represent another kind of focus. Rather than a physical sharpening of information, the inset represents conceptual focusing on information at a closer range and in greater detail.

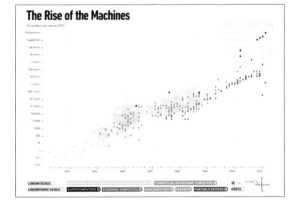

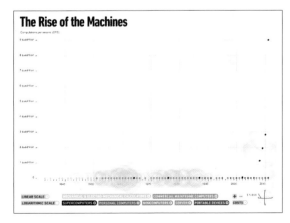

Figure 3.51
The Rise of the Machines, 2011
Popular Science
Design: Catalogtree
Realization: Systemantics
Research: Ritchie King
Catalogtree's design shows the increase in computational processing speeds from the earliest invention of mechanical calculators to today's portable digital devices. Users can focus on information at a linear or logarithmic scale, toggling between two views. Cost is reflected in the large bubbles.

LAYERING

Layering creates the illusion of depth in the two-dimensional picture plane, literally and metaphorically. Overlapping forms, illusions of transparency, sizes of elements, and locations within the picture plane create the perception of layers. In dynamic media, things can be layered in time. Elements can move between background and foreground along an imaginary Z-axis, passing in and out of time.

While messages typically take two-dimensional form, designers often create the illusion of depth through layering. Where things are positioned in the illusory depth of the picture space communicates their importance and expresses meanings associated with location. Designer Chip Kidd's cover for the book, *1Q84*, layers a translucent veil over the photograph of a woman's face (Figure 3.52). Author Murakami tells the story of a young woman who enters an unreal, imaginary world. Kidd's design translates the theme as a hardcover image of the woman covered by a translucent vellum book jacket that diffuses her face in a white, parallel existence. The typographic title switches from white type on the hardcover to unveiled portions of the woman's face on the jacket. The layered illusion is both material and metaphorical.

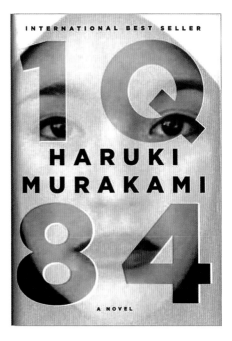

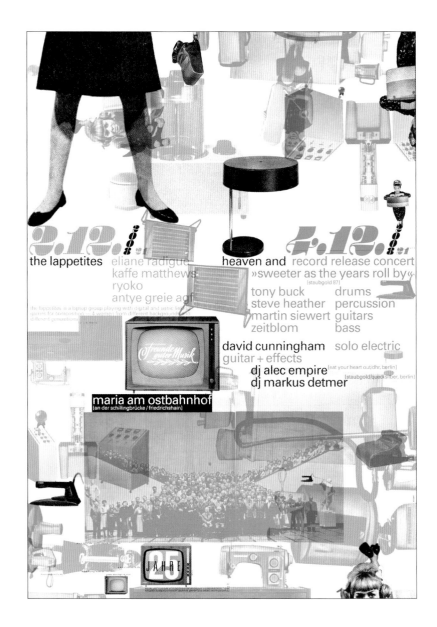

Figure 3.52
***1Q84* book cover, 2011**
Chip Kidd
Kidd's design for Haruki Murakami's story of a woman passing into an alternate reality, existing in two planes simultaneously, uses layering to describe the narrative. The text is printed on a translucent vellum book jacket, while the woman's face is printed beneath on the book's hard cover.

Figure 3.53
25 Jahre Freunde Guter Musik poster (Twenty-fifth Anniversary of Friends of Good Music), 2008
© Cyan Berlin
The poster by Cyan uses transparency to layer a collection of everyday household appliances from the past. Color establishes a visual hierarchy among the items and typographic elements, deepening the illusion of space and keeping the composition from becoming an overall pattern.

We perceive things that are closest to us as more important, more recent, or more aggressive than things in the distance. They demand our attention. Things that appear as transparent overlays are elusive, ethereal, or transitory. These meanings result from both our physical and cultural experiences. For most of us, the past is "behind us" and the future is "ahead." But in other cultures, the past is what we can see—what is known and in front of us—and the future is yet to be seen. In this sense, the illusion of layers is an *embodied* concept that has much to do with our own physical location in space; we attach cultural significance to these positions (Figure 3.53).

Layering can override other spatial cues. For example, we generally think that smaller things are farther away in space than things that are large. Several words set in different point sizes, for example, could be perceived as close or far based solely on their sizes. Absent of any other cues—such as overlap, focus, or color—we judge distance by the size of letters and placement in vertical space. But by layering one word on top of another, the smallest type moves forward, overriding the other positional cues (Figure 3.54).

The development of design software, such as Adobe Photoshop and Illustrator, made it simpler to layer elements than under photomechanical processes of the past. Prior to design software, images were layered photographically in the darkroom through sandwiched negatives, overprinting (one ink on top of another), or reversing out of one image and printing back with another. These were complicated processes that were often unconvincing. The spatial complexity of work since the 1990s is due, in large part, to the layering capacity of technology. It represents a contrast to mid-twentieth-century approaches to imagery, which frequently used flat geometric shapes or simple overlapping elements that could be silhouetted easily.

The design firm 2x4 uses layering to create a surprising union between historical artwork in the Isabella Stewart Gardner Museum collection and contemporary visitors, interpreting the campaign theme of "Art Comes to Life" (Figure 3.55). In this example, attention is drawn to a "not so perfect" assemblage that, on the surface, appears to be a complete whole. This is not simply an attempt to increase the illusion of depth in the two-dimensional surface of the posters, but a deliberate construction of experience through the integration of discrete forms. The layering successfully collapses time as well as space—the art of the past with the museum viewer of the present.

Layering, therefore, can present us with an implied hierarchy of elements for our attention. Elements that "rise to the top of the pile" in the illusion of depth or assert themselves ahead of others in time (for example, in interactive media) typically demand that we process them first. Layering can also build connections, a "third meaning" that arises from the assembly of an image that is significantly different from those of the single elements alone. In this sense, layering demands that we visually process the structure of the composition to get through the competing levels of meaning.

**Figure 3.54, below
Layers**
The two compositions contain exactly the same elements in the same colors and sizes. The composition on the left flattens space because no elements overlap. The composition on the right pushes some elements forward, even when color or size suggests they are more likely to be in the distance.

**Figure 3.55, bottom
Isabella Stewart Gardner Museum Campaign
2x4**
The campaign by design firm 2x4 uses layering to integrate the contemporary audience with artifacts from the museum's collection, expressing the theme "Art Comes to Life."

SYMMETRY/ASYMMETRY

Symmetry is a correspondence in the size, shape, and arrangement of parts on opposite sides of a plane. Conversely, asymmetry is a lack of correspondence between the elements on opposite sides of a plane.

Symmetry and asymmetry describe spatial arrangements of elements in a two-dimensional visual field. Perhaps the most common understanding of symmetry is *bilateral* or *reflective* symmetry. If you fold a piece of paper, creating an axis, you have bilateral symmetry (Figure 3.56). People are strongly attracted to such arrangements, in part, because the human body and those of other organisms are bilaterally symmetrical. It has been shown that people considered "most beautiful" have faces that show high degrees of bilateral symmetry.

Other forms include *translational symmetry* (moving successive lines or objects in a certain direction by the same distance each time; *rotational symmetry* (an object that looks the same from any position when rotated); and *helical symmetry* (as seen in springs and drill bits)

(Figure 3.57). These types of symmetry are more complex and less easily recognized, but they can order compositions in ways that achieve similar perceptions of balance.

Symmetry/asymmetry is not just a visual concept. It exists in mathematics, physics, music, rhetoric, politics, and social behavior. We can think of reciprocity and gift giving as forms of symmetry. Many musical compositions use reflective symmetry and even conversations between two people can be considered either symmetrical (when each has a full and proper turn) or asymmetrical (when one speaker dominates). Because we understand these relationships in various realms of human experience, it is possible to link content with form through such spatial arrangements (Figure 3.58).

**Figure 3.56
Symmetry**
Perceptions of human beauty have a high degree of bilateral symmetry.

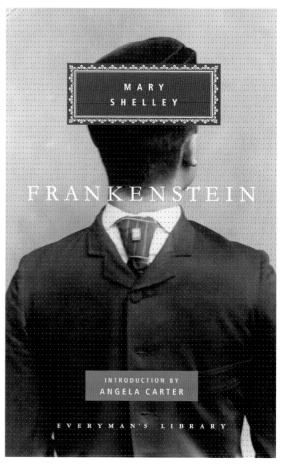

**Figure 3.57
Translational, rotational, and helical symmetry**
Translational symmetry successively moves shapes in the same direction and distance from their locations in the previous row. Rotational symmetry looks the same from any position. Helical symmetry rotates around a central axis.

Figure 3.58
Frankenstein **book cover, 2009
Everyman's Library
Barbara de Wilde**
DeWilde's cover for Mary Shelley's Frankenstein uses the symmetry of the clothing to set up the visual logic for the typography. The position of the head is surprising and communicates the content of the book.

Symmetrical compositions tend to be rather static. The implied axis acts as a fulcrum that anchors the elements in stable, balanced positions and is so rigid that it often commands more attention than any single element in the composition.

Asymmetry is the absence of symmetry. When used effectively, it can communicate qualities of dynamism, energy, and motion because elements imply some instability in their arrangement. *Informal balance* is the perceived equilibrium among elements in an asymmetrical composition; the character and placement of some elements compensates for the size, weight, or motion of others (Figure 3.59). When well designed, informal balance overcomes the tendency for dissimilar elements in the same composition to appear chaotic. Elements in random compositions pay no heed to an axis; the only plane is a single continuous one defined by the edges of the page. They imply that the behavior (or position) of each element operates according to its own logic without regard to any organizing principle. Asymmetry—and informal balance, in particular—implies a force (such as a need for equilibrium) that determines the position of elements. When a single element fails to respond to this force while others do, it stands out and attracts our attention.

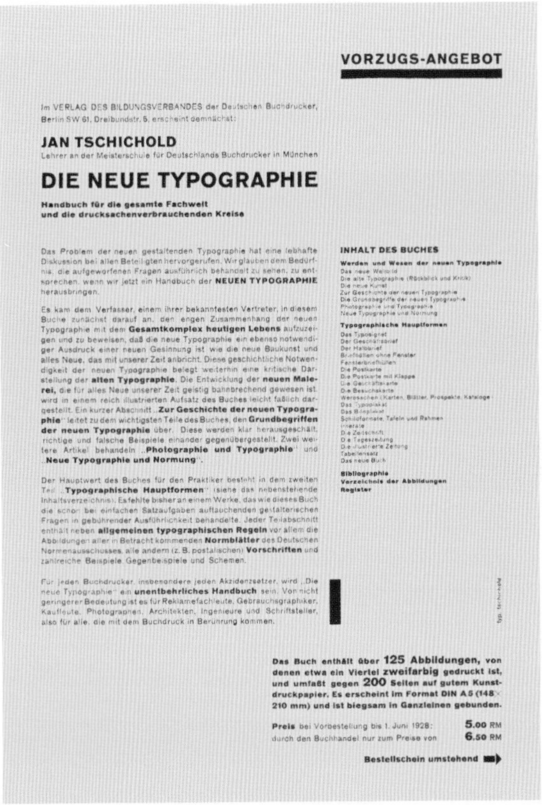

Figure 3.60
Prospectus for *Die Neue Typographie*, **1928**
Jan Tschichold
(1902–1974)
Tschichold's prospectus for his book on new typography illustrates the modernist preference for asymmetrical compositions. Tschichold wrote, "The liveliness of asymmetry is an expression of our own movement and that of modern life" (p. 68, English translation).

In a quest to be more modern and less reliant on classical composition strategies of the past, twentieth-century designers embraced asymmetrical compositions. Designer Jan Tschichold, in his seminal works, *Asymmetrical Typography* and *The New Typography*, argued that, "the liveliness of asymmetry is also an expression of our own movement and that of modern life; it is a symbol of the changing forms of life in general when asymmetrical movement in typography takes the place of symmetrical repose" (Tschichold in McLean, 1995) (Figure 3.60). This view became prevalent in mid-century European modern design and is evident in posters and publications of that period.

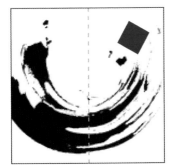

Figure 3.59
Compositions with informal balance are equal in "visual weight" on both sides of a central axis but are different in the color, shape, or size of the elements. Asymmetrical arrangements are typically more visually active than symmetrical compositions.

CLOSURE

The Gestalt principle of closure describes our ability to see incomplete forms as whole. Our minds react to shapes that are familiar and fill in the missing information.

On a dark evening, when looking up into the sky, we may notice a bright curved line. We have learned that this is the new moon, or the fingernail moon from ancient stories and songs (Figure 3.61). We see the moon in partial outline but we interpret that outline as representing the entire sphere. This is because our experience in moon watching teaches us that there is a larger form, even when much of it is not visible. It is also because we tend to perceive geometric shapes as complete, even when parts are missing. Closure is a perceptual process—whether conscious or unconscious—through which we fill in the missing information for familiar or regular shapes where only partial ones exist (Figure 3.62).

The principle of closure often operates in figure-ground relationships that are unstable. Armin Hofmann's poster on "good form" relies on our knowledge of complete letterforms in order to read the primary message (in this case in German). At the same time, positive and negative forms reverse back and forth, calling additional attention to black rectangles that are formed entirely by the way in which the designer interrupted the letterforms (Figure 3.63). Closure allows us to see these as geometric shapes in addition to the letterforms themselves and figure-ground moves them forward and backward in the picture plane.

Figure 3.61
Perception of the moon as a complete sphere, regardless of partial visibility during some cycles, is an example of the Gestalt principle of closure.

Figure 3.62
The Gestalt principle of closure states that when presented with fragmentary stimuli forming a nearly complete image, the mind tends to ignore the missing parts and perceives the figure as whole.

CHAPTER 3 / GETTING ATTENTION

Closure is important to the design of many logos. It allows open forms to integrate successfully with a variety of surfaces—the pattern of a building façade or the ridges of corrugated packaging, for example—without having to add a background shape that could be overly complex at small sizes or that would conflict with the familiar shape of the subject itself. In some cases, the incompleteness of form reads as highlights. In other cases, it heightens the expressive attributes of the object by eliminating features (Figure 3.64).

Understanding the power of the mind to complete images allows designers flexibility in how they represent subjects. If the shape is simple or the object familiar, then the designer can take liberties with its representation, removing unnecessary detail. It also allows designers to manipulate parts-to-whole relationships, substituting simplified or abstracted parts and letting the viewer complete the figure.

Figure 3.63, above right
Die Gute Form
(Good Form), 1954
Armin Hofmann
Hofmann's poster for an exhibition at the Swiss Industries Fair calls attention to the concept of form by leaving letterforms incomplete. Viewers complete the letterforms in their minds.

Figure 3.64
Range Design
and Architecture
Graphic Identity
Thirst
Designer:
John Pobojewski
Creative Consultant:
Rick Valicenti
The designer carefully eliminates portions of the letterforms in the logotype. The defining strokes of each character remain and the overall effect is one of "constructing the word," consistent with the activities of the firm.

CONTINUITY

Continuity is the perception of visual similarities across time and space. It implies repetition and consistency in the application of elements, stylistic qualities, or compositional structures across formats that include multiple components.

Figure 3.65
SPIN Magazine, 2012
Design: ETC (Everything Type Company)
SPIN Creative Director: Devin Pedzwater

ETC's redesign of *SPIN* maintains continuity through the use of theme and variation in treating recurring elements. Frames, overlapping photography, color, and common typographic treatments hold together a diverse set of images and articles. The design provides enough invention to make it interesting without sacrificing unity.

Imagine that you are watching a film and the action in a scene moves from one camera angle to another. You notice that when the angle shifts, the main character in the film is now wearing a different shirt, the sky outside the window indicates a very different time of day, or there is a new object on the table that was not there before. These are breaks in the visual continuity of the film and they attract attention precisely because they are unexpected and inconsistent with the viewing experience at the beginning of the scene. They interrupt the narrative and take you out of the experience of the film.

On the other hand, we can tolerate interruptions in continuity if they move the story forward. Film editors splice together scenes shot at different times and angles for expressive impact. A well-placed shift in the action of a film (a jump cut) heightens the drama. Even though it

is a change in viewpoint or content, it rarely breaks the continuity of the viewing experience or our understanding of the story.

Designing series and sequences of images and/or text, therefore, requires maintaining some features across the reading or viewing experience and using breaks in continuity for expressive purposes or to garner attention. In the design of multi-page documents—books and magazines, for instance—typographic and graphic systems determine how designers treat recurring elements. Folios (page numbers), column widths, and caption-to-photograph relationships may be consistent from spread to spread, regardless of content. Grids maintain proportional relationships even though elements change. This approach allows readers to focus attention on the information that is particular to the article, interpreting

the recurring elements through "habit." The specific content of each spread may be different, but the repeating visual characteristics hold the publication together as a single experience.

Designers strengthen continuity through other visual strategies. For example, gradually increasing the scale of objects or the playfulness of layouts can build predictability and anticipation in how elements will be treated in the next spread. Readers notice a break in this gradient and interpret it as significant to the overall narrative. Visual similarity among images (for example, colors, shapes, focus, or repeated content) recall earlier layouts in the publication, thereby linking content that is otherwise separated in time and space.

Everything Type Company's redesign of *Spin Magazine* is an example of establishing continuity through *theme and variation* (Figure 3.65). Repeating visual elements are familiar but slightly reinterpreted throughout the publication. The large open rectangle repeats at a smaller scale in the same color in a later spread. The designer reinterprets the overlapping photographs on an early spread as overlapping color blocks in a later layout. The alignments of square blocks of caption type are offset from the article in the same way that pictures extend beyond the perimeter of the open boxes. And centered quotes echo centered headlines, while the rest of the text is justified.

Website users look for continuity in behavior as well as visual form. Designer Matthew Peterson's website (http://textimage.org), for example, consistently uses vertical scrolling to produce changes in content categories and horizontal scrolling to explore individual projects and essays in greater depth (Figure 3.66). Supporting diagrams "hide" behind examples and open like drawers. Interaction with the site feels like continuous movement over a single, large landscape of information, despite the changing imagery, and users access sections through repeating behaviors that are reserved for specific types of information. This is in contrast to website interaction that changes content only through menus or clickable sections of the homepage—that is, in which one screen disappears and is replaced by another that looks completely different from the first.

Continuity, therefore, is not only a strategy for maintaining visual similarities from one page or screen to the next, but also a means for reinterpreting the form in ways that surprise and delight. The task for the designer is to develop a vocabulary of form that uses recurring elements in different combinations to speak with different inflections.

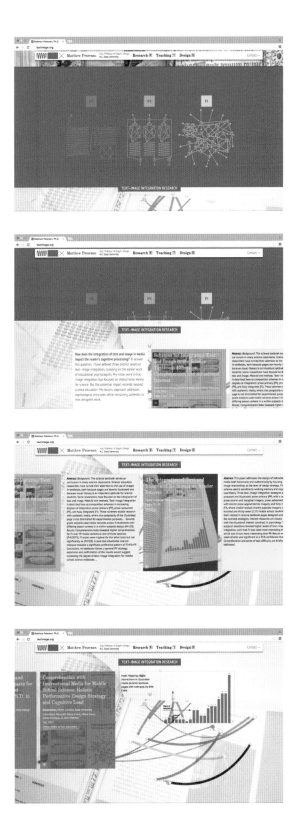

Figure 3.66
Research Website, 2016
Matthew Peterson
College professor Peterson achieves continuity in his research website through a consistent vocabulary of navigational movement, despite very diverse content elements. Vertical scrolling moves readers through topical sequences, each preceded by an explanatory diagram, while horizontal movement drills down into the textual detail of articles. The result is continuous travel across a landscape of information, rather than flipping among sequential screens.

SERIES AND SEQUENCES

A *series* is a collection of images or elements that share something in common. The content or qualities that hold them together (and that distinguish them from other elements or images) do not suggest a particular order. A *sequence*, on the other hand, exhibits a specific order of related elements or images. Sequential order is suggested by some organizing principle, such as numbers, time, gradation in size, cause/effect relationship, or a story with episodes directed at achieving a goal.

Series and sequences rely on repetition and difference; some element must make reference to the initial or preceding image so the linkage between images is clear. But there must also be distinctions among images or a meaning larger than the collective content of the individual images does not emerge (Figure 3.67).

The use of serial imagery is a common strategy for establishing continuity and commanding attention across time and space. Because a series does not imply a particular order among the images, visual characteristics must hold them together formally or conceptually. In the design of an identity system for the Biennale di Venezia International Art Exhibition by Stockholm Design Lab, elements of participating nations' flags form a visual language that is applied to publications and other components of the system. The serial strategy maintains visual continuity across applications; however, each component is different and need not be seen in a specific order. This clever approach honors national identities without giving priority to any single country (Figure 3.68).

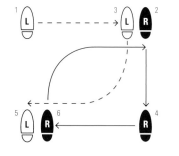

Figure 3.67
Series and sequences
The members of a series share something in common but there is no implied order for their arrangement. A sequence not only includes members with similar characteristics, but their form also suggests an order for their arrangement (large to small, simple to complex, and so forth).

Figure 3.68
Biennale di Venezia catalog covers and dissection of flags
Stockholm Design Lab
The Stockholm Design Lab *translates the exhibition theme, "Making Words," in a series of graphic components. Just as the flags of participating countries comprise members of a series with no implied order or hierarchy, so does the visual language of the identity system.*

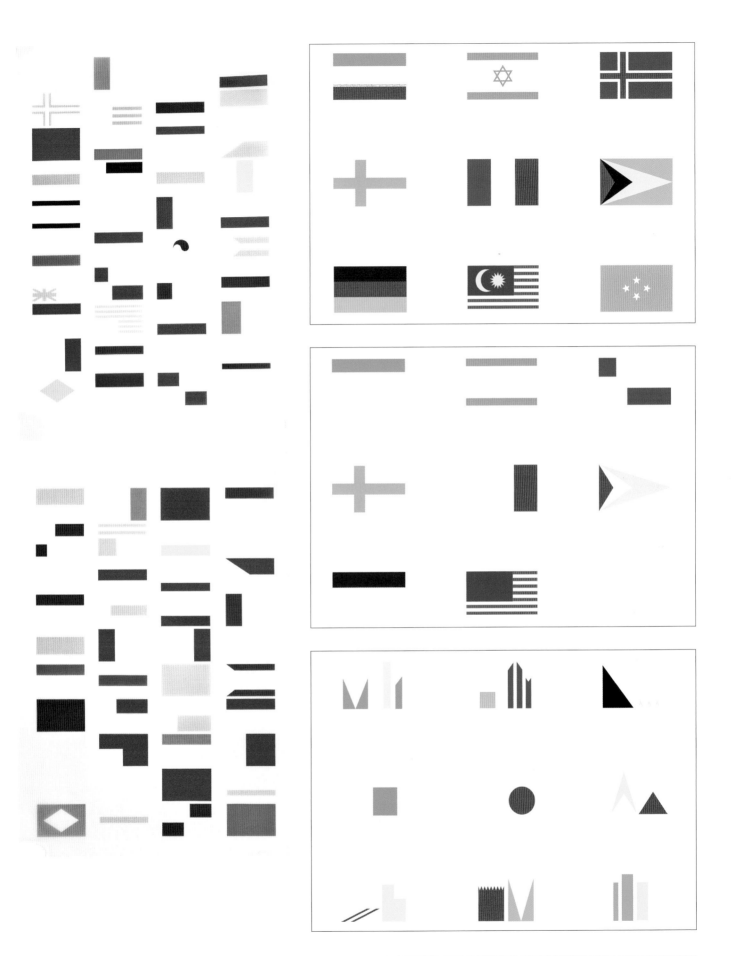

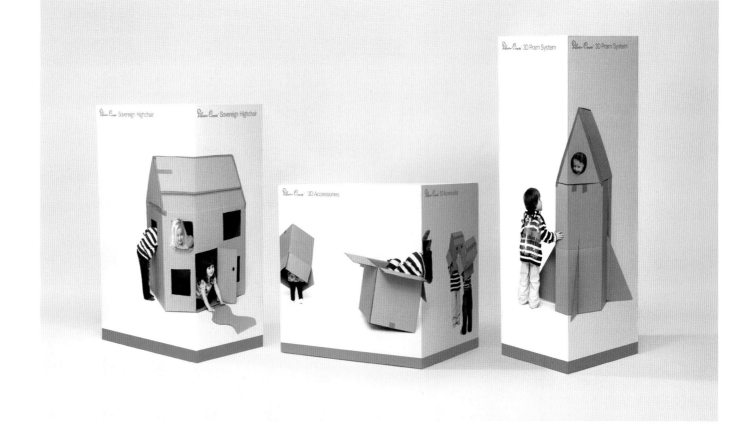

Figure 3.69
Small Kids, Big Boxes
**Silver Cross toy
packaging, 2015
Emma Morton for Love
Photography:
Ben Wedderburn**
In her design for
children's product
packaging, Morton
remembered the joy of
playing with the box. The
package clearly identifies
the product in text and as
one in a series through
the visual language.
When lined up on store
shelves in no particular
order, the boxes express
the playfulness of
children in a landscape of
ad hoc structures.

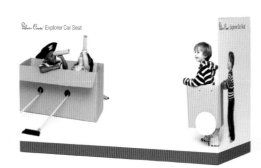

Emma Morton's series of packages for Silver Cross Toys
are necessarily different sizes and shapes, depending
on the product. As a series, they are recognizable by
photographic images of children using the discarded
box in play. The clean white backgrounds emphasize
the children's activity in transforming the boxes. When
the packages are lined up on shelves, they create an
imaginative playscape, yet no specific order is required.
This quality is important in packaging. Customers need
to recognize different objects in a single product line, but
stacking and shelving by store employees is unpredictable
(Figure 3.69).

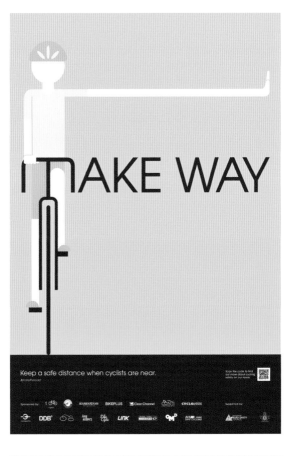

Figure 3.70
MAKE WAY/RESPECT/ CYCLISTS/SHARE THE ROAD, 2012
Road safety campaign
Singapore Road Safety Council
DDB Singapore and 100Copies Bicycle Art
Designer: Thomas Yang
The poster series for this safety campaign uses a common visual language and a repeating band at the bottom of each poster that aligns with the next, regardless of the order.

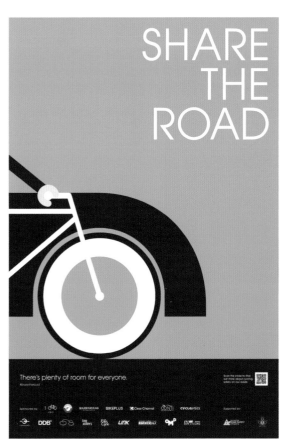

The members of a sequence depend on each other for their position; their ordering is significant (Figure 3.71). Sequences explain processes, show the evolution or construction of things over time, illustrate cause and effect, and tell stories (Figure 3.72). In the 1960s, drivers along US highways saw periodic and somewhat puzzling roadside billboards with slogans such as, "You'll love your wife/You'll love your paw/You'll even love/Your mother-in-law/If you use/Burma Shave." No single billboard had the same impact as the rhyming sequence built as drivers traveled long distances. Repetition, as well as the sequential completion of the message, worked together to hold the driver's attention.

Book design is naturally sequential, with the page-to-page experience furthering the communication of content (Figure 3.73). In a catalog titled *Earthquakes and Aftershocks*, California designers Jon Sueda and Yasmin Khan created a layout structure that follows the unfolding of an earthquake event. The spreads build as a sequence of increasingly frenetic layouts, then subside with intermittent moments of activity as aftershocks. Unlike a series, the sequence communicates something more than is apparent in a mere collection of images. The ordering of images is meaningful and does not depend solely on the content of the individual images, but also on their position within the overall sequence.

Available time sets the upper limit of the audience's attention span. Advertising campaigns often build audience interest or understanding across weeks and months. Serial campaigns use redundancy to reinforce the same message over and over again. Individual ads may use slightly different characters or visual styles but there is enough similarity to alert audiences to repetition of a consistent message. Other campaigns are narrative and build a story, one chapter at a time. In any case, if there is too much time between messages, the audience fails to see them as a series or sequence.

Figure 3.71
Desktop spine totems, 2016
© Paul Garbett
The playful spines of these journals keep the periodicals in order of their publication by assembling a face when aligned.

CHAPTER 3 / GETTING ATTENTION

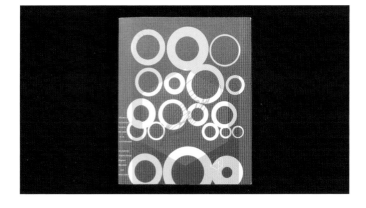

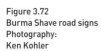

Figure 3.72
Burma Shave road signs
Photography:
Ken Kohler
Signs advertising shave cream appeared on the American landscape in 1926 and were a major effort of the company's advertising campaign until 1963. The signs represented a complete, often rhyming sentence, assembled sequentially as motorists moved down the highway.

Figure 3.73
Earthquakes and Aftershocks: Posters from the Cal Arts Graphic Design program 1986–2004
Designers: Jon Sueda and Yasmin Khan
Editor: Jérome Saint-Loubert Bié
The sequence of spreads in the publication follow the pattern of an earthquake, from quiet to chaos, followed by lesser aftershocks. In this way, the design is consistent with the narrative in the text.

PATTERN

A pattern is a recurring set of objects, elements, or events, repeated at regular intervals (which is known as *periodicity*). Patterns exist in both space and time and are often based on relationships that can be described as mathematical formulas.

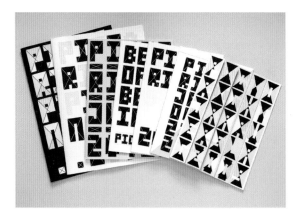

Visually, we experience patterns over time (sequences of flashing lights, for example) or through space (as in the alternating squares on the chessboard). Patterns can be simple and easy to discern or, as in the case of many mathematical sequences, deep and highly complex. We discover patterns in nature (Figure 3.74), and seem to be pattern-seeking animals, even when the absolute periodicity of obvious repetition is missing.

While mathematical patterns follow precise rules, we accept more variation in visual patterns, still recognizing recurring approaches to form among the elements despite subtle changes. De Designpolitie's system for Pictoright, a service that deals with copyright infringements for artists, reveals a paradox at the heart of the modern use of the term *pattern*. Not only does pattern reflect rules-based repetition but also a collection of elements we perceive as a whole that exhibits logic from one to the next. The Pictoright system varies slightly across applications but seems consistent in principles for their composition (Figure 3.75).

Figure 3.74, below
Patterns occur throughout nature.

Figure 3.75
Pictoright, 2008–2016
Concept and Design:
De Designpolitie
Pictoright deals with copyright infringements for artists. De Designpolitie's solution to the graphic identity was to repeat patterns with small variations across formats, a visual reference to duplication of artists' work.

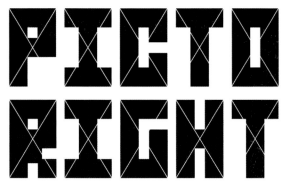

Dutch designer Harmen Liemburg creates very large, multicolored silk-screen posters comprised of signs and symbols collected from his travels (Figure 3.76). Like the previous examples, these complex designs have an underlying structural logic that allows dissimilar forms to appear as repeating patterns. Not only do we perceive the overall layout as patterned, but we find many smaller repeating patterns within the larger composition. This second level of patterning holds our attention, inviting a "second reading" of the form in the details.

Figure 3.76
Aurora, 2011
Garbage In, 2011
Harmen Liemburg
Liemburg collages images in his large silk-screen posters from ephemera collected on his travels. His work includes repeating patterns that serve as an organizing structure for the complex array of elements.

Figure 3.77
Platform Summit
identity, 2013
Pentagram
Partner and Designer:
Eddie Opara
Associate Partner and
Designer: Ken Deegan
Designer: Pedro Mendes
Pentagram's Opara
branded Platform, an
organization dedicated to
increasing participation
by underrepresented
groups in entrepreneur-
ship and technology. The
ThreeSix II font, designed
by MuirMcNeil, conveys
technology and is the
basis of a set of icons
developed by Opara
for the organization's
summit. Similar units
are recombined to form a
consistent pattern when
used together.

Eddie Opara's design for the Platform identity also shows slight variations in icons composed of the same elements. When arranged in a line, they appear as a pattern despite their individual differences (Figure 3.77). To read as a pattern, it is important for each icon to occupy similar space and to appear roughly the same in the distribution of black and white. The identity continues the idea of pattern in other design applications in its conference setting.

Type design relies on pattern. The twenty-six letters of the alphabet are made up of recurring forms (strokes, counterspaces, ascenders, descenders, angles, and so forth). The general goal in typeface design is to create an optically even distribution of these elements so that no single character draws attention over others in typeset text. Fixation on single letterforms interrupts the flow of reading and distracts readers from the content of the message. The pattern of these typographic elements determines the texture and value in blocks of text.

Pattern in text is created not only by the repetition of elements in the design of letterforms but also by the recurring intervals of space between elements. As with the design of typefaces, the goal in decisions about point size, line spacing, and column width is often to create an even distribution of black elements and white space. When type is justified on too narrow a column, however, the spaces between words are often uneven as the computer program attempts to reconcile differences in the number of characters in each line of type. These "white rivers" interrupt the regularly patterned distributions of black and white in text, arbitrarily drawing unwanted attention that slows down reading (Figure 3.78).

In protest of the modernist preferences for highly refined typographic form, designers in the late decades of the twentieth century used irregularities in letterspacing for expressive purposes, often referring to pre-digital technologies and handcrafted work. These unpredictable spaces are reminiscent of spacing problems that arose in letterpress printing. In metal type, spacing could not be controlled between certain letter combinations. When digital technology overcame this limitation, adjusting spaces optically with increasing levels of perfection, designers chose to introduce exaggerated interruptions in the regularity of typeset patterns (Figure 3.79). These irregular interruptions in pattern brought attention to the designer's presence by referring to the unique qualities of an older handset craft.

Pattern, therefore, is more than decorative. It identifies formal similarities and differences among elements in a composition, determines reading flow, and attracts attention to elements that represent a break in the regularity of the pattern.

Typefaces are designed so set text produces an even gray. When type is set on too narrow a column width and justified, the line lacks enough words between which to distribute the additional spaces in lines with fewer characters than others. As a result, the distances between words are noticeably different and interrupt evenness in the pattern of text and the rhythm of reading.

Typefaces are designed so set text produces an even gray. When type is set on too narrow a column width and justified, the line lacks enough words between which to distribute the additional spaces in lines with fewer characters than others. As a result, the distances between words are noticeably different and interrupt evenness in the pattern of text and the rhythm of reading.

Figure 3.78
White rivers
Justified type (in which both sides of the column align) often creates uneven spaces called "white rivers" when the column width is too narrow.

Figure 3.79
Color; Future
Agency: F/Nazca Saatchi & Saatchi
Creative Directors: Fabio Fernandes/Pedro Prado/ Rodrigo Castellari
Art Director:
Rodrigo Castellari
Copywriter: Pedro Prado
The very simple typography in these posters gains interest through variable letterspacing. The designer separates one typographic unit from another through patterns achieved through spacing, rather than changes in size or typeface.

RHYTHM AND PACING

Rhythm is movement, or the appearance of movement, through a patterned recurrence of weak and strong elements. Rhythm is present in patterns that we experience across time and space. *Pacing* is the speed or rate at which something, such as successive spreads in a magazine or a story, moves to completion.

Rhythm lives deep within us in the syncopated pulse of our heartbeats. It is a fundamental aspect of our everyday perceptual experience. Whether in our bodies, in the pattern of bricks in a building that moves across a wall, or in the lapping waves that roll over us at the beach, a regular rhythm provides predictability and structure; we anticipate the next beat. A syncopated rhythm conveys energy and activity; we respond to contrast among the elements. An irregular rhythm creates interruption and anxiety; we notice the break in pattern. In other words, rhythm in design is a powerful means for communicating emotional experience.

Rhythm starts with the repetition of an element across space and time. A solitary element has no rhythm; it needs additional elements, or beats, to become rhythmic. One clap does not make a rhythm. We hear rhythm in music through the passage of time, with intervals between contrasting notes. But as the repetition of details in the chairs, railing, balustrades, and window sashes in Mark Havens's photograph of a tourist motel in Wildwood, NJ shows, we also experience rhythm across space (Figure 3.80).

While rhythm involves recurring changes in pattern among elements, pacing is our perception of the tempo or speed at which we experience those elements. The tempo can be even, but narratives tend to have events that lead to actions that are then resolved in a conclusion. Design can mirror those shifts in pacing across the layout of a publication. Imagine a book composed of spreads with full-page photographs that randomize the shapes and numbers of objects. If the layout maintains these layouts throughout the entire publication, there would be no perceived change in tempo. But if the design of the book gradually increases the size of photographs and the viewpoint of images as the layout progresses to the center of the book, we read that change in tempo as meaningful to the content of the narrative, as building to some sort of climax or focus (Figure 3.81). In other words, visual pacing in the layout can support literary pacing in the story.

A 1976 issue of the design journal, *Visible Language*, was devoted to French Écriture (writing) (Figure 3.82). Designed by graduate students at Cranbrook Academy of Art at a time when the school investigated ideas about the

Figure 3.80
Untitled (Toledo & Atlantic)
Mark Havens
Havens photographs the rhythm of a motel out of season. The pattern of chairs and windows is interrupted at regular intervals.

Figure 3.81
Rhythm and pacing
Layout can establish rhythm and pacing in multipage formats. In the top sequence of spreads, there is no change in the pattern of layout strategies. In the bottom sequence, tempo is established by a sequence of layouts that build to a climax with the narrative.

nature of authorship and singular interpretations of text, the publication starts with straightforward layouts that resemble any scholarly journal. As the text progresses from the front to the back of the journal, however, the layout and typography "fall apart," breaking down the traditional structure of columns and paragraphs, and emphasizing words not likely candidates for highlighting under traditional typographic hierarchies. The spatial disintegration of the text and typographic emphasis on words places ideas contained within the original text in new juxtapositions with each other, illustrating the theory that there are many possible interpretations. The pacing is one of progressively disintegrating compositions in which the designer (and by implication, the reader) overtakes the author in "writing" the meaning of the text. In this case, the pacing of the design alone gradually builds a new concept not present in the original text—that the reader "writes" the text. The layout resembles the rereading of text that is often the case in scholarly work.

To control rhythm and pacing in multipage publications, designers must establish a working strategy that overcomes the limitations of software and that acknowledges the visual understanding of reading patterns as horizontal experiences over time. Programs, such as Adobe InDesign, typically display one spread at a time and illustrate the relationships from spread to spread as tiny icons too small to read or through vertical scrolling. This visualization is unlike how we read a book—left to right across the spread, leading horizontally to the next spread as we turn the page. To overcome this vertical bias in the software, designers print out spreads and assemble them in horizontal arrangements during the design process. The practice of seeing all spreads in a horizontal row makes rhythm and pacing immediately apparent, much as we follow musical notes as they move along a musical staff.

Figure 3.82
Visible Language,
Volume 7, Number 3:
*French Currents of the
Letter,* 1976
**Art Director:
Katherine McCoy
Designers: Richard
Kerr, Jane Kosstrin,
Alice Hecht**
The layout of the design journal's issue on French Écriture (writing) begins with fairly conventional typography that becomes increasingly dispersed as the text progresses. This pacing illustrates the emergence of French critical theories of interpretation regarding the stability of text and meaning.

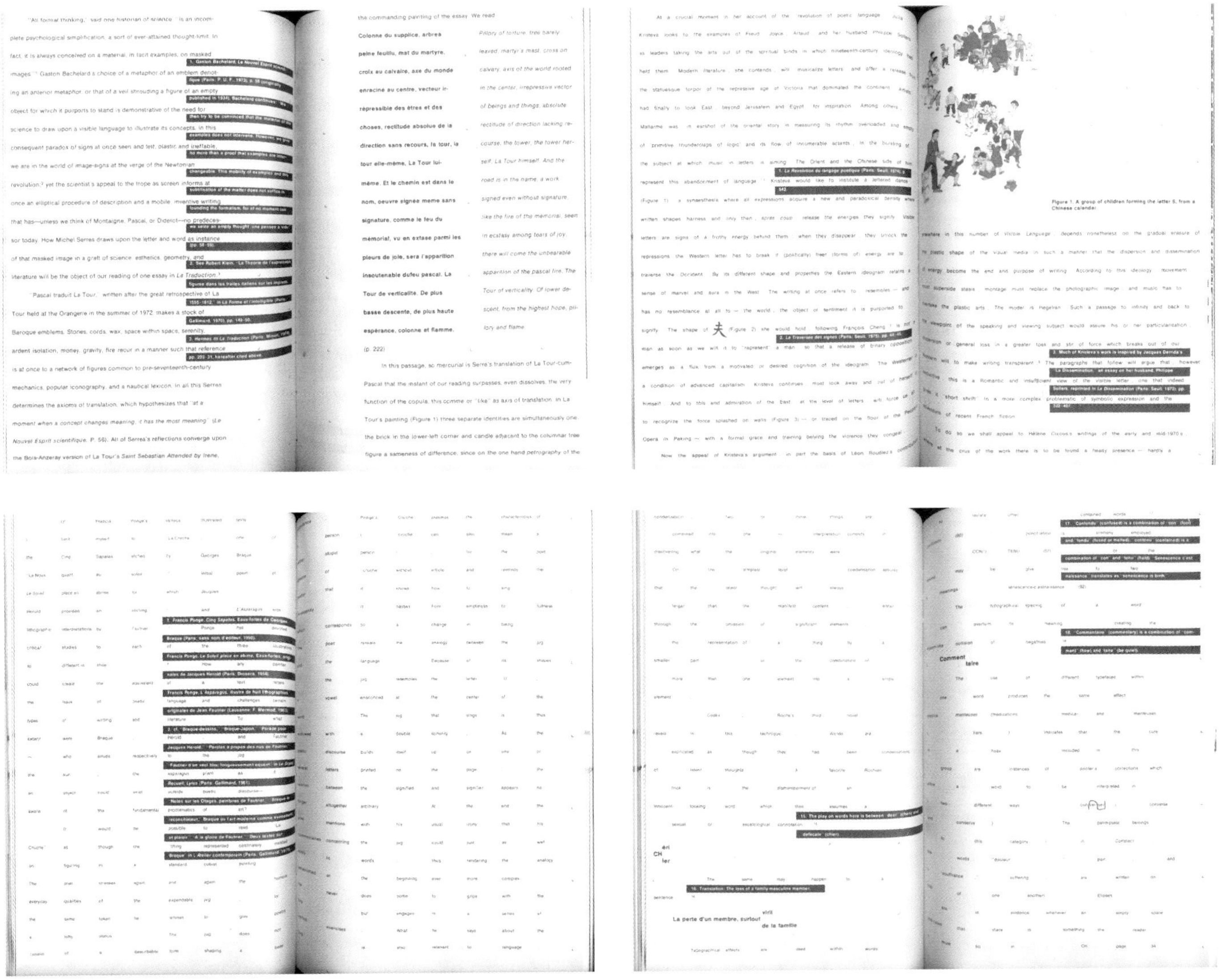

MOTION

Motion is the action or process of changing place or position. Assumed to be the domain of film and animation, motion can be represented in print as well. In all three media, the simulation of motion is achieved through a series of still images.

Motion is a primary means for attracting attention. Many species recognize threats or prey by movement in their environment. And the quality of motion tells us something about the thing moving. A rubber ball bounces differently from a wooden one; a teenager moves differently from a senior citizen; a colored leaf falls differently from a pinecone. We are attracted to things that move and we make judgments about their nature based on the type of motion.

Our perception of motion in a sequence of still images depends on timing. A Gestalt principle call the *phi phenomenon* is the optical illusion of perceiving a series of still images as motion. Film requires a quick succession of still images to convey motion that is convincing to human perception—twenty-four frames per second is the current movie industry standard. Slow down the film rate and movement becomes choppy; the illusion is lost. In screen-based motion graphics, for example, the same element is redrawn at different locations on the screen, one element at a time. If the intervals of time between elements are too great, we interpret them simply as random objects and do not perceive them as a single element moving.

Matt Checkowski's typography for the main titles of the movie *Bicentennial Man* moves in syncopation with the mechanical assembly of a robot. Each of the segments includes a slight variation in the position of the credit line to accomplish this choreography of image and text (Figure 3.83). In this case, the movement of type draws attention to the gestures of the various machines.

Motion is also an important attribute of interactive media. Early web design resembled print layouts, erasing one static screen and replacing it with another or scrolling to reveal more of a fixed page of text than could be seen within the real estate of the screen. Today, interactive websites involve an array of behaviors that use motion; text "opens up," telescopes, and moves across the screen to define shifting relationships between the content and actions of the user. These movements serve different purposes. Some grab our attention, others serve as feedback, confirming that our execution of an action has produced the expected results. In other cases, motion changes the state of the screen as we move through information. Text or images necessary at the beginning of a reading experience move to less important locations on the screen once we finish with them. In this way, motion shifts our attention to things that are immediately relevant.

Animation also expands the content of screen-based media by adding motion to the visual repertoire. There is a temptation under the capabilities of software to make things move simply because it is possible. In the best use of motion, designers bring meaning to complex ideas through dynamic form. Motion, in these instances, reveals things that are not apparent in static images. The *New York Times* innovation portfolio (www. nytinnovation.com), for example, includes animated diagrams and illustrations that support its news articles. A modular robot disassembles and puts itself back together again. Animated illustrations break down tennis player Roger Federer's match-winning footwork. A driving simulation illustrates response times when distracted by texting. Motion, in this sense, expands our understanding of content in ways that a printed newspaper never can. It communicates change over time.

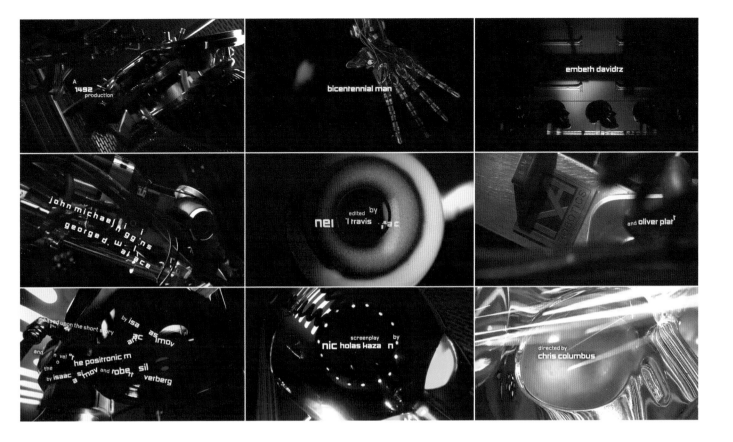

Figure 3.83
Main title for
Bicentennial Man, 1999
Touchstone Pictures,
Columbia Pictures,
1492 Pictures, Laurence
Mark Productions, and
Radiant Pictures
Art Director:
Mikon van Gastel http://
www.artofthetitle.com/
title/bicentennial-man/
Designer:
Matt Checkowski for
Imaginary Forces
Type in the opening
credits of the feature
film *Bicentennial Man*
replicates the movement
in assembling a robot,
the story of the film. Main
title designer Checkowski
used the motion of
typography and sound to
emphasize to the actions
of different machines.

Static media also create the illusion of movement through conventions we have learned through our experiences with various visualization strategies. Comic artists and graphic novelists use the multi-panel format to depict the physical action of a story. In our minds, we fill in the gaps between frames. Frames of the story need not be in a linear sequence: we assemble an understanding of the action of the narrative regardless of arrangement. Speed lines, optical blurs, and techniques such as close-ups and shifting viewpoints replicate the qualities of motion we find in film.

Single compositions can also communicate the potential for motion, even in abstract shapes. We assign the laws of the physical world to the conceptual world of two-dimensional space. A piano positioned above the head of a pedestrian passerby on a city street implies the precipitous descent of the piano and the imminent danger to the pedestrian. The audience reads this motion into the scene based upon the laws of physics (gravity), but also consistent with a tradition of falling pianos in slapstick films, advertisements, and comic strips.

Abstract shapes also imply motion by their orientation to the edges of the page. A square standing on its corner seems likely to fall, whereas one resting on its side does not. There is visual "tension" between two shapes that almost touch but don't; we anticipate future movement toward one another. A dotted line appears to "go somewhere," even when there is no arrow at its end. Motion, or implied motion, is a powerful tool for attracting attention. It not only draws the eye to certain elements but also communicates their character through representations of behavior.

SUMMARY

As the previous discussions illustrate, the designer's toolbox includes a number of formal strategies for gaining audience attention. When used effectively, they not only create interest that competes well in an environment of sensory overload, but they also support the informational goals of the communication. Contrast—in both the differentiation of figure from ground and in color—establishes the importance of some elements over others within a composition. Relationships of size and distance reinforce the roles various elements play and our interpretations of their consistency or inconsistency with actual experiences in the physical world. How designers organize elements in space also influences what we see first and the meanings we assign to their locations. And the linear ordering of multiple elements in time and space can reinforce the stories they tell. The attention-getting qualities of form constitute an essential first step in the communication experience, but it is critical that design delivers on the promise of being worthy of our interest. Design must also orient the audience to appropriate interpretive behaviors, engage us in compelling interactions, and extend meaning beyond the momentary encounter with the message.

Orienting for use and interpretation

Design facilitates people's interactions; that is, it sits between our desire to engage with our environment or other people and the actions necessary to do that. We want to accomplish things, such as learning about an important issue so we can vote responsibly, finding our way in a new setting, or persuading others to join a group activity. The physical products of communication design—websites, maps, and posters, for example—help us to achieve our goals. They support the activities that satisfy our motives for interaction with the world around us.

The attention-getting properties of design shape our first judgments about how relevant communication is to reaching our goals. These properties separate the objects of our attention from the competing background. But once design has our attention it must orient us to the actions and thinking necessary for deeper interpretation. Orientation is a way of adjusting to new conditions and aligning attention to a particular position or point of reference within those conditions. It orders our interactions with a message and guides us through the interpretive process.

The physical qualities of form communicate what objects are for and how we should engage with them. The materials and shape of a saw, for example, indicate where and how to hold it (Figure 4.1). The serrated teeth on the cutting edge not only suggest the right direction and angle for sawing, but also the nature of the materials for which it is appropriate. The wicked nature of the form reminds us to keep tender body parts at a safe distance and recalls related concepts in our interpretive repertoire, such as "going against the grain." In other words, the design of the saw orients us to its general purpose, suggests the action required for its use, and recalls other experiences with similar concepts that provide a point of reference for our interpretation.

In communication design, a successful web interface orients users to the logic of the navigation system and how it works. It signals what our interactions with the interface should be to produce changes in the computer's state of being. We can navigate from one screen to another, for example, by buttons, rollovers, scrolling, swiping, or bumping the cursor into the sides of the screen. Links indicate exit points from the primary content to something likely authored by someone else. While we bring to our interaction with the website our past experiences with computing conventions, our first exploratory attempts either confirm or deny our perceptions of the system and we adjust our behavior when early assumptions prove incorrect.

A 2005 experimental site by the Institute for Interactive Research (dontclick.it) demonstrates how difficult it is to let go of screen-based conventions for navigation. The site uses track pad or mouse movement and rollovers to change the information. It penalizes users for clicking through virtual explosions on the screen. While the site deliberately orients users to alternate navigation strategies through large, typographic instructions, the conventional clicking behavior is so strong that users focus disproportionately on navigation rather than on information to avoid the habit.

Printed communication typically orients readers to its purpose and information structure through the use of a grid and a typographic system. For example, layouts encourage the scanning behavior we use in reading periodicals. Contrary to behavior with books, we don't read magazine articles one at a time in order from cover to cover. Instead we determine interest in particular articles by quick assessments of subject matter assembled from headlines, pictures, and captions. Captions have specific typographic characteristics and appear in particular locations with respect to images, distinguishing them from the feature article. Sidebars and advertisements look different from the main body of text. Page numbers appear in the same place from spread to spread. This systems approach to layout not only keeps readers from having to adjust to the design of each issue or spread, but also makes production of the magazine more efficient by establishing the form of recurring elements. Designers don't make new decisions about the system with each issue, only about the content that changes from issue to issue.

At the level of the individual page or spread, however, there can be additional visual cues that orient reader behavior. The arrangement of text and image can lead us from left to right so we are likely to turn the page, expecting the continuation of an article. The typography can tell us whether the two pages represent continuing content or the juxtaposition of more than one discussion. And the relationship between text and image can make us see something particular in the image that we might miss if the formal alignments consisted only of boxes of type and the edges of rectangular photographs.

Figure 4.1
Orienting for use
The design of a tool often communicates what it is for and the action required for its use.

Principles for orienting readers to the interpretation of information

There are different principles for ordering information that orient readers or viewers to the nature of content. Their use by designers as visual strategies signals the relative importance among elements and tells readers how elements are alike or different. The *alphabet* is a common strategy when there are many equivalent elements. While we assume some general similarity among components of alphabetic lists—all entries in the dictionary are words, and all phrases in the book list are titles—we expect no other special relationship among the items in the list that would recommend a different order. We recognize the alphabetic ordering principle when elements are treated visually alike and arranged in a left-aligned list or in a repeating format across multiple pages—for example, with a headline of the entry name at the top of the page. Imagine trying to use a dictionary if all type was set flush right!

Time is another common ordering principle that designers utilize in orienting readers or viewers to information. We recognize recurring chronological formats, such as timelines and calendars, but we also understand the structure imposed by time-based media—that is, with one visual element or group of elements deliberately following another in a presentation. A book releases information page by page in a fixed sequence experienced across time. When the visual ordering of elements reinforces the chronological ordering of content, the layout of the book orients readers in ways that assist in the interpretation of any single element. Consider a book on the history of war. If the descriptions of individual battles (text, maps, photographs, and so forth) are dedicated to discrete spreads, rather than presented as a continuous narrative that starts and stops anywhere on the page, the reader better understands a particular battle and its time-related position in the course of the war. The map of one battle doesn't wind up on a spread that is mostly about another battle that took place months later in a different location. In visual terms, the book becomes a timeline of discrete military encounters, a pattern we recognize as meaningful in the unfolding of history.

We also understand when an artist or designer plays with our perceptions of time. The flashback, for example, is a commonly used strategy in film. It breaks the chronological sequencing of events. Formal characteristics inform viewers of this break in continuous time: photography switches from color to black and white; focus blurs; or the action returns to a familiar configuration of elements at a different time of day. Through some manipulation of form, the filmmaker signals an interruption.

Time is especially important as an ordering principle in interactive media. In a poster, everything in the message is present at the same time and elements are fixed in their locations. The design of interactive media, however, releases information sequentially and elements no longer necessary to a specific action often disappear. How things come and go is important; transitions (the spaces between events) are designed. Early editions of interactive software used the print metaphor of turning pages, with one screen completely replacing another through clicking or swiping. Scrolling and zooming made stronger references to continuous experience, but greater computing capacity now supports more variations in how information appears and disappears (a fade, for example) and adds meaning through the action itself.

Categories are also useful in orienting readers or viewers to the structure of information. A category is a grouping of members that have something in common but that are different from members of other groups. Designer David Small's interface for the North Carolina Museum of Natural Science allows visitors to place an animal specimen on a blank white table (Figure 4.2). The table reads the RFID-tagged specimen, launching interactive information under topical categories, with one category being no more important than another. Organizing the system by category tells the visitor where to go for certain kinds of information. Museum visitors would not expect to find mating habits under the category of "diet," for example. Further, recurring categories from specimen to specimen invite visitors to consider the frameworks researchers commonly use to study natural history. Because all specimens yield similar categories for investigation, visitors gain insight from the structuring of information into general concept groupings of the ways in which species are different.

Location can be important in providing a point of reference for information—You are HERE! Maps locate an element within a context—a building within a city, a city within a state, a state within a country, and so forth. They use standard conventions for representing location—for example, orienting the map so north is at the top—and our language for describing the location of things corresponds to these conventions. People in Atlanta, Georgia might refer to "going up to Richmond, Virginia" for a vacation. Labeling China and Japan as the "Far East" has nothing to do with the configuration of the globe but is the result of representing geography in flat form and who made the maps—that is, the cartographers who elected to make the United States and Europe the "center of the world."

Figure 4.2
Interactive naturalist tables, NC Museum of Natural History Small Design Firm
Visitors to the museum place RFID-tagged specimens on the table to activate digital information on the species. Users access information by category, seeking explanations of diet and habitat, for example.

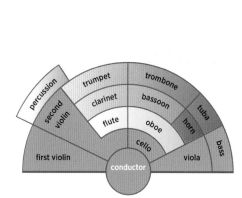

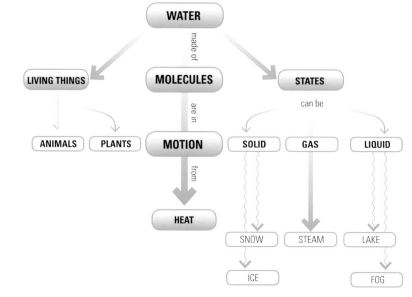

The periodic table image with legend:
- alkali metals
- alkaline earth metals
- transitional metals
- other metals
- nonmetals
- noble gases

Figure 4.3, above
Map of the orchestra
While all maps use location as an orienting structure, many represent things other than geography. The map of the orchestra locates various instruments, explaining somewhat the quality of musical sounds and the gestures of the conductor.

Figure 4.4, above right
Periodic table of the elements
Originally developed by Dmitri Mendeleev (1834–1907)
The periodic table of the elements has a formal logic that allows users to make assumptions about an element and its relation to other elements, based on its location in the table and grouping with other elements of the same color.

Figure 4.5
Concept map
Concept maps describe the relationships among elements or ideas through their hierarchical location within a field of ideas or objects.

Not all maps are about true geography. Some illustrate other concepts in which location matters. A map of the orchestra, for example, is a loose standard across musical groups and orients us to the actions of the conductor and the contributions of various instruments to the character of the music (Figure 4.3). Mendeleev's 1869 *Periodic Table of the Elements* is also a map in which the location of each of the 118 elements reveals something about atomic structure (Figure 4.4). Mendeleev organized elements from the top to the bottom of the table by atomic number. Elements with the same number of electrons in their outer orbit appear in a vertical column or *group* and color designates elements with the same general characteristics (metals versus noble gases, for example). In other words, location within the table allows us to draw conclusions about the properties of any single element based on its position within the chart.

Concept maps locate components or concepts within a nodal network of relationships. Some concept maps are hierarchical with general concepts at the top and more specific concepts following as the map expands downward. The map in Figure 4.5, for example, illustrates concepts related to water.

Other concept maps imply non-hierarchical relationships among concepts. The cultural influences of communication devices, such as a radio or smartphone, may be no more important than their technological lineage. Understanding that these two categories of information (culture and technology) can have related historical timelines, however, may be apparent through their proximity and linked nodes in the map.

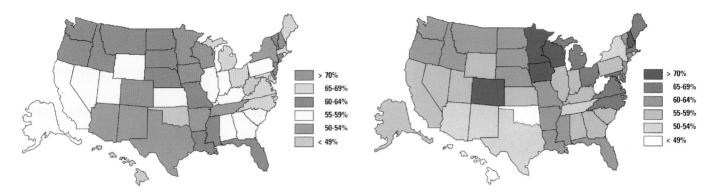

Figure 4.6 Voter turnout maps legend:

> 70%
65-69%
60-64%
55-59%
50-54%
< 49%

The previous example points out that the distinction among information components may not always be exclusive. It may be difficult to define the boundaries between categories and locations or to identify when something starts and stops in time. In these cases, form can orient readers to some gradation of magnitude, amount, or importance among elements. Cognitive psychologist Donald Norman cites the form of maps as either getting in the way or supporting our orientation to information. Figure 4.6 shows voter turnout (by percentage of eligible voters) in the 2012 United States presidential election. Because the color representing different percentages of participation changes with each percentage in the map on the left, it is impossible to look at Colorado and Georgia and understand which state had greater voter participation without going to the legend. Neither can we make easy judgments about overall participation nationally. Because no single color dominates another visually, it is difficult to see pattern in the data. In the map on the right, the darker the value of a single color, the greater the percentage of voter participation. As a result, there is a perceptual logic to representing magnitude in the form of the map on the right that orients us to its use in making judgments about voting behavior.

Consequently, an important role of communication design is to direct reader or viewer behavior in the use of communication systems. The following discussions suggest visual strategies for organizing recurring functions or types of content and ordering the interpretation of elements within individual compositions or messages.

Figure 4.6
Voter turnout maps
Psychologist Donald Norman describes a principle for information design that asserts that perceptual and spatial representations are preferred if the mapping between the representation and what it stands for is natural. If voter turnout is calculated in percentages by state, then a gradient of a single color is better understood than random colors.

AFFORDANCES

Affordances are "action possibilities" present in objects or the environment. Coined by psychologist James J. Gibson, the term describes how we learn from the things around us. Rather than assume that all understanding happens only in the brain, Gibson suggested that physical environments and objects incite certain kinds of perceptions and support particular types of experiences. The capacity to accomplish or interpret something is as much a consequence of our interaction with a physical context as it is a function of thought.

When we come across an object with which we are unfamiliar, we typically use multiple strategies in figuring out what we can do with it or what it means. What is its shape? How much does it weigh? What material is it made of? We examine its properties, making assumptions about how it might work. A flat stiff leaf is good for fanning ourselves in hot weather. A clamshell is good for digging up wet sand. And a small round rock with a sharp edge is good for chopping. If the rock has a point it may also make a good spear tip or be useful for incising marks in stone. In other words, the physical qualities of the object orient us to certain possibilities. We read the tangible properties of the object as enabling or constraining certain meanings and actions (Figure 4.7).

Cognitive psychologist Donald Norman, in his book, *Things that Make Us Smart* argued that designers too often ignore designing with affordances, and therefore, lose the advantage of specific qualities in the object that encourage user recognition of possibilities (Norman, 1993). Instead, designers frequently disregard the full range of opportunity, and they do so at *their* peril and *our* peril.

The importance of communicating affordances in consumer products is clear—the object's form should tell us how to hold it, where to turn it on and off, and how to direct its action. How we design the affordances of visual communication to orient people in its interpretive possibilities and use, however, is often less obvious.

The attributes of typography, for example, determine the affordances of printed communication. Designers widen the audiences for a text by their choices of point sizes. Large-type books serve more readers than traditional books because they provide an affordance for seniors who have reduced vision and for younger readers with impaired eyesight. A similar objective inspired Natascha Frensch's typeface, *Read Regular* (Figure 4.8). The typeface uses subtle shaping cues in the design of letterforms that are often mistaken by dyslexic readers because of the similarities in their shapes. Technology, such as electronic book readers, also overcomes the problems of diminished vision by an affordance that allows the user to resize text for comfortable reading. It is adaptable.

Figure 4.7
Affordances
Human beings perceive possibilities for action in the form of objects and environments.

abcdefghijklmnop
qrstuvwxyz
ABCDEFGHIJKLMNO
PQRSTUVWXYZ
(0123456789) [\]

aeou b d

o a e c b p

Figure 4.8
Read Regular typeface,
2001–2004
© Natascha Frensch
Read Regular was
designed with particular
affordances for dyslexic
readers. Unlike typical
typeface designs that
apply a general strategy
of form to all characters
for a uniform look,
Frensch's design took
particular approaches
to individual letterforms
that are easily confused,
such as the lowercase
"b" and "d."

Different media have different affordances that guide our general perceptions of what they are good for, how to use them, and what they mean. Photography captures a scene mechanically. While we can manipulate aspects such as lighting and pose, we generally assume photography to be more objective than drawing because the camera lacks the affordance for making choices about what to include or exclude in a scene once framed. For that reason, designers use photography when they want to communicate something accurately and in a particular setting. And when the design uses lighting and other visual effects to manipulate the content of the image, the audience assumes that the purpose is more than simple decoration.

Knowing that drawings exclude some details and retain others, we expect it to be subjective or to focus on a specific kind of use, such as instructions for assembling furniture. Illustrated instructions show views that are not possible in photography, eliminate distracting information that is not relevant to the task, and shift the scale of parts to make sure we can identify components correctly. Imagine trying to assemble IKEA furniture from photographs only. The challenge for the designer is to select the right medium for the task: that is, to match the affordances of the medium to the audience's need for orientation to a particular action.

Conventions in various media direct our perceptions of possibilities and our follow-through interactions with the system. New technologies, however, often demand new behaviors and their affordances are unknown to users. Before touch screens, most of our interactions with computers happened through typing. Smartphones and tablets required different kinds of interaction—such as swiping, tapping, and pinching—but also added the affordance of drawing on the screen with our fingers and activating the system by speaking into the device. More recently, tangible user interfaces (TUIs) read the presence of physical objects, allowing users to manipulate them as digital forms on the screen. Our interactions with these interfaces are meant to be more natural and intuitive, building upon our interactions with physical objects rather than with language or code. As the affordances of media expand, interaction relies less and less on visual and verbal devices, such as buttons and menus.

The affordances of various media and formats, therefore, invite a narrow range of appropriate actions. The attributes of the object or system predetermine what is interpretively possible.

CHANNEL

A channel is the route the message travels to its intended audience. While a channel can communicate a stimulus along any of five sensory paths—vision, hearing, taste, touch, or smell—in design the primary communication channels are visual, auditory, written, or electronic. Different channels bring types of interruption that distort or amplify communication.

Figure 4.9
Newsmap, 2004
Marcos Weskamp
News aggregator Newsmap provides users with the affordance for making quick judgments about news articles through more than one channel of information. Color indicates the category of information; the brightness of color designates how recent the story is. Typography delivers the headline and its size tells readers how many articles exist on the topic. Readers can customize their news stream, receiving only information relevant to their interests.

Spoken clearly, the pronunciations of *dah* and *bah* are easy to distinguish. Yet if you play a film clip in which the actor says *dah* but the image shows a mouth saying *bah*, people will say they heard *bah*. If you ask people to count the number of times a light flashes and you flash the light seven times but accompany it with eight beeping tones, people will say the light flashed eight times.

At a time when multitasking is an everyday practice, we feel skillful at navigating and believe we thrive under simultaneous input from a variety of media channels. We have the radio playing in the background while we read a book and type on the computer. Yet research shows that multitasking is less efficient and has risks that affect outcomes (APA, 2006).

Traditional printed newspapers deliver information through the channel of written text. Television depends on images and spoken words. Both communicate the news but with distinctively different characteristics. Media theorist Marshall McLuhan discussed the implications of these two channels in his book, *Understanding Media*. Before Gutenberg's invention of printing with movable type in the fifteenth century, people received information about their world from storytellers and town criers (McLuhan, 1994). Reading and the spread of literacy changed things. Reading is a solitary activity; individuals determine what and when they read. McLuhan credited television with returning us to some aspects of an oral culture through which we gain something socially by everyone hearing the same message at the same time (McLuhan, 1994).

Today it is common for online news to include text, video and animated diagrams, and sound, providing different channels of information in the same communication experience. If our goal is to understand the emotional significance of an event, for example, we expect to gain more insight from the visual and auditory channels of a video interview than from written text, where intonation and body language are not available. If we want to understand patterns in complicated statistical data, verbal explanations are probably less appropriate than visual representations. An affordance of electronic media is that multiple channels are available at the same time and audiences can choose how to access information.

The luxury of multiple channels has its challenges, however. The abundance of electronic information requires management. Marcos Weskamp's *Newsmap* is an effective combination of two channels that orient users to the search process. The site looks for news topics and represents them visually as well as verbally (Figure 4.9). The size of text blocks signifies the relative number of internet articles on the topic. Hue orients users to the general category to which content belongs (for example, entertainment or business) and color saturation (intensity) indicates how recent the information is—the brighter the color, the more recent the information. Users either customize their search or allow the system to dictate the breadth of topics. In this example, the orienting value of various channels lies in reserving certain visual qualities of form for specific purposes. Users quickly learn what different properties of the two channels mean and trust that the system will deliver consistently on that meaning.

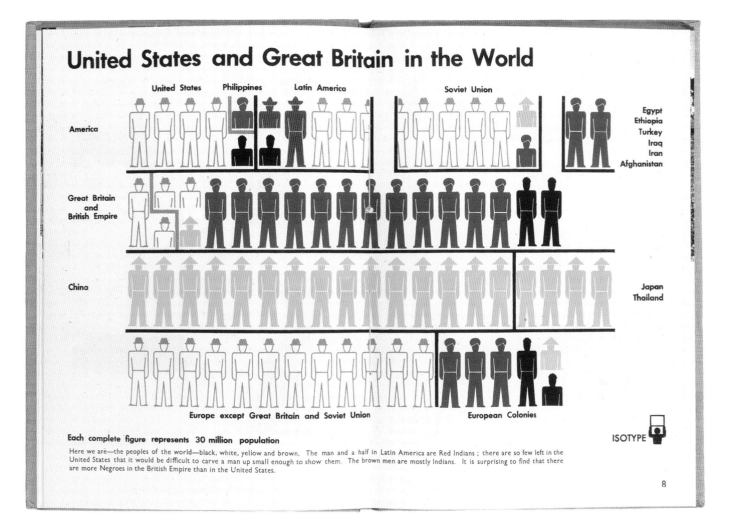

United States and Great Britain in the World

Each complete figure represents 30 million population

Here we are—the peoples of the world—black, white, yellow and brown. The man and a half in Latin America are Red Indians ; there are so few left in the United States that it would be difficult to carve a man up small enough to show them. The brown men are mostly Indians. It is surprising to find that there are more Negroes in the British Empire than in the United States.

8

It is important for the designer to select the right channel for the type of message and desired communication outcomes. Pictorial instructions may help in assembling furniture but not in taking the correct dose of medication. Text may tell us a good story about a journey but fail in helping us to locate a city within a region. In the 1930s, designer Otto Neurath developed a picture language for the communication of statistical and scientific information (Figure 4.10). Called ISOTYPE (International System of Typographic Picture Education), Neurath's system translated complicated concepts that readers might not otherwise understand in numbers or verbal narratives. This tradition continued throughout the twentieth century in business and science magazines and can still be found in contemporary news publications, such as *USA Today* and the *New York Times* (Figure 4.11).

Figure 4.10
ISOTYPE, 1936
Otto Neurath
(1882–1945)
Neurath developed ISOTYPE (International System of Typographic Picture Education) in the 1930s as a translation of statistical and scientific information from numerical to pictorial form. Other applications included travel symbols that oriented visitors to unfamiliar settings.

REBUILDING PROGRESS IN NEW ORLEANS

BEFORE HURRICANE KATRINA   1 YEAR LATER   2 YEARS LATER   3 YEARS LATER

Households Actively receiving mail in Orleans Parish

198,232
98,141
137,082
142,240

Buses Operational in Orleans Parish

368
61
69
76

Unemployment Rate in New Orleans metropolitan area

5.6%   4.1%   3.5%   3.3%

Average daily transit riders For the New Orleans regional transit authority

71,543
17,936
20,462
28,590

Labor force In New Orleans metropolitan area

636,886
482,163
507,548
511,471

Air passenger traffic Arriving and departing at Louis Armstrong Airport, June

869,156
580,539
638,261
715,155

Child care centers Open in Orleans Parish

275
63
98
120

Public schools Open in Orleans Parish

128
53
79
87 (Projected, fall 2008)

Permits for new residential construction In Orleans Parish, May

85 (June 2005)
30
323
387

Fair-market rent Two-bedroom apartment in New Orleans metropolitan area

$676
$940
$978
$990

Unoccupied addresses March 2008, Orleans Parish

Vacant or abandoned homes **71,657**

Total addresses **213,780**

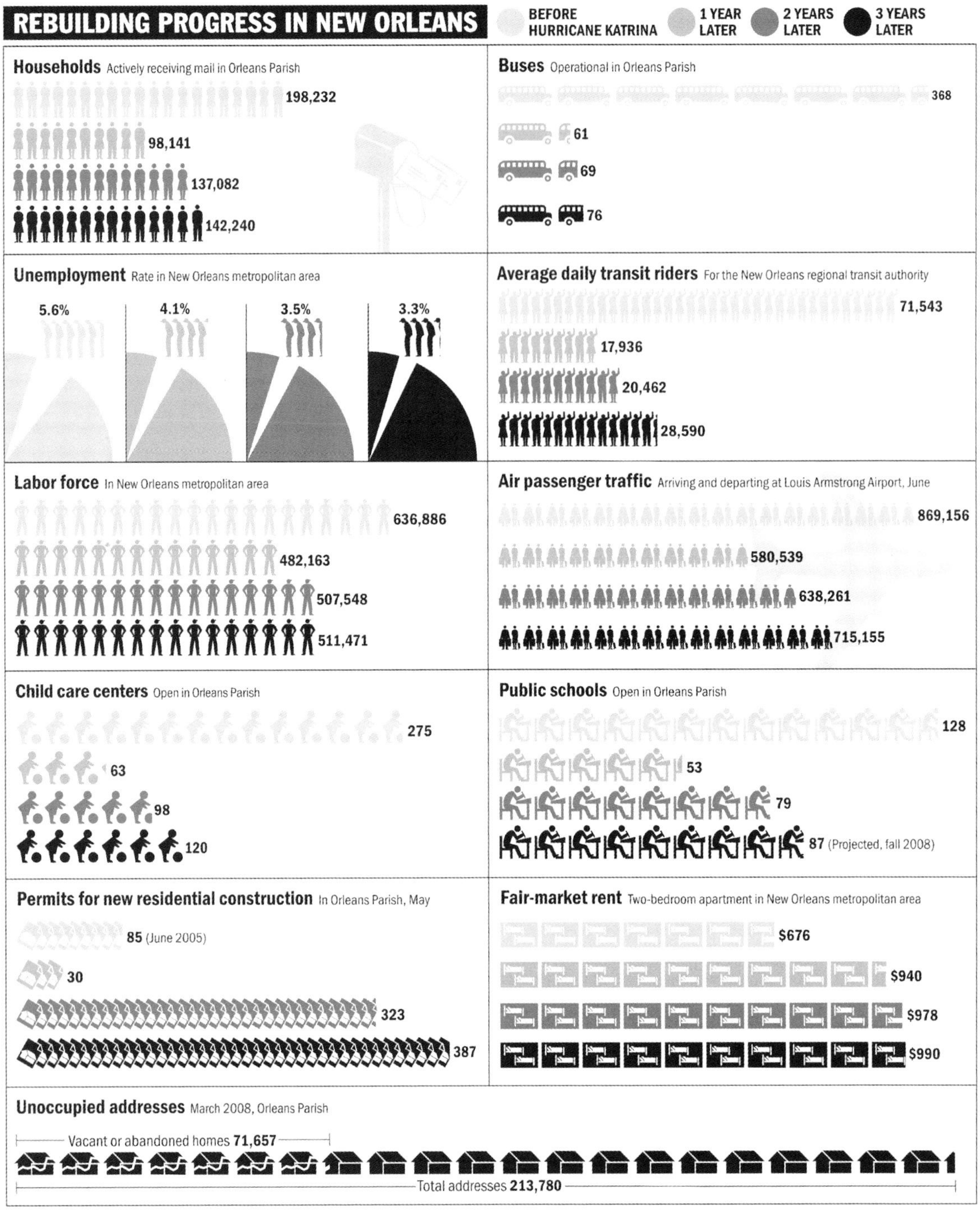

In some cases, the choice of channels includes or excludes particular audiences. Digital media provide captioning services that describe screen information for people with hearing impairments. Braille uses touch as an information channel for some audiences (Figure 4.12).

The breadth of channel options means audiences make choices among ways of accessing certain kinds of information. Overall, newspapers are declining as a primary news source, while internet use soars, especially for the 18 to 29-year-old demographic. This shift not only reflects preference for constantly updated information versus a channel that requires considerable production time, but also audience interest in moving across media at will (for example, from text to video). The use of multiple channels allows the designer to reinforce content through redundant messages (in which the text echoes what images illustrate); ambiguity (in which the text is only vaguely connected to images); or even playful subversion (in which the text actively contradicts images). These possibilities open multiple paths for creating meaning and reinforcing it through distinctive sensory channels.

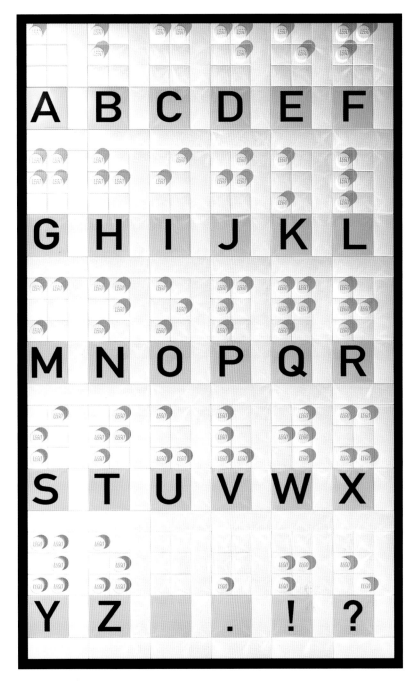

Figure 4.12
Lego Braille
Rocket & Wink
The Braille constructed from plastic Lego blocks uses the channel of touch to communicate the alphabet.

MEDIUM/FORMAT

A medium is a mode or system of communication that extends our ability to exchange meaning. It determines the means through which we craft messages. Film, drawing, offset printing, photography, cartoons, and typography are media. Media are distributed through formats. A format is the material form, layout, or presentation of information within the medium. Brochures, magazines, websites, and posters are all formats.

As our work and lives increasingly depend on electronic channels, the dominance of print media and formats changes. Designers must consider an ever-expanding set of options with a wide array of characteristics and affordances. Digital screens, for example, range in size from tiny watches to jumbo stadium displays and populate devices as diverse as mobile music players, automobile dashboards, refrigerators, and the sides of buildings. And if we imagine all the purposes these screens serve, who uses them, and for how long, we realize how complicated the designer's tasks are.

A medium is a material means for transmitting information via a channel. Historically, media for communicating the written word ranged from typography carved in stone or clay and ink applied to papyrus, linen, or paper with a brush, pen, or raised metal type. Today we have e-ink, as well as LCD screen displays—the unit is the pixel, not the stroke. Increasingly, designers create messages that travel through multiple media, presenting the challenge to choose forms that adapt well to an array of technological constraints. Colors that read well in print may vibrate on screen or get washed out in bright sunlight. Ideas that require the motion capabilities of electronic media may not translate well in print applications.

We attach meaning to the use of particular media. Our choice to write a letter by hand rather than in email is viewed as significant. We expect objectivity in journalistic photography and emotional persuasion in television advertising. These expectations build over time through our experience in culture and they influence how we approach similar media presentations in the future.

A comic book orients reading in a way that is particular to that medium. Scenes and actions are divided into frames and released over time. When the gutters between frames are missing, we don't misread the scene as one in which everyone speaks at the same time, but instead, understand it as an evolving conversation. This orientation to the depiction of time and space is inherent in the medium and through experience we deploy the appropriate interpretive behavior, regardless of the specific content of any single comic.

The medium of cartography also has characteristic ways of orienting our interpretation that are repeated from map to map, regardless of the geography depicted. A grid of coordinates and a corresponding index locate specific points on a flattened landscape. On the other hand, an isometric map allows us to see the highs and lows of the built landscape to predict what might block our view from a particular location (Figure 4.13). Google Maps offers a variety of viewpoints, including street-level photography and zooming between views. In all cases, these are orienting conventions that are characteristic of the medium (Figure 4.14). They tell us what behavior is required for interpretation and we make choices among them depending on our specific needs for wayfinding.

Formats are the physical structures through which a medium delivers its communication to audiences. The medium of offset printing, for example, can be used to create publications in many different formats: 4" × 9" accordion-folded brochures; 8½" × 11" letterheads; 18" × 24" posters, and so forth. Formats orient us both to their use and to the structure of information. We know books are organized in chapters so we expect a change in content when there is a chapter break. The binding tells us that sequence matters. Multi-panel brochures are less clear. Do we read one panel at a time as it unfolds, or are we to open all panels and read one side of the printed sheet and then the other? Loose cards in a sleeve seem to indicate no specific sequence in reading and content that varies from card to card.

The resolution sizes of computer screens, flat-screen monitors, and digital projectors suggest using a standard proportional relationship in formatting media presentations for projection (for example, 1024 × 768 or 1280 × 800 pixels). Internet browsers determine how much readers see on the screen without scrolling, however, the majority of online communication today is formatted first for mobile phone screens, then adapted for tablets or desktop computers. Google made the decision to privilege sites configured for cell phones in the order of its search engine listings. As technology and cultural practices change, so do the dominant formats for information.

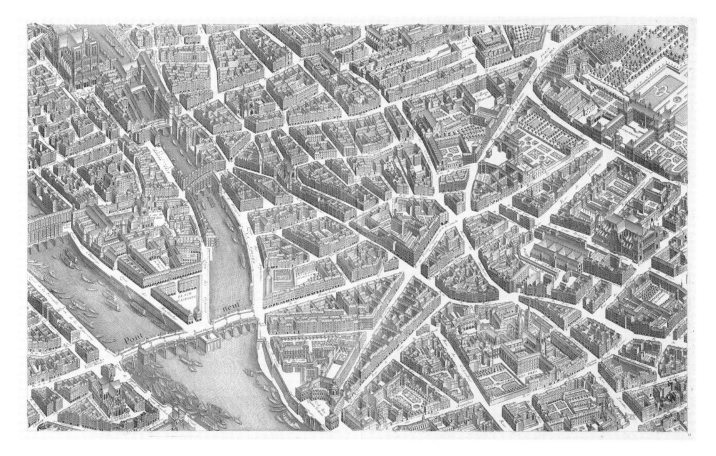

Beyond the content of communication, therefore, media have certain characteristics that influence how audiences approach interpretation. Our cultural experiences orient us to what interaction with a medium will be like; we don't expect sound from printed books but we know electronic text can "talk." Formats vary and also guide interpretation. We know that reading a book releases ideas over time in a way that a poster does not. These cues allow us to focus on content, not on the method of delivery.

Figure 4.13
Turgot map of Paris, 1739
Michel-Etienne Turgot, Louis Bretez
Turgot, chief of the municipality of Paris, asked Bretez to draw a faithful plan of Paris and its suburbs to promote the city. The resulting isometric map was remarkably detailed and showed a pedestrian what the view was likely to be from any place in the city.

Figure 4.14
Google Maps
Google offers many ways to view a city, combining still photography, videos, and cartography with graphic notations. As digital technology advances, it collapses traditional media.

FEEDBACK

Feedback is information given in response to an action or communication that serves as the basis for extending, ending, or improving communication performance. Feedback may take the form of an action, conversation, or other observable pattern in behavior.

In the evolution of the telephone, there have been many small but significant changes made in the way the phone works. These dramatically affected the experience of using the phone. A small tactile click was added to the push of a button for dialing so that the user knew it had been properly engaged. An audible tone was added so that each press of the dialing button registered a distinct sound in the user's ear. Sound was piped from the mouthpiece to the earpiece so that the speaker could better modulate his or her own voice while speaking. Each of these transformations incorporated feedback that confirmed an appropriate action by the user.

In the interaction with products, feedback occurs once a user initiates an action in a system and the system responds by providing signals that the action took place. It can address any of the five senses: the depression of a computer key feels as though it snapped; a finger tap on a touch screen emits an audible beep or click. Feedback tells the user that an action has changed the state of the system or that the system is still processing the command. Icons such as an hourglass, wristwatch, or spinning wheel tell us that an operation has not yet been completed, thus discouraging us from initiating additional commands that would further slow the processor as it completes its first routine.

Wayfinding systems orient us to movement through physical space and are usually composed of signage units that serve various purposes such as identification, direction, and regulation. The challenge for designers of these systems is to decide where and when particular kinds of information are needed (Figure 4.15). Users can determine from a directory that their destination is on the fourth floor, but somewhere along the path between the lobby and the room they need feedback that confirms they are still going in the right direction. The classic "You are here" maps orient people to their current location with respect to a destination. Strategically placed signs at decision-making points along the route confirm the correct path and reduce anxiety.

Printed communication and some products lack the affordance of traditional feedback. Because they are fixed in their attributes, there are no changes in the state of the object that allow readers to judge the appropriateness of actions. Instead, designers rely on conventions—such as the traditional ways in which newspapers articles jump pages or the organization of a book into a title page, table of contents, and chapters—to ensure proper use.

At the same time, designers often anticipate where improper use could occur in objects with fixed properties and provide visual cues that allow users to confirm appropriate behavior. Deborah Adler's design for Target prescription bottles standardizes the format of printed instructions for all prescriptions, unlike other pharmaceutical practices in which any narrative is typed into a blank label (Figure 4.16). But more importantly, Adler's design also addresses possible confusion among members of the family regarding whose medication they are taking. Noticing her elderly grandmother mistake her husband's pills for her own, Adler designed differently colored rings for each member of the family that fit over the top of the bottles. Redundancy in the labeling system—names on the labels and rings on the bottles—compensates for the lack of feedback opportunities in the medium.

As more and more communication takes place through digital media, the role of feedback is crucial. Conventions play an important part in orienting users to interactions that confirm the state of the system, but new technologies introduce novel demands on users and alternative methods for providing feedback. The challenges for designers are to determine when feedback is necessary and to develop responsive form that is meaningful to users.

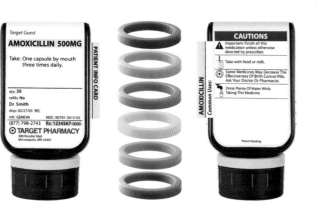

Figure 4.15, above
Wayfinding system for BRIC House
Poulin + Morris
Photography: Deborah Kushma/Deborah Kushma Photography
The Poulin + Morris design of signage not only labels rooms but also provides narrative instructions for reaching other locations. Rather than relying on arrows alone, the system provides the right kind of information at the right time (when orientation decisions are made), giving visitors feedback that they are on the correct path to their destination.

Figure 4.16, below left
ClearRx medication system
Design: Deborah Adler
Industrial Design: Klaus Rosberg
Noticing that her aging grandmother confused her medication with that of other family members, Adler designed a system that labels an individual's prescription by colored rings. The system provides feedback that confirms the individual's right medication has been chosen.

WAYFINDING

Wayfinding refers to all the ways in which we orient ourselves in space and navigate pathways from one place to another. We find our way in both physical and virtual environments, with the latter using much of the former as a metaphor in many of its navigational strategies.

**Figure 4.17
London Underground
map, 1933
Henry Charles Beck
(1902–1974)**
Technical draughtsman
Beck drew the London
Underground map in his
spare time. It departed
from previous maps,
which had been drawn
over geographic maps
of the city. Beck's map
shows stations equally
spaced on a grid of 45°
and 90° angles. Riders
of the subway are not
driving the train and need
only to know the order of
the stops for orientation.

Cities, buildings, and parks are clients for wayfinding systems. With the advent of themed environments, global events, and an emphasis on corporate branding, wayfinding emerged in the second half of the twentieth century as a formal means for helping visitors navigate complex environments while reinforcing a consistent brand for the city or organization in the process. In many ways, wayfinding is like mapping in that it orients visitors to possible pathways for experiencing the environment. In other ways, wayfinding is more dynamic, offering its directional guidance one sign at a time in response to visitors' movements through a specific place.

The term "wayfinding" comes from *The Image of the City*, an important urban planning book by Kevin Lynch. Lynch identified five elements perceived by people as they navigate any city: *districts*, *nodes*, *paths*, *edges*, and *landmarks* (Lynch, 1960). Districts are medium to large sections of the city that have some identifying character, such as arts, financial, and warehouse districts (Lynch, 1960). In physical wayfinding systems, districts may be called out by changes in the shape or color of signs or by some identifying aspect of the environment, such as architectural detail representing an historic district or a boat representing the harbor district. We can also think

of the content categories in the top-level navigation of the menu bar in websites as "districts." They contain a cluster of related topics, often displayed as pull-down menus, as the user drills down.

Nodes are specific destinations that we enter, such as plazas or museums (Lynch, 1960). Nodes are often the primary attractions of a city. In a website, a node may be a specific page within a category of information or commonly expected content, such as a section on "frequently asked questions."

Paths are the routes along which people move (Lynch, 1960). Paths are critical in the navigation of the physical environment and we need repeated confirmation from signage or some other indicator (a line on the floor, for example) that we are on the right path. In virtual environments, however, the path is often invisible or difficult to represent. Imagine tracing the path of an internet search or movement through a non-linear website. In some cases, a progress bar that visualizes the steps for executing a process online—for example, completing the purchase of a plane ticket—can be helpful in telling us where we are in the site and how far we have to go to the next step in completing the task.

Edges are boundaries between two things. In the city, the edge may be a visible boundary—a train track or harbor boardwalk—or an invisible boundary in which we sense by architecture or activity that we are leaving one district and entering another.

Landmarks are reference points that orient us to our location, but we do not enter them (Lynch, 1960). Clock towers or famous statues often serve as landmarks in urban environments. Wayfinding frequently depends on landmarks, especially when the environment has no orderly arrangement of paths or we don't know the city. The street view of Google Maps allows us to confirm our location through landmarks; before setting out on our journey, we determine what is visible from our destination, as well as the route for getting there.

The first priority in the design of wayfinding systems is to orient the user to the spatial environment, either by identifying the user's location on a map or by providing signs in the environment. The aim of wayfinding, as different from other uses of maps, is to identify a *particular* sequence of paths through the environment rather than to represent the entirety of navigation options. So while a city map attempts to describe all streets equally, with no

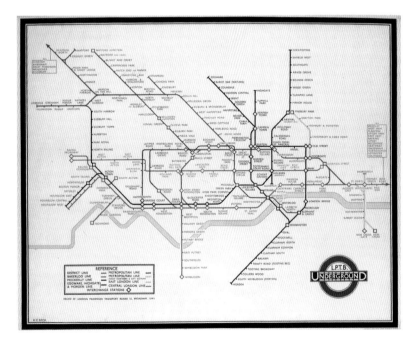

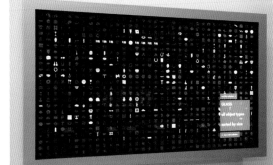

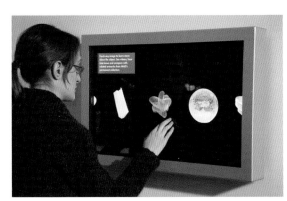

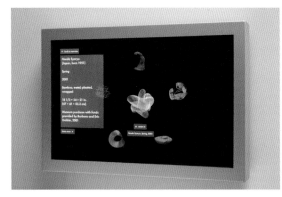

preferences for route or emphasis, a wayfinding system likely stresses streets that are most significant for visitors, avoids streets that are unremarkable or dangerous, and calls out streets that are good connectors between significant points of interest. In this sense, wayfinding tends to be quite intentional, whereas mapmaking has a broader range of uses.

Additionally, wayfinding systems often take liberties with geography to distort spatial scales in order to simplify the experience for users. A classic example is the London Underground map, designed by engineer Henry Beck in 1933. The map forsakes geographical precision in favor of a more approachable and easily navigated diagram (Figure 4.17). Beck ignored actual distances between stops and created uniform angles to make the map easier to read for subway riders. Subway riders aren't driving the train, so the only relevant information for orienting their behavior is to describe the system as a sequence of stops.

More recently, augmented reality collapses the wayfinding functions of signs and the GPS affordances of cellphones. Users aim their phones at a particular view of the city and the system adds typographic details, showing points of interest and services. As the user moves through the environment, the information changes to correspond to the new setting, serving much the same purpose as a signage system but without the visual clutter in the actual environment. Some systems overlay pedestrian pathways on top of visual data, functioning in the same way as GPS systems in automobiles. This annotation of the physical environment orients users in direct ways and is updatable through programming.

The directory for New York's Museum of Art and Design, designed by Lisa Strausfeld and colleagues is another example of electronic wayfinding (Figure 4.18). The display simultaneously shows all items in the museum's collection on a touch screen. Visitors select and enlarge any item and then find its location and details normally reserved for labels in museum exhibitions. This approach not only orients visitors to physical locations within the building but to specific content in the collection and exhibitions.

Today, technology embeds information in the environment and responds to our location dynamically. Wayfinding, therefore, is not just a means for getting from point A to B. It orients us to a landscape of information, visual cues that add distinctive qualities to the experience of navigation, and ultimately, the place itself.

MAPPING

Mapping is the activity of representing information spatially. The relationships among parts are expressed by proximity and location and often linked directionally.

While mapping has existed for millennia, it emerged as a powerful practice with the rise of information technologies and the internet. Historically, maps have represented physical and conceptual relationships in two-dimensional space and at scales that are easily accessed. A map of a campsite, for example reduces the scale of the site from acres to inches; it focuses on key features, such as lakes, parking lots, and paths, rather than attempting to render the complexity of the site in realistic detail. It typically stresses direction and orientation. It is schematic, which is to say that it simplifies form, reduces the overall information load, and focuses specifically on orienting us to the information necessary for action.

Older maps described the nature of space—features of the landscape configured by relationships and human activities. Today's maps describe the shortest routes between destinations, a focus on place. Lines connect cities with little detail about what we might see to the left or right as we drive down the highway. We understand something about the scale of the road and likely speed of travel but little about the quality of the journey.

Maps also tell us something about who made them. In drawing a map for a close friend to get to a concert hall, you know what your friend knows. You eliminate unnecessary details and choose landmarks your friend will recognize. The map is a story that tells your friend the sequence of steps for arriving at the venue. The automobile club, on the other hand, anticipates more general use and includes all streets, depicted accurately at a particular scale.

The Mercator Projection is the most common cartographic representation of the globe and probably the one most of us recognize as the map of the world. Developed in 1569 to aid in straight-line navigation that corresponded to the compass directions, the map distorts the sizes of landmasses to illustrate them on a flat plane (Figure 4.19). The Peters Projection was drawn in 1974 and shows landmasses of equal sizes equally. If governments use a map to make policy decisions, the Mercator Projection clearly favors countries in the Northern Hemisphere, which appear more equal in size to countries in the Southern Hemisphere. If we really want to understand how much larger Africa is than North America, or the distance between New York and Rio de Janiero, the Peters Projection provides a more appropriate representation. Both versions are accurate under their respective mathematical logic, but they serve different purposes.

The level of detail in maps depends on the distances we expect to travel. Architect Richard Saul Wurman produced maps of major American cities at two scales: 250 miles outside the city (which is typically the limit on driving people will do in a day) and 25 miles outside the city (which is when the names of streets become important to finding a destination). Wurman also produced a well-known set of access books for major cities in the world. Rather than illustrate the entire city in a single map, Wurman organized the books by walkable neighborhoods, believing visitors tend to spend time in discrete sections of the city, one neighborhood at a time. And instead of listing restaurants and other points of interest in a single alphabetical index at the back of the book, he located them within neighborhood maps so visitors could exit a shop or museum and know the dining options to the left and right. The books were designed for experience, not for information.

**Figure 4.19
Mercator Projection
(top), 1569
Gerardus Mercator
(1512–1594)**

**Peters Projection
(bottom), 1973
Arno Peters
(1916–2002)**

Both projections are accurate representations of the world within the limits of their respective mathematical models. However, they can lead to different conclusions regarding distance, landmass, and other geographical factors that inform policy and travel expectations.

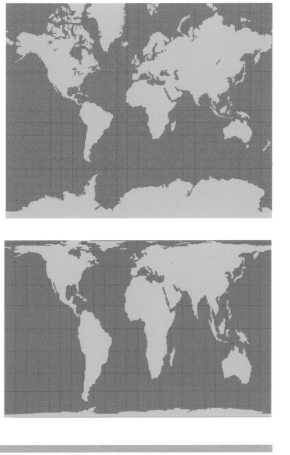

We think of maps mostly for their ability to chart geography and topography, but we can map concepts as well. Social interactions, plots of novels, the course of a war, and spheres of political influence can be represented in map form (Figure 4.20). Concept maps explore and communicate complex affiliations among units of information. Directional lines and phrases connect labeled cells or nodes, giving shape to abstract content and communicating dependent relationships. Concept maps are less literal than geographical maps. They show parts of systems or bodies of knowledge, simplifying complicated concepts in digestible form. These maps allow collaborators to build a common understanding of a problem, setting, or activity and to orient tasks around specific territories within the map.

Site maps show relationships among information units in networked media. They answer the question: "How do I get there from here?" They use visualizations in space to show possible paths through information and how many clicks it will take to get there. Designers often develop site maps through *scenarios*, stories of how a variety of specific users (*personas*) might search for and use information. This practice overcomes the limitations of a single viewpoint.

With greater and greater amounts of available data mined through sensors and other technologies, the human mind seems to be reaching its processing capacity. Mapping, when done effectively, allows us to see patterns in data and leverage points where action can yield positive results. Whether mapping territories or concepts, maps are a means for reducing the complexity of information into simplified schemas and for orienting the user toward important and useful connections.

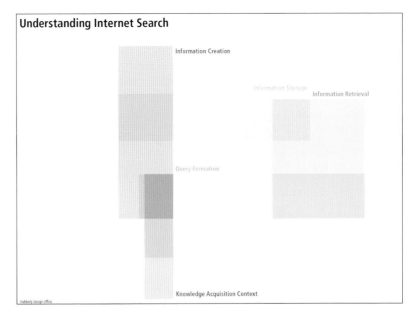

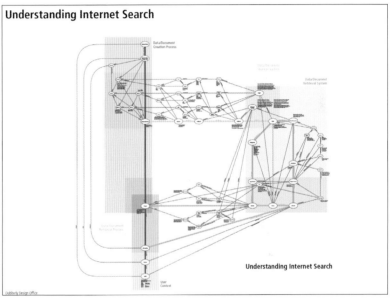

Figure 4.20
Understanding Internet Search: Concepts, Systems, and Processes, 1999
Designer: Matt Leacock
Design Director: Hugh Dubberly
Dubberly's map of an internet search clusters actions related to major systems in blocks of color, matching actions to a primary task. There is a hierarchy among nodes in the map, designated by size, and nodes are connected by phrases indicating the nature of the relationship.

HIERARCHY

Hierarchy is the arrangement of elements according to importance. Designers use contrast to establish the order in which we read or process units of information. Elements need not be arranged sequentially; readers can determine their relative importance by other attributes, such as size, color, or position.

Hierarchies organize all kinds of knowledge, experience, and actions in everyday life. For example, the officer ranking system in the military is a hierarchy. A general ranks above a colonel in authority, a colonel above a captain, a captain above a sergeant, and so forth. We study members of the animal kingdom through the hierarchical classifications of phylum, class, order, family, genus, and species. Restaurant menus organize information hierarchically, typically treating the name of the entrée with greater emphasis than the description of its lesser ingredients and isolating prices for comparison at some distance from the dining options. These hierarchies orient and direct our interpretive behavior. We have yet to determine the meaning of particular elements, but we understand relative importance in their ordered arrangements.

It is easy to understand the expected order of interpretation when things are arranged sequentially or in a list. But the visual world would not be very interesting if everything looked like a set of instructions or a shopping inventory. Pages in books and screens on the web order the release of information across time and space, but the simultaneous viewing of information in formats such as posters and diagrams relies solely on the contrasting visual characteristics of elements—size, weight, color, complexity, direction, position—in achieving varying levels of emphasis.

While we typically assign importance on the basis of visual contrast, too much contrast reduces our perception of any hierarchy. Think about a busy city street in which every shop controls its own signage and storefront design or the visual landscape of magazines at the newsstand. When everything is entirely unique in its characteristics, nothing stands out. Our detection of hierarchy among elements in a visual field depends on a controlled gradient of difference. Similarly, if the design applies too many contrasting variables among elements, some characteristics can undermine those intended to determine emphasis. For example, if the designer signals importance between two elements by contrast in size, then applying a striking color to the less dominant element shifts the subordinate role in an otherwise black-and-white composition (Figure 4.21).

Control of visual hierarchy was particularly important to the work of mid-twentieth-century designers, for whom clarity and accurate representation of the author's informational intention were paramount. Modernist work typically established obvious levels of importance among elements, using only one type family and a limited color palette to maintain continuity among contrasting units of text. We presume that elements of the same size and/or color relate in significance, as well as content.

Figure 4.21
Berthold type series
Erik Spiekermann
Spiekermann's design for a series of type specimen booklets carefully controls hierarchy. In some examples, elements dominate by size, in others by color, direction, or position within the visual field.

Figure 4.22
Barbican International Theatre posters, Why Not Associates
Why Not Associate's Theatre posters establish a clear hierarchy among the elements through the size and visual eccentricities of type and the diffused imagery in the background.

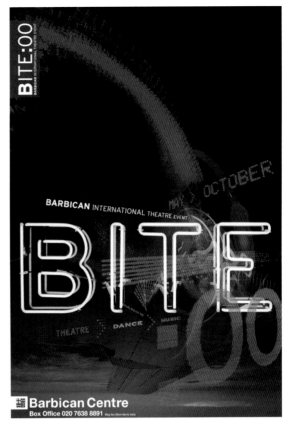

British design firm Why Not Associates' posters for the *Barbican International Theatre Event* include text and imagery (Figure 4.22). The most important element for reading at a distance (BITE) is both large and shows the greatest contrast with its background—it clearly rises to the top of the information hierarchy. The imagery, in this case, is somewhat atmospheric so its diffused form does not compete with the more important text. As discussed earlier in this book, the lack of sharp contours in the imagery reduces the level of attention it commands. Detailed information (date, location, etc.) is smaller and requires a closer reading. In other words, despite the minimal number and diversity of elements in the compositions of these posters, the reading order is clear. Like the earlier modernist work, the hierarchy is apparent, but it does not rely on the rigid application of a grid or limited palette of typefaces.

There are recurring diagrammatic structures that imply a hierarchy among elements. Branching diagrams, for instance, place the most general concepts at the top or left of the diagram and lead to increasing detail in successive layers of the diagram. Others nest concepts like Russian dolls, with detailed or original concepts in the center and more general concepts in the outer rings. In other instances, we read the position of elements in deep space as an indication of their importance. An interactive map, for example, not only describes the hierarchical organization of content but also tells us where we are in the information system—what we will encounter first, second, and third in our movement through the site.

Designer Herbert Bayer's 1953 diagram of the *Succession of Life* orders complex information using several of these strategies simultaneously, but also allows readers to enter content systematically (Figure 4.23). Color separates information about animals (red) from plants (green) and environment (black). A hierarchy among typographic elements corresponds to the content hierarchy; changes in weight, color, direction, and uppercase versus lowercase letters distinguish information at different levels of detail. Divisions of space demarcate zones of time and categories of content. Bayer cleverly "rolls up" the first half of a timeline when no significant life likely existed on Earth, thus conserving space and directing the reader to relevant information. And changes in the world population of various species, labeled by images, appear as changes in the width of a line. This is an ordered visual coding of an enormous amount of data that orients readers to its interpretation. Unlike the posters by Why Not Associates, this example doesn't direct the reader to one thing first, another second, and so forth. Instead, it zones information and makes apparent the significant relationships among different kinds of data.

The order in which we read something determines what we think it means. Hierarchy is critical in orienting us to the importance of certain content in the interpretive process.

**Figure 4.23
Succession of Life
and Geological Time
Table, from *The World
Geographic Atlas*, 1953
Herbert Bayer
(1900–1985)
© DACS 2016**
Bayer used visual characteristics to orient readers to this complex diagram. Line thickness indicates the relative population of species across time on Earth; color separates plants from animals; and typographic orientation distinguishes individual entries on mountain building from general divisions of time. This restrained use of different visual variables for each type of information creates a clear hierarchy in what would otherwise be a confusing diagram.

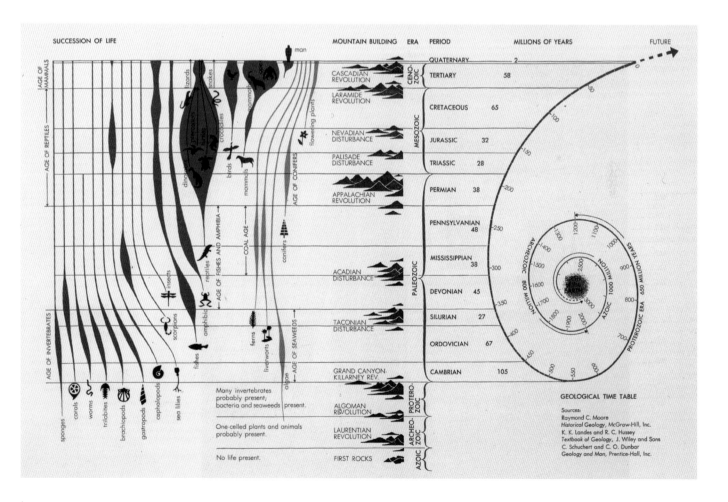

READING PATTERN

The experience of reading in a particular language shapes the way we orient ourselves to a visual field. Reinforced across thousands of examples in our lifetimes, reading order influences how we confront a page.

The Gutenberg Diagram, articulated by newspaper designer Edmund Arnold (1913–2007), describes how Western readers typically approach a printed page. The diagram divides the visual field into four quadrants, each attracting attention in a particular order (Figure 4.24). A visual sweep of the composition begins at the upper left of the page and moves horizontally to the right along aligned elements, such as lines of text. Readers work their way to the lower right of the page in subsequent scans. Fallow areas attract less attention unless a dominant element pulls the eyes in that direction. This pattern is often referred to as *reading gravity* and explains why compositions with the same top and bottom margins sometimes appear bottom heavy (Figure 4.25). A slightly larger bottom margin tends to make the vertical orientation of the composition read as optically centered.

Paula Scher's poster for the Public Theatre makes successful use of the top-left-to-lower-right reading pattern, reinforcing it through the large type and a stair step arrangement of secondary information (Figure 4.26). Other examples are less explicit in their application, yet the emphasis among elements and their location in space correspond to the typical reading pattern. An arrangement of visual form however, can undermine this typical orientation to content. Michael Bierut's *Inner City* poster subverts the normal reading pattern, taking the reader into the center of the composition through a series of layered words (Figure 4.27). The altered reading pattern is consistent with the concept of urban infill.

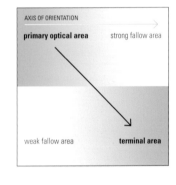

Figure 4.24
Gutenberg Diagram
Edmund Arnold
(1913–2007)
The Gutenberg Diagram describes the reading pattern in Western languages. Readers enter at the top left and work their way horizontally to the lower right, resulting in fallow areas in the upper right and lower left corners of the page.

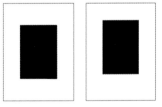

Figure 4.25
Reading gravity
The upper left to lower right reading pattern in Western languages tends to make images and text feel heavier toward the bottom of the page when mathematically centered (left). Adding slightly more space to the bottom margin than the top (right) creates the illusion of vertically centered elements.

SIMPATICO
BEVERLY D'ANGELO
JAMES GAMMON
MARCIA GAY HARDEN
ED HARRIS
FRED WARD
WELKER WHITE
WRITTEN AND DIRECTED BY SAM SHEPARD

STARTS
NOVEMBER 1
THE
PUBLIC
THEATER
425 LAFAYETTE STREET
(212) 598-7150

Figure 4.26
Public Theater, season poster, Simpatico, 1994
Paula Scher
Scher's poster for the Public Theater uses an obvious reference to the typical reading pattern in the stair-stepped typography. At the same time, the heavy border and large type in the background keep the smaller text from "sliding off the page."

Figure 4.27, opposite
Inner City Infill.
Poster for the 1984 architectural competition sponsored by the New York State Council on the Arts
Michael Bierut/ Pentagram
Bierut's poster undermines the typical reading pattern by stacking large type rather than aligning it with a single horizontal baseline. As a result, readers read *into* the space rather than across it, consistent with the topic.

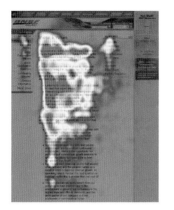
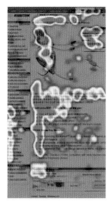
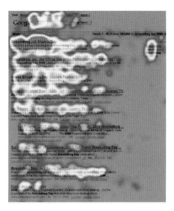

There have been attempts to describe how readers move through screen-based information. Usability researcher Jakob Nielsen, who tracked eye movement on several types of sites, describes a recurring F-shaped pattern of viewing. His studies indicate that we do not read online text word-for-word. We look for key words (subheads, bullet points, and so forth) at the left edge of paragraphs (Figure 4.28). What is not clear is whether this behavior is the result of natural reading patterns or a specific consequence of the configurations in the test presentations. There appears to be somewhat less predictable behavior in the areas of the second test devoted to image, suggesting that alternative configurations could produce different patterns, as they do in the Inner City poster.

Regardless of findings, it is obvious that how we read language is an orienting force to be reckoned with in designing information. Compositions can be consistent with dominant reading patterns or use attention-getting visual strategies to reorient readers' interpretive behavior. Designer Jonathan Barnbrook's book design

intentionally redirects the natural reading order to slow down interpretation for greater contemplation (Figure 4.29). In one spread, centered type with highlighted words encourages a staccato scanning behavior as well as a left-to-right, top-to-bottom pattern. Other spreads read first as shapes and second as text, encouraging an alternate approach to the page from more traditional layouts.

Shifting the orientation of text within the visual field or undermining a common baseline for letterforms in the same word or sentence further complicates orientation to the reading task. It slows down the speed of reading for some gain in reflection or reference to forms other than text.

Reading pattern, therefore, is an orienting force that determines perceptions of hierarchy in complex layouts. Subverting reading pattern for expressive means requires strong attention-getting characteristics in elements located in the fallow areas of the composition.

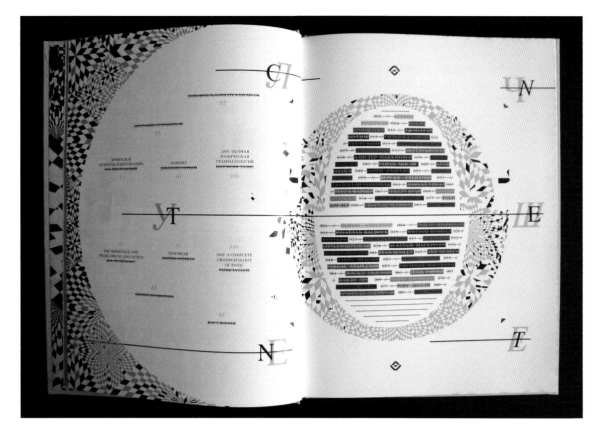

Figure 4.29
Newspeak: British Art Now, 2010
Booth-Clibborn Editions
Jonathan Barnbrook

Barnbrook's typographic layouts forgo traditional reading patterns in favor of more contemplative layouts that intentionally slow down reading.

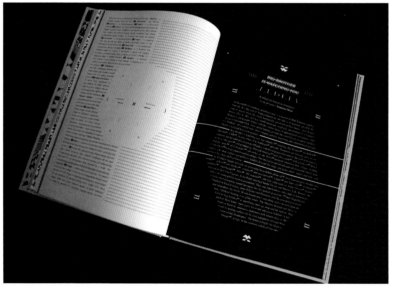

GROUPING

Grouping is an orientation strategy that uses elements in formal proximity or with visual similarity to indicate a relationship among them that is different from their relationship to other elements.

We have an almost instinctual need to group things together to create meaning where it might not otherwise be. The creation of constellations in the night sky by the ancient Greeks reflected a desire to make order out of a random array of stellar phenomena. In tests for color blindness, the ability to see numbers in an otherwise undifferentiated texture depends on the ability to group elements by color (Figure 4.30).

In a more complex task, Ladislav Sutnar redesigned a number of industrial catalogs for the F.W. Dodge Sweet's Catalog Service and RCA (Figure 4.32). Catalog design of the nineteenth century was not a project deemed worthy of great design and was usually left to printers. The classic Sears Catalog, for example, exhibited highly random layouts in which there was little control over hierarchy or continuity from spread to spread. Eccentric shapes—

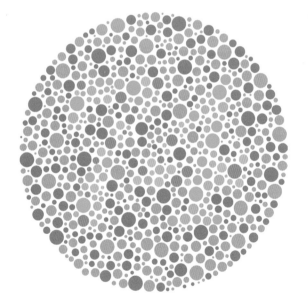

Figure 4.30
Ishihara color plate, 1917
Shinobu Ishihara
The Ishihara test for red-green deficiencies groups dots of different colors to form numbers. People with normal color vision can see the numbers; those with color deficiencies cannot.

Figure 4.31
Sears Catalog, 1918
Early catalog design showed little hierarchy among elements. Groupings of descriptions and images required separating lines to distinguish one from another.

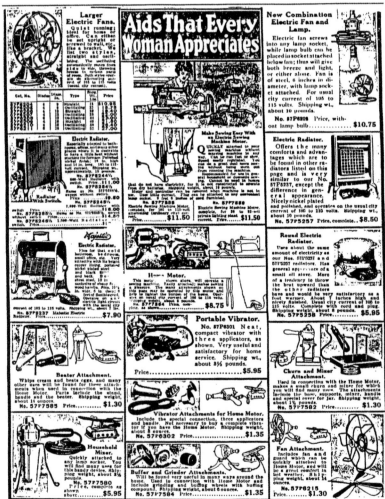

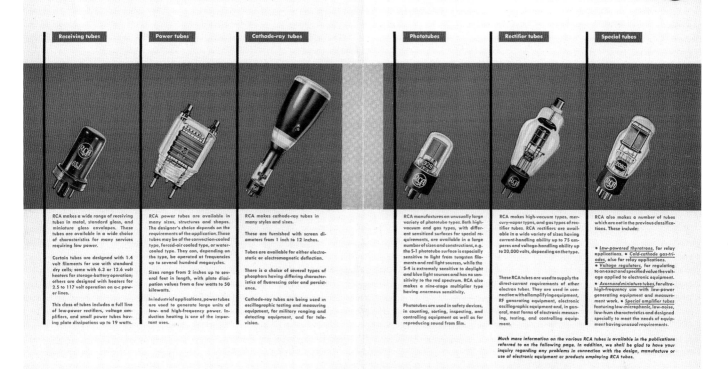

rather than a typographic system—contained discrete units of information and images often spilled over from one item description to another (Figure 4.31). Sutnar, in work from 1941–1960, applied a modernist grid to the design of publications and used groupings to cluster similar types of information. Geometric shapes still defined certain kinds of information, but they were used systematically to group related elements and to create larger forms that unified diverse photographs and statistical information. The generous use of white space allowed these groupings to be seen, unlike the crammed pages of nineteenth century catalogs in which the distances among elements were all the same, regardless of their content affinity.

Figure 4.32
RCA Electron Tubes Catalog, 1943
Ladislav Sutnar (1897–1976)
Sutnar brought design to industrial catalogs, which presented aesthetic and readability challenges in the shapes and sizes of objects in their inventories. Sutnar grouped elements, using blocks of color to minimize the eccentric silhouettes of industrial components.

The nature of the relationships among grouped elements varies with the intent of the designer, meanings of the individual elements, context of the grouping, and experience of the audience. Clustering the logos of high-tech companies, such as Microsoft and Apple, conveys commercial competition among computer giants. Adding the trademarks of General Electric and NBC television shifts the story to one of mega-mergers and the American entertainment industry. Adding the Camel cigarette image, Nike swoosh, and Playboy bunny changes the meaning to one of American business. Arranging these images on a blue field adjacent to red and white strips changes the meaning from one of commercial success to the corporate takeover of American politics and freedom (Figure 4.33).

Areas of color are also helpful in separating distinct discussions. The Cheapflights diagram of what is and is not allowed in luggage on an airplane clusters objects by content and procedure. Color blocking organizes many oddly shaped images and chunks of information into fewer explanations, and separates them by procedures to be followed at the airport (Figure 4.34).

Grouping also directs our behavior with information in highly pragmatic objects, such as forms and questionnaires. Completing applications or surveys and compiling responses can be confusing if answers are not grouped in particular locations and aligned on the left and right sides of the page regardless of the line lengths of the corresponding questions. Likewise, forms can be difficult to tabulate if workers have to search across the page for responses. In these instances, the context of use argues for particular groupings among elements.

Grouping, therefore, breaks complex information into fewer, more manageable units and reinforces content affinities that orient interpretive behavior.

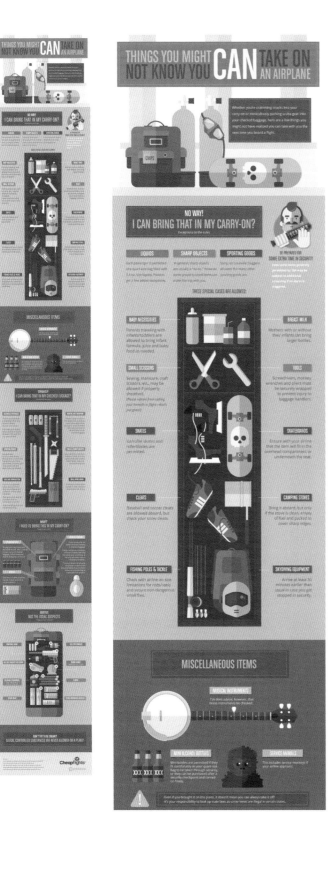

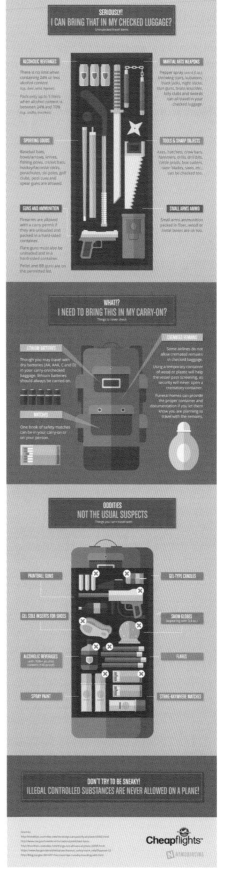

Figure 4.34
Things You Might Not Know You Can Take on a Plane, 2016
©Cheapflights Media (USA)
Designed in conjunction with NowSourcing
Cheapflights uses grouping to illustrate items that can and cannot be taken on an airplane. The clustering of items responds to the nature of the regulation and blocks of color contain dissimilarly shaped objects.

EDGE RELATIONSHIPS

An edge defines the boundary between two things: between the object and its environment, between an element in the composition and its background, and between two elements. Some edges are clearly defined, while others are fuzzy. Elements can interact with the edges of an object or they can echo the edge elsewhere in the composition.

There has always been a mistrust of the edge. We know that under test conditions, small children and animals avoid a precipice. There is an instinctual backing off for self-preservation. To go over an edge requires a willful decision, an overcoming of an aversion. No one steps off a diving board casually.

Designers can orient us to meaning by placing elements on or adjacent to the edge (Figure 4.35). This relationship does more than simply extend the image beyond the obvious perimeter of the object. Rather than serving as a frame that encloses some things and excludes others, the edge exerts influence on our perception of how elements behave within the composition. Elements either submit to the edge or challenge its confining qualities, contributing to the dynamic nature of the composition. In cases where single elements span the visual field and touch the opposite edges of the page—much like a clothesline—the effect is to anchor the element in space, undermining any possible action. In other cases, locating elements on opposite edges creates tension through an implied line between the two sides of the composition (Figure 4.36).

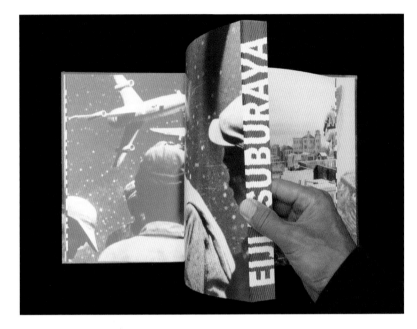

Figure 4.35
Eiji Tsuburaya, Master of Monsters: Defending the Earth with Ultraman, Godzilla, and Friends in the Golden Age of Japanese Science Fiction Film
Designers: Jon Sueda and Gail Swanlund, Stripe
Stripe's design for a book on Japanese science fiction films prints on the edges of pages. More than color, the edge printing builds and deconstructs typography as part of each spread's composition.

**Figure 4.36
AIGA Humor Show
poster, 1986
Design: M&Co.
Creative Director:
Tibor Kalman
Art Director and
Designer:
Alexander Isley
Writers: Alexander Isley,
Danny Abelson**

Isley's poster splits
elements, assigning
half of the images and
text to opposing edges
of the composition. The
color bar in the center
is typically printed on
the edges of an offset
press sheet to calibrate
color registration and is
trimmed off when the
job is completed. The
humor in Isley's design is
that the poster appears
"mis-trimmed," placing
what would normally
be on the edge in the
center. The banana peel
is a slapstick icon for
"slipping," a metaphor for
the trimming mistake.
The designer audience for
this poster knows these
printing conventions.

Elements within the composition can also draw attention to edges as ways of organizing different kinds of content (Figure 4.37). In a poster for SF MOMA, the division of space by photographs and color areas sets up a number of internal edges. Typography passes over and through different shapes, changing its orientation within space to yield to the power of the edge. These shifts demarcate changes in the type of information and move our eyes around the space and the planes of architecture, the subject of the poster.

In certain formats, the characteristic edge of the format controls design decisions. The gutter of a book or the fold of a tabloid newspaper, for example, represents an ever-present edge in spreads. Although design software minimizes the assertiveness of the edge during the design process, in bound form these edges exert a strong influence on how the reader perceives elements in the composition (Figure 4.38). Likewise, interactive media sometimes use the edge as navigation: bumping the cursor to the edge scrolls content to the left and right, sometimes panning a "landscape" of information and diminishing any perception of a "page."

In her design of oversized books, Dutch designer Irma Boom plays with the edge as a printing surface (Figure 4.39). We normally expect printing on the width and height of pages but not on the very narrow depth. Because Boom's books include hundreds of pages, the edge dimensions are significant. In her design of a book for the Cooper Hewitt Smithsonian Design Museum, Boom prints the page edges of the book in color and then calls attention to them through a white border on the covers. The white ink glows in the dark, defining the object only by its edges when the lights are out. The result is heightened perception of the book as a three-dimensional object.

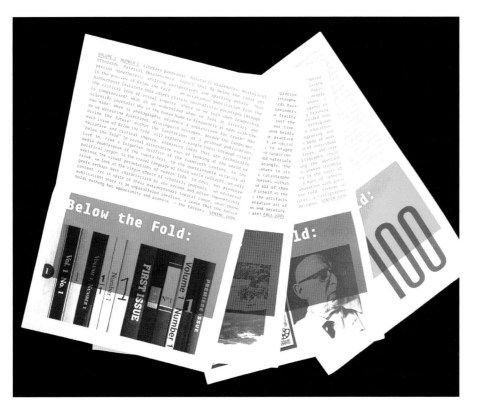

Figure 4.38
Below the Fold
Winterhouse
Below the Fold inverts
the typical news tabloid
design by locating
images in the lower half
of the publication and text
at the top. In this case,
the fold edge is not only a
design element but also
a reference to journalistic
practices.

Figure 4.39
***Making Design,* Cooper
Hewitt Smithsonian
Design Museum, 2016
Irma Boom**
Boom is known for her
over-sized book designs.
In this example, she
further emphasizes
the book as a three-
dimensional object by
printing on the edges of
the pages and a border
on the perimeter of the
cover. The border and
type glow in the dark,
creating an outline of the
book.

Edges are also important in how we read things. Figure 4.40 is an example of a *close edge*. Imagine this as advertising a variety of entertainment media. Although we normally read text horizontally, the wide word spacing between "free" and "book" and close vertical edge between "free" and "film" creates some ambiguity regarding which medium will require payment. The close edge phenomenon is especially important in maintaining the clarity of titles or quotes in which words are stacked in several lines. If the visual spaces between words are greater than between lines of type, the design encourages vertical reading, thus slowing down our interpretation of the text.

Edges, therefore, are powerful devices for orienting us to the interpretive task and in creating tension. They establish the limits of the visual field and function as a stable architecture with which other elements interact.

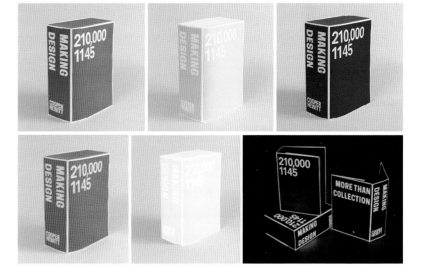

FREE BOOK
FILM FOR SALE

Figure 4.40
Shared edges
Although sentences
read horizontally, shared
edges and wider spacing
between words than
between lines of type
create ambiguity in
whether a book or
film is free.

DIRECTION

Direction is the line along which something appears to be moving with reference to a future point or region. It is a visible or invisible vector that connects a path to a goal. Unless specific cues argue otherwise, we tend to assign the laws of nature to the directional movement of elements in two-dimensional compositions. For example, a rectangle standing on its corner is more likely to "fall" than one resting on its side. We imagine the direction of the fall to correspond to the laws of gravity.

Gunther Kress and Theo van Leeuwen, in the book *Reading Images*, discuss how images direct our interpretation of narrative. The *authors* describe elements in a composition as actors that are connected by *vectors* in transactional relationships. Vectors may be visible or invisible; the gaze of a person toward an object may constitute a vector when there is really no line present. Such images are narrative because the directional quality of the vector tells us something about the potential for interaction among the elements (Kress & Van Leeuwen, 2006).

For example, Lewis Hine's 1931 photograph of a steelworker on a beam establishes a narrative in several ways (Figure 4.41). Despite the strong vectors of the steel cables, our attention is drawn to the steelworker's extended arm and pointing finger. It is the building in the distance with which the steelworker appears to have a transactional relationship, not the other elements. The precarious nature of his position is undermined by the illusion that the Chrysler Building in the distance helps him to maintain balance and avoid falling. In other words, the converging directional vectors in the image (the lines of the arm and the spire of the building) counter the facts of the image.

Sometimes directional cues and vectors are explicit. They indicate a path or direction something travels. In the safety illustrations by German "electropathologist" Stefan Jellinek, the path electricity travels appears in red (Figure 4.42). The directional line connects the action to the dangerous consequence.

In orienting ourselves in space, we confront six possible directions based on the human body—left, right, up, down, forward, and backward. All other directions can be derived from these six. Maps and coordinate-defined spaces determine direction in relation to these guides. A flat or two-dimensional map of a multistory shopping mall, for example, must not only indicate where stores are located on a flat plane, but also show the position of floors in relation to each other. In other words, they must direct how we move vertically as well as horizontally.

Joel Katz Design Associates in Philadelphia considered pedestrians' relationships to space and direction in navigating unfamiliar cities. His *Walk! Philadelphia* orients street maps to the directions in which pedestrians currently face, rather than to north at the top of all maps (Figure 4.43). *Walk! Philadelphia* offers a more user-centered approach to wayfinding and simplifies the process of street orientation. Pedestrians unfamiliar with the setting don't have to guess about compass directions.

Figure 4.41
Empire State Building Construction Worker, 1930
Lewis Hine
In Hine's photograph a construction worker balances on a beam by reaching out to "touch" the Chrysler Building in the distance. The directional vectors created by his arm and the distant building overcome the precarious reality of his physical position.

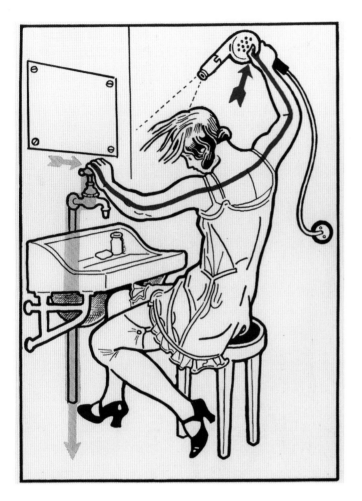

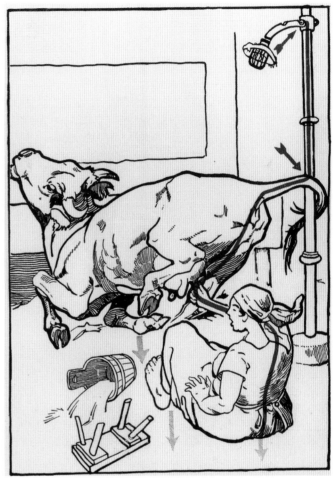

Figure 4.42
Electroschutz in
132 Bildern, 1931
Stefan Jellinek
(1871–1968)
Illustrations:
Franz Wacik
These humorous
illustrations in a
book by a German
"electropathologist"
describe safety
dangers in the 1930s.
The directional lines
establish a relationship
between an action and
a consequence.

Finally, directional cues can orient us to the order in which to interpret elements within a composition (Figure 4.44). Nigel Holmes shows a diagram for completing a task, ordering movies on Netflix. Elements of the diagram indicate necessary physical actions, eliminating the need for step-by-step verbal instructions across multiple images. Elements in a poster for the Cooper Hewitt Smithsonian Design Museum serve a similar function in moving us through the composition while encountering elements in a specific order (Figure 4.45). In this case, the ordering of elements works against the traditional top-down reading pattern and relies on numbers and graphic symbols to suggest an alternate bottom-to-top route through information.

Directional elements and composition cues, therefore, orient us to the content of the communication. They tell us where to look and imply the order of events or cause/effect relationships among elements in the visual field.

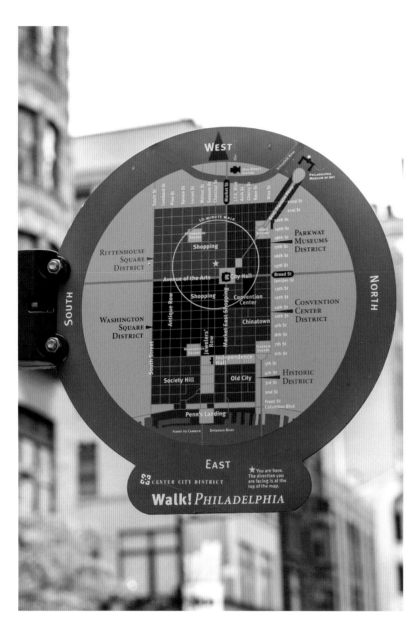

HOW NETFLIX WORKS

Figure 4.43
Walk! Philadelphia
Joel Katz
Katz's signage design for Walk! Philadelphia orients the pedestrian to the direction in which he/she is moving, not to the conventional compass locations.

Figure 4.44
How Netflix works
Nigel Holmes
Holmes's "explanation graphics" tell subscribers how to use Netflix to rent films. The illustration uses frames that order the sequence of steps in the process and arrows that indicate the action taken in each frame.

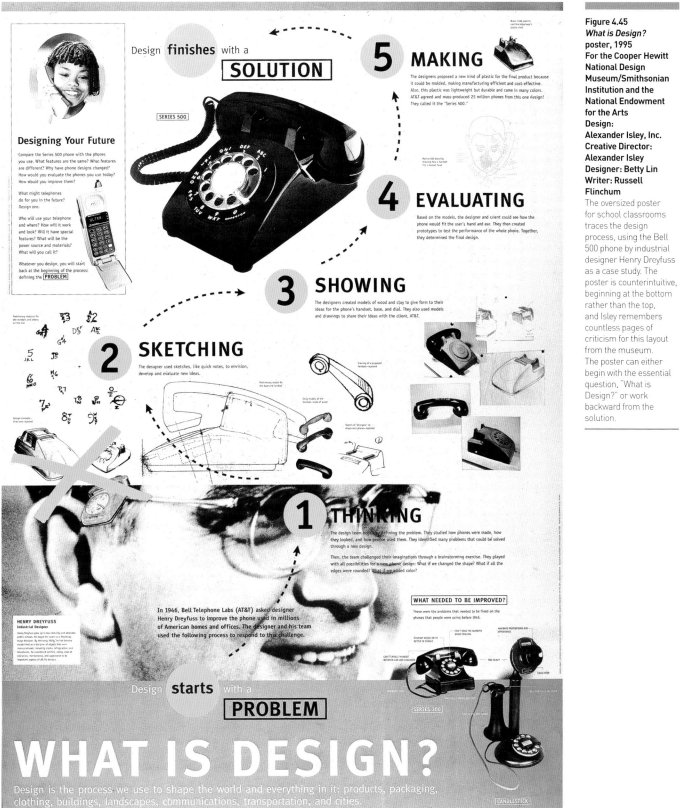

Figure 4.45
What is Design?
poster, 1995
For the Cooper Hewitt
National Design
Museum/Smithsonian
Institution and the
National Endowment
for the Arts
Design:
Alexander Isley, Inc.
Creative Director:
Alexander Isley
Designer: Betty Lin
Writer: Russell
Flinchum

The oversized poster
for school classrooms
traces the design
process, using the Bell
500 phone by industrial
designer Henry Dreyfuss
as a case study. The
poster is counterintuitive,
beginning at the bottom
rather than the top,
and Isley remembers
countless pages of
criticism for this layout
from the museum.
The poster can either
begin with the essential
question, "What is
Design?" or work
backward from the
solution.

POINT OF VIEW

Point of view is the position from which something or someone is observed. Point of view can frame events, scenes, or information in radically different ways. It tells us where we are positioned with respect to the objects or people in the image.

Point of view influences our perception of events and information. It determines whether we are a participant or a spectator, an actor or observer. It is not only another way of seeing, but also another way of knowing. The first edition of the *Whole Earth Catalog* in 1968 (a year before man landed on the moon) featured a picture of Earth as seen from space. What made this picture so powerful—revolutionary, even—was that for the first time we could see our world as an object floating in space. Small, fragile, and alone, the vision of the Earth from space changed our perception of the environment we inhabit. In a less profound sense, Google Earth gives us satellite views of our own neighborhood, allowing us to see familiar things from a new viewpoint.

But a photographer does not have to leave the planet to surprise us with viewpoints other than the ordinary ways in which we perceive our environment. Russian photographer Aleksandr Rodchenko was known for his dramatic compositions, often shot from a high or low

position and an oblique angle (Figure 4.46). The framing of these images reduced detail to graphic pattern, consistent with modernist preference for essential form and stripped of any overt cultural or historical references. Rodchenko's abstractions were more important than the literal subject matter of the photographs. His goal was to make the familiar seem unfamiliar—to reorient viewers from their ordinary habits of viewing.

Explanations of a three-dimensional world often require multiple viewpoints to fully understand an object or environment. *Plan views* illustrate things from above. *Elevations* depict things from the side and *sections* cut across the object or environment at some informative place. The *section* in Figure 4.47, for example, shows us layers of the Earth that we could not observe in real life. *Isometric projections* show three-dimensional views in two-dimensional drawings. Isometric maps are helpful to pedestrians because they indicate what might be obscured by a building or landform in reaching a street location.

Figure 4.46
Steps, 1930
Aleksandr Mikhailovich Rodchenko (1891–1956)
© Rodchenko & Stepanova Archive, DACS, RAO 2016
Rodchenko was known for his unusual photographic viewpoints in compositions that were less about narrative and more about the position of objects in space.

Figure 4.47, opposite
Section
Scientific diagrams show a variety of views from plan, to section, and elevation. They can illustrate structures and processes that are invisible to the human eye.

How we use images in publications can establish whether our viewpoint is that of a participant or spectator in the action of the image. When an image extends to the perimeter of the page, as viewers we are in the same figurative space as the people or objects in the image. When framed by white space or a border, however, the frame sits between us and the activity in the image. We are spectators watching from outside, figuratively peering through the frame. Nothing about the image itself has changed between the two layouts, but our position with respect to the scene has.

Point of view asks us to self-consciously adjust our visual perspective, but in doing so, it may also ask us to take on dispositions and cultural assumptions that are different from our own. Artist Fred Wilson uses this technique to masterful effect in gallery installations and catalogs. For his exhibition, *Mining the Museum*, Wilson exhibits cigar store Indians with their backs facing the audience. This change in our customary physical viewpoint on the object raises questions about racism and historical attitudes toward Native Americans by a dominant white culture.

As these examples show, point of view orients us to both the physical and conceptual content of an object or scene. Just as we use the phrase "point of view" in everyday language to communicate the distinctly different perspectives that two or more people might have on an issue, point of view in design affords the designer the opportunity to reveal fresh insight into otherwise familiar material. It tells us where we are in relation to the things shown and how to think about the act of viewing.

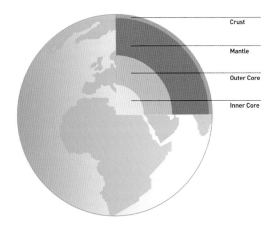

Crust

Mantle

Outer Core

Inner Core

SUMMARY

Orienting the audience to the use of the designed object is a critical task for designers. When readers or users don't understand the system well enough to access the message, they struggle with interpretation. We all have culturally determined preconceptions of how various objects work to construct meaning. Designers must be aware of the affordances that enable or constrain certain kinds of actions and the codes or conventions that guide interpretation. Books tell us, by design, that content will be released in a linear and sequential manner over time. Interactive websites update specific fields of information or even change their states of being to confirm that our actions produce the desired results. Signage indicates by variations in its form when it is identifying, directing, or regulating our behavior.

The designed object also orients us to the meaning of specific elements, and once we confirm that our perception of the system and how it operates is accurate, we react and take action. Form defines the relationships among information elements and leads us to certain interpretations.

Interacting, interpreting, and experiencing

Interpretation is the process of finding meaning in the things we see and hear. In interpreting visual communication, we assign particular significance to the elements of visual and verbal language and their arrangement with consideration of the surrounding context.

Previous theories of interpretation held that authors and designers of messages created meaning—that they could impose meaning on form—and that the obligation of the reader or viewer was to interpret that meaning accurately. Historically, the goal of designers throughout most of the twentieth century was to overcome the distractions of culture seen as obstacles to interpretation and direct experience; to eliminate elements and stylistic devices that required particular cultural interpretations in favor of simple, undecorated forms that designers thought were universally human.

Since the last decades of the twentieth century, *constructionist* theories of design have held that the reader or viewer is the primary creator of meaning, influenced by the surrounding context and past experiences. Critics argue that inherent differences in cultural positions—that is, the idea that our cultural backgrounds and past experiences shape interpretation—mean that multiple meanings to the same message are always possible. It is likely, for example, that teenagers respond in much different ways to symbols of authority than do their parents, or that immigrants and natives assign distinctly different meanings to signs of patriotism. It is also likely that interpretation depends, to some degree, on the setting in which we encounter the message. The Stars and Stripes on a picnic cooler is less likely to inspire feelings of national pride than the American flag waving in an Olympic athlete's arms. Form, therefore, does not exist in an interpretive vacuum but is contextually dependent. Meaning emerges from the audience's surrounding physical and cultural environment and from social use. This view of interpretation challenges designers to go beyond their own assumptions about what things mean and to consider the possible novel interpretations that viewers and readers may generate on the basis of their own rich and varied experiences.

Interpretation, therefore, results from the designer's choices about form and message; the physical, social, cultural, and technological circumstances surrounding the message; and the characteristic thinking behaviors and past experiences of the interpreters.

The nature of signs

The smallest unit of meaning is the *sign*. A sign is something that stands for something to someone in some respect. In English, the letters C-O-W constitute a sign for a large farm animal that gives milk. For some a hand gesture with the thumb pointing upward is a sign of approval. And a photograph of the Eiffel Tower is often taken as a sign for the city of Paris. In all cases, the relationship between these signs and what they stand for is *arbitrary*—that is, a matter of tacit cultural agreement rather than any natural relationship between the sign and its meaning. The sign for the same animal in Spanish, for example, is V-A-C-A and the letter combination C-O-W appears in many other English words with different meanings. The sign of the raised thumb for approval originated with Roman gladiators but now also refers to social networking and internet applications. And it is the frequency with which messages use the Eiffel Tower to represent Paris that joined the landmark and its location.

In the early part of the twentieth century, Swiss linguist Ferdinand de Saussure and American philosophers Charles Sanders Peirce and Charles Morris developed new insights into *semiotics*, the study of signs. Saussure's work represented a significant break with previous studies of language by focusing on the act of communication in the present, rather than on the history of words and changes in language over time. Saussure believed interpretation depends not only on the individual meaning of signs, but more importantly, on the structural relationships among them in use. All the same words appear in the two sentences: *The car hit the boy* and *The boy hit the car*. The different meanings of these two sentences depend on word order, not on the words themselves. As discussed in previous sections of this book, the arrangement of elements in a visual composition is crucial in how we interpret them.

Saussure described two components of a sign, the *signified* (the person, thing, place, or idea for which the sign stands) and the *signifier* (the sound or image that represents the signified) (Saussure, 2000). It is this idea—the separation of the concept and its physical representation in words or images—that allows us to consider the contribution of form to meaning (Davis, 2012). Had Saussure not seen these two components as distinct we could not discuss how the meaning of typography is different from spoken language, photography is different from drawing, and information that moves is different from information that stands still.

Figure 5.1
New York Times Sunday Review, "Don't Show Me the Money," 2013
Martin Venezky
Venezky's layout plays with syntax—the ordering of elements. Words appear in many different typefaces and in different spaces throughout the composition. The text defies linear reading, building meaning instead from the juxtaposition of ideas without an obvious hierarchy.

American philosopher Charles Sanders Peirce was interested in types of signs and how they perform. His classifications were typically expressed in groups of three: *icon* (a sign that physically resembles what it stands for); *index* (a sign that points to something else or that refers to a cause/effect relationship); and *symbol* (an abstract sign whose meaning must be learned through association with what it stands for). This triad is the most frequent of Peirce's groupings referred to by designers.

Peirce also argued for the importance of the *ground*, the pure abstraction of a quality. The signs for men and women on restroom doors represent gender by physically resembling people: women in dresses, men in trousers. They are iconic in their resemblance to human form but indexical in "pointing to" a specific use for the room. The seemingly neutral, institutional form of these icons, however, is their ground. They are not, for example, photographs of Russians in folk costumes, comic book drawings of surly teenagers, or some other quality of specific people. Because they lack detail or historical references, designers often call these icons "Helvetica Man and Woman," referring to a sans serif typeface having the same undecorated qualities and developed in the same period. This quality or ground is what Peirce meant when he said a sign stands for something *in some respect*. It represents expressive opportunities for designers. It means that simply choosing appropriate content isn't enough; that designers must think beyond the subject matter of the sign to its visual properties as well.

American Charles Morris's contribution to semiotics was identifying three ways of thinking about the nature of signs: semantics, syntax, and pragmatics. *Semantics* is the relationship between signs and what they stand for. Think about the concept of "dog" and how different the meaning is when represented by a Yorkshire Terrier or a Great Dane. In a literal sense both are dogs but neither may be a best example for the general concept of "dog;" their extreme sizes may better signify "tiny lapdog" and "big regal dog" than "dog." Asking which sign, if either, best represents the desired concept is a question of semantics.

Syntax is the relationship of one sign to others, the ordering of elements within a message. When typography is involved, there is both the syntax of verbal language (grammar) and the syntax of visual form (composition). In some cases, the visual arrangement of words departs from the one-word-after-another verbal syntax of text. Sentences can be interrupted by other forms or appear as words dispersed across the visual field, but the typographic characteristics of each word allow us to reassemble the individual signs as a complete thought (Figure 5.1).

Syntax is crucial in the interpretation of time-based media. The order of episodes in a narrative, for example, determines what we think a story is about. Early twentieth-century filmmaker Lev Kuleshov experimented with scene sequencing. He alternated a picture of a famous actor with images of a bowl of soup, a girl in a coffin, and a woman on a sofa. Despite all four photographs being exactly the same in each sequence, viewers reported very different expressions on the actor's face depending on the order of the images (thoughtful following the forgotten soup, sorrowful following the coffin, and lustful following the woman on the divan). This study demonstrated the power of editing and that the interpretation of any single image relies on its position with respect to others.

Pragmatics concerns the relationships among signs, their interpreters, and context. It addresses the effect of people, settings, and use on the interpretation of meaning. Red type has a negative connotation in a financial report—signifying "being in the red" or "red ink" as a deficit—but not in a textbook. We notice when a fashion magazine uses snapshots rather than dramatically staged fashion photographs or when the camera movement in a film is jerky and amateurish. We consider the makers' intent in the use of these signs as "realism" or signifying a particular person's point of view, only because they appear in contexts that otherwise use slick professional photography.

There are many theories, therefore, about interpretation. We can see these ideas gain popularity at various times in the history of design and designers need to understand how they shape assumptions about the effects of form.

The nature of interaction and interpretation

Interaction is a back and forth relationship between two things; an action by one produces a response by the other. Today, the term *interaction design* often describes the design of digital systems and products, such as websites, games, and software. In these examples, physical activity by the user is necessary to communicate with the operating system of the computer. Changes in the display and sound provide feedback that lets the user know the device did or did not get the message.

All design, however, involves some level of human interaction with messages, products, environments, or services. There need not be a computer involved to think about design in terms of interaction among the intent of message originators, the qualities of objects and systems, and the behavior of people for whom they are designed. The printed *Audubon Field Guide to Birds*, for example, allows readers to search for birds by an alphabetical listing of species, family (there are eighty species of wrens, for example), appearance (by color, silhouette, or size), or habitat, much as they would search a digital database. Recognizing that birdwatchers have different needs in different contexts—reading at home versus observing in the field, for example—the book accommodates different types of interaction with information (Davis, 2012).

Feedback to the source of the communication may be less direct in printed communication than in digital interactions, yet if we don't attend, don't buy, or don't join, someone gets an idea about how we feel. Designers who think of their work as creating conditions for people's experiences—rather than crafting the physical characteristics of artifacts as an end in itself—design with people's behavior and emotions in mind.

If the qualities of interaction go beyond the practical—that is, if they are poetic, transform our understanding or beliefs, or surpass the ordinary in some way—we describe the experiences they make possible as *aesthetic*. They add value or beauty to the everyday. Design can attract attention and orient people to its use, but if it doesn't deliver a compelling experience it may fail in its mission to meet people's expectations or be memorable. And designers often take the opportunity to turn actions that are simply functional into something memorable. Automotive designers lavish surprising attention to the sound of a car door closing, recognizing that even such a banal moment can signify meaningful things (luxury or precise engineering, for example).

The standards for a compelling interaction are cognitive, emotional, and cultural. On the cognitive side, design can enhance or diminish the accuracy or efficiency of our thinking by its form. When form is not appropriate to the task or doesn't correspond to the structure of the information, the interpretive process is not very satisfying. For example, a recipe book that embeds ingredients in a paragraph of narrative instructions, rather than in a separate list, makes it difficult for the cook to plan grocery shopping and assemble the necessary cookware before preparing the dish. And if the steps of the recipe aren't clearly separated one from another, it is easy to get lost when moving back and forth between the cookbook and the task.

Emotion plays an important role in interpretation. We respond to some messages viscerally—at the gut level and bypassing logical reasoning. Advertising makes strong use of this approach and sells us things we normally couldn't buy, such as love, status, or masculinity. Visceral images convert objects to emotions. We want a special perfume or cologne because we believe it makes us as sexy as the model. We want the newest technology because advertising associates ownership with cutting edge status. We want a beer because the foaming, frosty mug appeals to our senses of touch, smell, and taste, not to rational thought.

Other messages require reflection and judgment to elicit our emotions. We are inspired by the documentary of an accomplished statesman. We find endless fascination in the work of artist Georgia O'Keeffe. We are continually motivated to master a game that requires strategy and skill. In these cases, our emotions result from careful consideration of information or the desire for competency at a particular task. We think about these things long after our initial encounter, while visceral images disappear quickly from our consciousness because they aren't processed rationally.

On the cultural side, we live in a visual world that not only exposes us to an enormous number of stimuli but also assigns status to them based on style and context. We know when something feels current, official, and for us or for someone else. The qualities of form position information in history, tell us something about its source, and speak the languages of various social groups. We know from cultural experience what procedures and time are required to publish in noteworthy publications—we judge the credibility of information on this basis. Action movies, sports magazines, and heroes in computer games influence our perceptions of masculinity. Our experience associates neon with urban nightlife, camouflage with the military, and pink and blue with gender. In other words, we draw upon our history of interpretation *in a cultural context* to make sense of what form means, though that cultural milieu is never set in stone and can, itself, change.

Designers often borrow or appropriate form from other cultures, repurposing meanings from one time or context in another. Interest in vernacular form—that is, form produced by people not trained in design—dominated graphic work at the end of the twentieth century. Often as a commentary on the belief that all messages can be interpreted in more than one way, vernacular form introduced cultural references that had little literal relationship to the content of the message. In this way, form expanded the range of connotations. For example, Art Chantry's poster for the King County Department of Public Health uses humor to remove the stigma from condom use (Figure 5.2). Chantry's poster reminds us of workplace safety posters from the 1950s. In today's climate of political correctness, the poster borrows the direct communication style of blue-collar work environments of another time.

In other ways, the interpretation of contemporary messages actually produces new cultural meanings. It is through communication technologies that we participate in the conversations and activities that shape and define our social environment. Designers yield increasing control to users in a digital world. Collectively, we generate the content and form of messages that influence what we think things mean. And new technologies often arrive before we know what they are really good for; through use and interaction we explore their communicative possibilities and contributions to shaping culture. Originally conceived as a means for sharing information among scientists, public use of the internet redefined concepts of identity and privacy, authorship and publishing, and service. The "truth" of images is challenged in a culture in which "photoshop" is a verb, not just the name of a software application. Information, therefore, gains cultural meaning through the means of production and circulation.

The concepts in Chapter 5 focus on how we construct meaning in visual messages. They address the roles that cognitive processing, emotion, culture, and language play in creating compelling experiences.

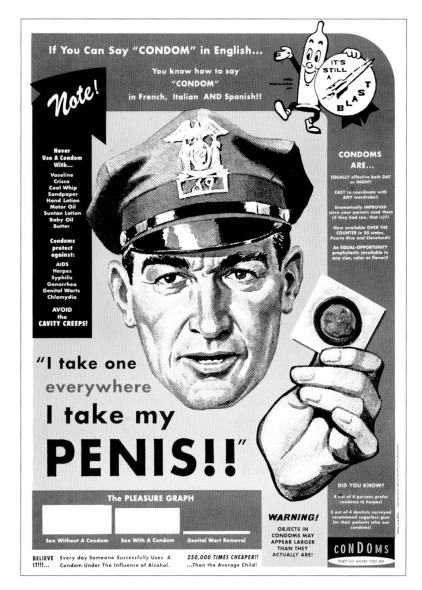

Figure 5.2
Penis Cop poster for King County Department of Public Health, 1993
Art Chantry
Chantry's poster appropriates the style of workplace safety posters of the 1950s for a contemporary message.

LEGIBILITY/READABILITY

Legibility describes whether something visible is easily discernable. Legible typography, for example, is of sufficient size and spacing to be seen and to allow one letterform to be distinguished from another. When the design of text provokes our desire to read it and determine its meaning, we say it is readable.

When we complete federal tax forms we want to do so with efficiency. We expect the form to tell us what financial and personal information is necessary to report, how taxes are to be calculated, what expenses offset the amount owed, and how to file the final outcome of our labor. The design of the form should orient us to these various activities. The *Simplification* division of design firm Siegel+Gale was asked by the United States government to redesign the 1040 tax form for print and screen (Figure 5.3). The designers addressed the language and configuration of the form, reducing error rates and completion time. Ultimately, a more legible design improved taxpayer attitudes.

Likewise, the nutrition label on food packaging carries important information that, when previously left to food producers, was not legible and varied from company to company. In 1992, Burkey Belser designed a label for the United States Food and Drug Administration that standardized the representation of caloric and nutritional content for all food packaging in the United States (Figure 5.4). The design of the label uses type weight, indents, and ruled lines to communicate legible information that encourages consumers to make healthy choices.

If typography is too small, too tightly spaced, or not arranged in a manner conducive to deciphering the important relationships among elements, it is ultimately illegible and fails us in executing the task and making appropriate judgments.

Typographic legibility is important in environmental applications as well. In the 1990s, the United States Federal Highway Administration addressed the problem of an aging population driving on America's roads, making the legibility of signs an important safety issue. Environmental communication designer Don Meeker and type designer James Montalbano proposed new typeface called *Clearview* (Figure 5.5). The design of the typeface addressed the small counterspace problem of Highway Gothic, which had been used since the Eisenhower administration and took its form from the mid-century technology for die-cut letters. It had never been tested.

Figure 5.3
1040 EZR
Design Director:
Mike Scott
Digital Designer:
Sierra Siemer
Siegel+Gale
Siegel+Gale designed an e-file tax form for mobile devices. The system pulls information from the taxpayer's W-2 form and shows the calculations simply in a legible sequence.

Figure 5.4
US Food and Drug Administration Nutrition Facts Label, 1990
Burkey Belser
The US Food and Drug Administration nutrition label arose from government concern over the obesity epidemic in the United States. Designer Belser set the label in eight-point type and surrounded it with a border to keep food manufacturers from interfering with the legibility of the label.

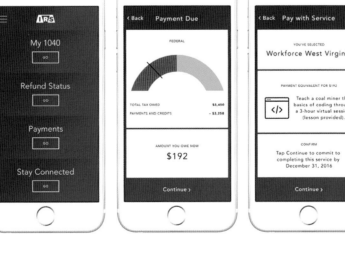

Positive Contrast Version	Negative Contrast Version
Clearview-6-W	Clearview-6-B
Clearview-5-W	Clearview-5-B
Clearview-4-W	Clearview-4-B
Clearview-3-W	Clearview-3-B
Clearview-2-W	Clearview-2-B
Clearview-1-W	Clearview-1-B

Figure 5.5
Clearview highway signage, 1992
Top: ClearviewHwy™ cascade of weight in both positive and negative contrast versions
Bottom: Proportion-based grid system for layout of freeway and expressway guide signs
Meeker and Associates, Inc.

The Clearview typeface was originally designed to help older drivers. The typeface improves legibility for all drivers by about 20 percent with no change in the size of the sign. It creates greater distinction between similar letterforms (the lowercase "I" and "l", for example), which improves legibility in poor light conditions and at high speeds and long distances.

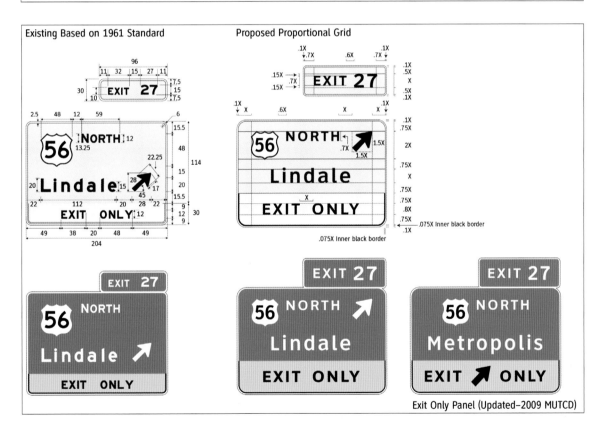

Existing Based on 1961 Standard

Proposed Proportional Grid

Exit Only Panel (Updated–2009 MUTCD)

Verdana

Figure 5.6
Verdana typeface, 1996
Matthew Carter
Microsoft
Carter's Verdana was
designed for computer
screens. It has wide
letterspacing and a large
x-height to ensure that
letters are legible on a
backlit screen.

A major study in 1994 recommended a 20 percent increase in letter height to accommodate the viewing distance and reaction time of older drivers (Terminal Design, Inc., 2004). But such increases meant a 40 to 50 percent increase in the overall size of the sign panel (Terminal Design, Inc., 2004). *Clearview* increases the x-height of lowercase letters without increasing the capital height, thus occupying roughly the same space as the older Highway Gothic. The typeface was developed through rigorous user testing. Unfortunately, the Federal Highway Administration quietly withdrew its support for the typeface in early 2016, returning to the 58-year-old Highway Gothic.

Type designer Matthew Carter designed *Verdana* to overcome the coarseness of computer screen displays of the time (Figure 5.6). He shaped the typeface on the basis of pixels, rather than pen strokes. The relationships among different types of strokes (straight, curved, and diagonal), large counterspaces, wide letterspacing, and large x-height ensure that letterforms are readable on backlit screens. Commonly confused characters, such as the upper and lowercase *i*, *j*, and *l* and the numeral *1* are carefully drawn for maximum contrast. Various weights in the typeface family are distinctive, making clear differences even at very small sizes.

It would be helpful if there were rules designers could follow to make things most legible, but typography is *relational*; change in one variable produces an entirely different relationship among the other variables. For example, we may improve our ability to read text set in Helvetica by increasing the space between lines of type, allowing us to better see the shapes of letters and words. But the same amount of space may be too much for Garamond, in which the height of lowercase letters is much smaller than in Helvetica. Too much space between lines of Garamond could make it more difficult to find the next line of text when our eyes return to the left edge of the paragraph. Bold white type on black paper may be perfectly legible, but bold white type on a black computer screen may produce a glow that fills in the tiny spaces inside and around letterforms. Legibility, therefore, depends on the particular relationships among typeface, point size, type weight, line spacing, and the surface on which letters sit.

Type designers typically classify typefaces into two groupings: text and display. Typefaces designed for body text are meant to function well at point sizes between six and fourteen points, and to ease the task of reading long, repeating lines of text. Display typefaces are optimized for larger point sizes. They often grab our attention successfully in small amounts, but are awkward to read in long lines of text. There are many typefaces that designers use for both text and display, and it is up to the designer's creativity to follow and to sometimes break these rules. The readability of typography has everything to do with context. We don't want to read the 560,000-word English translation of Tolstoy's *War and Peace* set in a Stencil typeface, but may be perfectly happy with a poster set in the same typeface. And we are likely to be comfortable with hand-drawn signs advertising a yard sale but find the individuality of the same letterforms awkward in regulatory highway signage. In other words, what we see as readable has much to do with the nature of content and the circumstances in which it is read.

Typography is not the only kind of form in which readability is important. Successful interpretation of charts and diagrams depends on the match between content and form. When design forces information into a form that is inconsistent either with the perceptual nature of the content or the task it supports, we spend extra effort in deciphering meaning. Over the years there have been many attempts to explain what constitutes a healthy diet. The United States Department of Agriculture Food Pyramid has undergone a number of transformations. Early versions

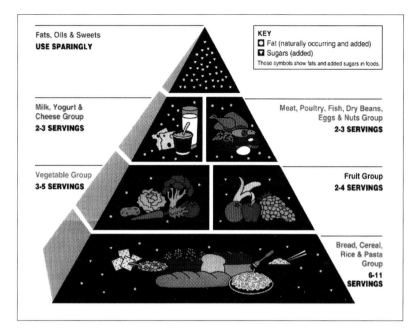

asked consumers to discriminate among differently sized wedges of a polyhedron (Figure 5.7). However, we don't plan meals first by volume. The truly useful information is in text in the margins describing the recommended number of servings in each food group (Davis, 2012). In this case, the use of numbers is a better match for the nutrition task. A more recent design attempts to integrate exercise with descriptions of food groups, another difficult perceptual task under a highly abstract form.

Legibility and readability are not the only criteria for success in design, however. But in cases where efficient and effective communication is paramount, designers must pay careful attention to the task of reading and processing information. Legibility, in the end, leads to readability. That is, well-set type draws the reader in and creates a fit between the design, the reader's expectations, and the task at hand.

Figure 5.7
Food Pyramid, 1992
US Department of Agriculture
This older version of the Food Pyramid presented food groups as differently sized wedges of a polyhedron. Few people, however, plan meals by volume or surface area, and the truly useful information is in the text outside the pyramid, which tells consumers how many daily servings of each food group are advised.

DENOTATION AND CONNOTATION

Denotation is the literal or surface meaning of a sign. It is an explicit and direct description of fact. Connotation is an idea or feeling that a representation invokes in addition to its literal meaning. Because connotative meanings are not factual but instead figurative descriptions, they generally arise from cultural and social experiences in which people, things, places, and events become associated with particular abstract ideas, emotions, or behaviors.

"I say what I mean and I mean what I say."

If only it were that simple. Most of us believe that language is an instrument of communication that transmits meaning from the communicator to an intended audience. Provided that we send the message without interference, then the meaning is clear and language has done its job. But as we know, sometimes what we say is misunderstood, taken out of context, or interpreted beyond its literal meaning by a listener or reader.

On the other hand, were language not capable of evoking a field of associations beyond the single word, we would find little reason to read a good book, listen to great music, or write poetry. A rose would be just a pretty plant with thorns, not an expression of affection, and the photo of the politician's family would be evidence of marital status, not a symbol of family values. The power of visual and verbal language lies in the ability to produce a variety of combinations, each with its own field of associations.

French critic Roland Barthes reminded us that photography is paradoxical. At the same time as it mechanically records exactly what is in the scene (its denotation), it is also subject to manipulation by pose, lighting, and the inclusion of other images that heighten its connotations. Denotatively, an image of a table of pasta and wine is simply that. Connotatively, says Barthes, it stands for "Italianicity" (Barthes, 1977). A Chianti bottle, checkered tablecloth, and red, white, and green references to the Italian flag are a connotative code for the experience of dining in an Italian restaurant. Further, the connotative association of Italy with food reinforces the meaning of the photograph. We would be less likely to represent Russia through a dining experience because other associations with that country are stronger.

The documentary photograph or film is presumed to be a denotative representation of fact. Yet because it requires decisions about how subjects will be shot, sequenced, and described, it, too, is open to interpretation. And as time passes, the documentation takes on connotative qualities associated with another time and place. The work of Dorothea Lange, a documentarian best known for her photographs of Depression-era labor for the Farm Security Administration, recorded the lives of displaced farm and migrant workers in the 1930s (Figure 5.8). Lange's photographs, denotative in their intent, came to stand for the heartbreak of homelessness, rural poverty, the Great Depression, and the role of photography in documenting social conditions. In other words, they continued to gain connotations long after they were made.

Typefaces also have connotations that arise from how they were created and where they are used. *OCR-A* connotes computer usage; *Courier* connotes twentieth-century typewriters; *Helvetica* connotes corporate design; and *Comic Sans* connotes informality. In and of themselves, these typefaces do not mean anything. When they are put to use, however, they contribute to the meaning of the text. In some cases, typeface selections reinforce the verbal meaning of the text. In other instances, they introduce additional or contradictory connotations.

Designers routinely weigh the relationship between the denotation and connotation of form. They anticipate how various audiences with different cultural experiences may interpret images and language. They must also think about how messages are interpreted connotatively in a variety of possible settings. The meaning of a message is always an interaction among content, context, audience, and use.

Figure 5.8
Migrant Mother, 1936
Dorothea Lange
(1895–1965)
Lange photographed
displaced American
farm workers during the
1930s. While her role was
one of documentation,
providing literal
depictions of workers in
the nation's heartland,
her photographs came
to stand connotatively for
poverty and suffering in
the Great Depression.

FRAMING

Framing is the construction of meaning through the designer's choices of what to include in the message. It is the designer's selective influence over audience perception that encourages some interpretations over others. In photography, images are framed first by the selection and viewpoint of a scene, and second, by any *cropping* that further narrows the number of elements in the visual field and changes the original composition.

**Figure 5.9
Raising the Flag on Iwo Jima, 1945
Joe Rosenthal
(1911–2006)**
The famous photograph of raising the American flag on Iwo Jima at Mount Suribachi is actually a cropping of the original image. In the cropped image, the flagpole divides the composition in half, anchoring it in the corner of the image. This makes the opposing physical force of the marines seem greater and more heroic than when the flag had no resistance in the open sky.

In the simplest sense, a frame creates a space that includes some things and excludes others. It draws attention to the framed content and elevates its importance as the focus of the composition. The frame around a painting separates it from the surrounding wall. A window frames a view from the interior of a building—we often buy or rent a space because it is a "room with a view." A browser window is a frame that isolates specific content from the Web and the desktop. A photograph frames a scene from a different moment in place and time. Such frames can be visual, conceptual, or both.

The sequence of photographs taken at the raising of the American flag on Iwo Jima at Mount Suribachi during the Second World War—and the subsequent cropping of the final shot—illustrates how framing influences interpretation (Figure 5.9). The heroic final image cropped extraneous elements from the image and created a composition with marines and navy corpsmen united in pushing against the strong angle of the flagpole. Their effort is more apparent in the cropped version because the top of the flagpole is anchored in the corner of the composition.

Media professor Robert Entman explains that framing elevates certain "aspects of a perceived reality" over others. Studies show that the most accessible components become those most used in making a judgment (Entman, 1993). So when designers limit the elements within the frame of the composition, they amplify particular interpretations of an image. Much has been written about photographs documenting President George Bush's speech on the Iraq War, delivered on the USS Abraham Lincoln in 2003 (Figure 5.10). With a helicopter landing on the ship's deck and a banner proclaiming "*Mission Accomplished*," the image was framed by White House public relations staff to create the illusion that the President joined the crew somewhere in foreign waters on the heels of victory in the war on terrorism. In fact, the ship was anchored not far from the beach in San Diego, California and the war continued for another nine years. In other words, the photograph was not altered—it was an accurate recording of the speech—but the angle of the shot and the elements included in the picture framed a message that was politically motivated.

Figure 5.10
President George Bush on the USS *Abraham Lincoln*, 2003
Associated Press
The framing of this image of President Bush was carefully staged to give the impression of victory at sea. The banner in the background proclaimed "Mission Accomplished" for a war that continued for nearly a decade. In fact, the ship was anchored off the coast of San Diego, CA.

Figure 5.11
India, Tamil Nadu, Nadurai, 1950
Henri Cartier-Bresson (1908–2004)
Cartier-Bresson's photograph focuses attention on the child by framing the image within the overall environment and positioning the hands of the mother who is largely outside the image. The image would have a different meaning were the mother fully included and other aspects of the setting included in the composition.

Framing can eliminate distracting content or direct our attention to something particular in the scene. The photograph by Henri Cartier-Bresson draws our attention to the face of the child through an unexpected framing of the scene (Figure 5.11). Were the mother fully included in the image or more of Tamil Nadu shown, our attention to the face of the child would be less likely. The photographer further frames the child's face by the position of the mother's hand and her body. The meaning of the image is that everything going on around the child is far less important than the child. The photographer is quoted as saying, "To take a photograph is to align the head, the eye, and the heart" (Cartier-Bresson, 1999).

In the case of cosmetics and fashion photography, close cropping not only focuses our attention on the relevant body parts (lips, eyes, hands, or legs, for example), but it also eliminates features of models that may not be as perfect. This creates the illusion of a flawless body necessary to suggest that the advertised product is responsible for such perfection. Historian Stuart Ewen calls this "the dream of wholeness," in which we piece together partial images of the perfect man or woman from fragments in the media (Ewen, 1988).

Framing, therefore, shapes our perceptions of the subject of the message by narrowing the number and content of elements in the image. Because we are usually unaware of what has been eliminated, we see only the designer's perspective on the scene or subject.

ABSTRACTION

Abstraction is a process of distilling general qualities from specific, concrete examples. To abstract something is to extract its essence without concern for literal depiction or imitation.

So common is abstraction in the contemporary visual environment that we often forget how adept we are at reading it. In an email message we come across a semicolon, followed by a dash, and then a closing parenthesis. Rather than reading these as misplaced punctuation marks, we recognize them as a small winking face, shorthand for an emotion. It takes only these three tiny marks, properly sequenced, to communicate a complex human emotion, illustrated through a distinct facial gesture. Emoticons substitute for intangibles (humor, irony, sadness) that are characteristic of human interaction and their use in text-based electronic communication is a study in creative abstraction.

Paleolithic cave paintings, such as those at Lascaux, France, include three types of signs: animals, human figures, and abstract symbols. Scholars offer a variety of interpretations for these symbols ranging from star maps, to visions seen during hallucinations, to predictions of successful hunts with abstracted wounds expressing the danger of various animals. In any case, it is likely that Stone Age humans were able to process their life experiences through abstract forms that went beyond imitation of the way things looked. It is notable that no geographic features or vegetation appear in the paintings, making it likely that the forms were more than a physical record of the environment and instead had spiritual significance.

Abstraction, therefore, is an overall reduction in the physical information about an object or concept that still carries the meaning of the thing or idea. Avant-garde artists and designers used abstract form to break with conventions. They recognized the twentieth century as significantly different from previous times and sought a visual language that expressed the concerns of a new age. Nineteenth-century art relied on illusionary techniques for representing depth in space and nostalgic subject matter (pastoral landscapes and heroic portraits) that seemed at odds with the social unrest of the new century and the technological advances made possible by the Industrial Revolution. In contrast, modern artists and designers advocated the direct experience of abstract form (purely geometric compositions, for example), unencumbered by artistic conventions such as perspective and style. They also rejected content that suggested the individual circumstances of the artist in favor of simple abstract forms thought to rise above any specific cultural experience. The Futurists, for example, used abstract symbols, letterforms, and diacritical marks—the marks over and under letters that tell us how to pronounce something—to visualize the mechanical sound patterns of factory machines. And Bauhaus designers created an abstract visual vocabulary in products, architecture, and communication that expressed German industrial prowess and modern manufacturing as the country recovered economically from World War I.

Figure 5.12
Library of Congress logo
Chermayeff & Geismar & Haviv
Sagi Haviv
The Library of Congress logo abstracts a book and the American flag. While the objects are recognizable, they are simplified to essential characteristics.

LIBRARY OF CONGRESS

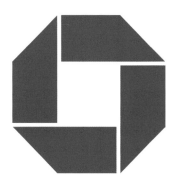

Figure 5.13
Chase Bank logo, 1961
Chermayeff & Geismar & Haviv
Tom Geismar
The Chase logo is one of the earliest purely abstract logos that made no tangible reference to an object or person. Throughout the twentieth century, such logos purported to embody the qualities of the organizations they represent. As the number of these logos proliferated it became difficult to differentiate one from another if not supported by a careful campaign to associate the mark with the company.

In these and other modernist movements throughout the first half of the twentieth century, artists and designers used abstract form in an attempt to achieve universal meaning, independent of particular cultural knowledge for its interpretation.

Since the twentieth century, abstraction has been the formal basis of communication strategy in more than one sense. First, there is abstraction in the use of a symbol or logo to represent all the things a company or organization does; the very idea of logos and corporate identity is an abstraction. Second, there is abstraction in the form of the logo, which not only represents the company and its activities but also the character of the organization. Some logos are *iconic*; they physically resemble the things they stand for. Chermayeff & Geismar & Haviv's logo for the Library of Congress not only signifies that the agency deals with books, but also evokes the American flag as a reference to its role as the nation's library (Figure 5.12).

On the other hand, the firm's logo design for Chase Manhattan Bank bears no obvious resemblance to banks or banking (Figure 5.13). As one of the earliest modernist symbols for an American corporation, its abstract form communicated the forward-thinking attributes of the company, a message that had to be learned over time by customers.

For a number of years, information designer Nicholas Felton abstracted his life in annual reports. With the cool objectivism of a corporation, Felton converted personal experiences into abstract representations of data including miles traveled, beverages consumed, and trips to the movies (Figure 5.14). Other years' reports recorded the number of Felton's face-to-face conversations, letters sent by mail, books read, and photographs taken. Numbers, in this case, are an abstract representation of a rich and complex life.

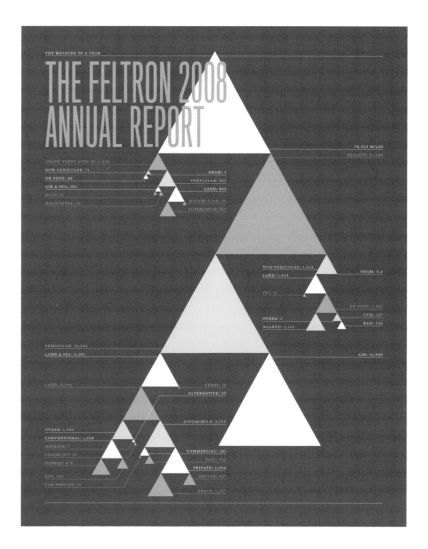

In simplifying or reducing something in the world down to a pictorial essence, abstract symbols and images can lead to more efficient communication. A small mark can stand in for a much larger entity (such as the golden arches standing in for the transnational corporation McDonald's) or intangible concepts not easily represented as pictures. Not all abstractions are universally understood. It is incumbent upon the designer to make sure that the use of an abstraction does not limit the overall effectiveness of the message.

Figure 5.14
Feltron 2008 Annual Report
© Nicholas Felton
Information graphic designer Felton designed personal annual reports that documented the content of his year of life. The reports abstracted the richness of everyday life as "data."

ICON, INDEX, AND SYMBOL

An *icon* is a type of sign that physically resembles the concept or thing for which it stands. An *index* is a sign in which the relationship between the sign and what it stands for is habitual or causal. Smoke, for example, is an index for fire. A *symbol* is a sign in which the relationship between the sign and its meaning must be learned and is governed by a code or cultural convention.

Historically, religions have used icons to represent spiritual figures such as gods, saints, and angels. Because many religions believe that the full glory of a spiritual entity is not easily depicted in concrete form, religious icons carry with them a general understanding that they are lesser versions of their subjects.

Icons had a role to play in modern times as well. Otto Neurath believed a picture language could overcome the difficulties of cross-cultural communication. He created international travel icons to serve an increasingly mobile population. His work continued under other designers, including Neurath's former pupil Rudolf Modley in the 1930s and Otl Aicher in the design of wayfinding strategies for the 1972 Olympic Games (Figure 5.15). Across time, travel icons became increasingly general, losing cultural and racial detail but maintaining their original intent to help people understand content without the support of text. Cook and Shanosky's 1974 design of icons for the United States Department of Transportation is used throughout the country and makes few cultural references to anything but gender (Figure 5.16). Today, the International Organization for Standardization (ISO) publishes a guide for industry, government, and the public that attempts to create an internationally agreed upon, standard set of symbols for everything from travel to safety and security.

Figure 5.15, opposite
Olympic symbols, 1972
Otl Aicher (1922–1991)
Aicher, a founder of the Ulm School of Design, had a long-standing interest in sign systems. The iconic pictographs for the 1972 Munich Olympic Games set the standard for the genre. Design work for the games that followed included a similar system.

Figure 5.16, right
US Department of Transportation travel symbols, 1974
Roger Cook and Don Shanosky
Cook and Shanosky's system owes much to the 1930s legacy of Otto Neurath, whose ISOTYPE system used icons to facilitate international understanding in unfamiliar settings. The symbols are copyright free and can be downloaded by designers from the AIGA website.

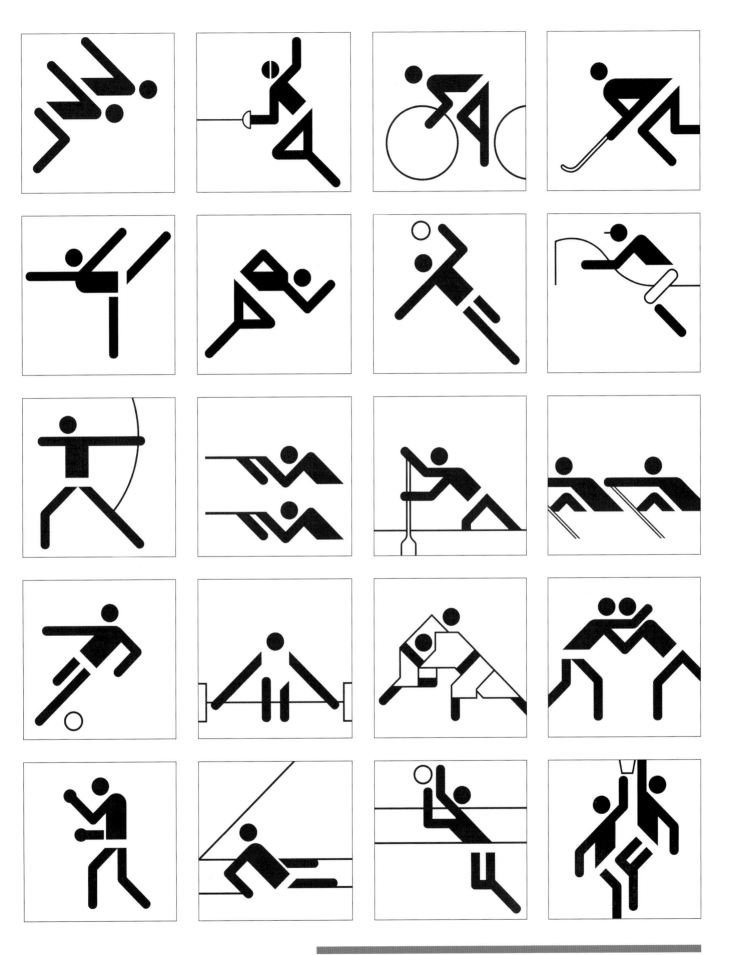

When Apple Computer introduced its graphical user interface in 1984, the term *icon* took on new meaning. Within the metaphor of the virtual *desktop*, icons were any small representations of computer functions (files, folders, disks, trash, etc.). Beginning computer users did not have to understand code in order to interact with the computer system, and over time, the visual vocabulary of these small images expanded beyond physical imitations of the things for which they stand (spinning wheels, for example). Smaller screen real estate in mobile devices and the global use of applications encourage the proliferation of these economical little signs.

An *index* is a bit more elusive a concept. We understand what it stands for by a repeated connection between the sign and its meaning or by some understanding of cause and effect. For example, when we hear a siren we know from experience that there is an emergency. When the leaves fall from the trees, we know the seasons are changing. When the light on our coffee maker is on, we know that the heating coil is warm. In this way, the communication is indirect; we use one thing to point to something else.

Electronic products use indexical signs to communicate the state of the system; a spinning wheel or an hourglass is iconic, but it also serves as an index that the computer is doing its work. The use of 0 and 1 for *off* and *on* in an array of electronic products is an index; it points to the binary code through which computers operate.

Indexical signs expand the inventory of available form in the designer's repertoire. For example, in today's culture, smoking has become synonymous with disease and early death. Anti-smoking campaigns make frequent use of this cause/effect relationship, not needing to show the cigarette to incite audience concern. A famous anti-smoking commercial in the United States showed body bags piling up at the ground level of a high-rise housing tobacco company Philip Morris, much in the way smokers cluster at the entrance to offices during a cigarette break. Cigarettes never appeared in the commercial, yet the bodies were an index for the dangers of tobacco and the company's disregard for public health.

Symbols have no apparent or natural relationship to the things they stand for. The association is learned and only significant in highly specific contexts; such meaning comes about through repeated experience that links the symbol to its meaning. The alphabet, for example, is symbolic. At one time in history letterforms may have had some iconic significance—for example, it has been suggested that the letter "A" has its origin as an ox head in Egyptian hieroglyphics. Today, however, the letters of the alphabet carry no meaning other than their role in replicating spoken sounds when combined in words. We learn that certain letter combinations in words mean certain things, but there is no physical resemblance between the words and these meanings.

During the heyday of freight train transport in the United States—between the Civil War and the Great Depression—homeless travelers, known at the time as *hobos*, marked their journeys with a series of evolving symbols that told others about safety, where to get food, and the best trains to hop. This same spirit inspires computer hackers to scrawl cryptic chalk marks on the sidewalk to identify open wireless hot spots and network nodes. Called *warchalking*, the practice uses symbols that mean something only to people aware of the code (Figure 5.17). In these examples, meaning depends entirely on cultural experience. There is little about the symbols that resembles the physical world.

Logos make frequent use of symbolic form. These small marks bear considerable responsibility for communicating the qualities of a company or organization. In many cases, it is too difficult to describe the complex activities of the organization in pictorial form and many companies do more than one thing. So abstract symbols without iconic references stand in for intangible attributes. In some cases, the name of the company is equally abstract and serves as symbolic identification of the business. Standard Oil became ESSO in 1911 and then Exxon in 1972. Texaco started in Texas and used the star from the Texas flag as its symbol. Today, few consumers connect the star logo to the state.

In practical use, signs can perform in more than one way. An icon can be used indexically, for example. The icons for men and women are used to point to gender-specific restrooms. The icon of a book can index the function of a shop as a bookstore. Likewise, an icon can be used symbolically. The mascots and logos of sports teams do not signify that tigers or pirates are on the playing field, only that players perform as fiercely as tigers or with the daring of pirates; icons, in this case, are used as metaphors for something else.

Figure 5.17
Hobo and warchalking symbols
Homeless travelers have used symbols to mark the environment since the 1800s. The abstract signs tell those who follow where to find things and safe places to rest. While some are iconic in origin and indexical in purpose, many are simply the result of cultural agreement regarding their meaning. These symbols inspired the contemporary practice of *warchalking* in which people identify areas with open Wi-Fi access through chalk marks on the ground.

MATERIALITY

Materiality is defined by the sensory qualities of an object that give it a particular character as part of its meaning. It includes the visual, spatial, tactile, auditory, kinesthetic, and temporal characteristics of form.

At a time when most things are digital—really just electronic patterns of *on* and *off*—it is easy to forget how much of communication design is the result of a very physical process. Desktop printing has reduced the practice to one of manipulating pixels on a screen, hitting "print," and watching the design emerge from the hidden innards of a laser or inkjet printer. But consider how much of the "stuff" of design has origins in much more material processes (by hand or by manufacturing) and what the residues of these processes contribute to meaning.

Serifs in type design likely had their origins in the tap of hammer to chisel when ending a stroke in carved stone. The thicks and thins in strokes of Old Style typefaces, such as Garamond or Goudy, reflect the gesture of the hand holding a flat-nib pen. The heavy horizontal and thin vertical strokes in Chinese woodblock letters reflect the strength in the vertical grain of the wood. In fact, with

almost every new technology we build new relationships to the materiality of its production. Even laser printing leaves a slight trace of its fused toner on the page, different from the spray of inkjet printers.

Much of modern design practice has been a back and forth between two opposing forces: the desire to make invisible the means of production in order to foreground the subject matter and demonstrate precision, and the celebration of production technologies that draw attention to how things were made and the mark of the designer's hand. What explains this tension and what is the impact on the interpretation of text and image?

It appears that in times when technology improves the precision or efficiency of production, designers often embrace manual processes that convey the human spirit. The work of William Morris and the Arts and Crafts

Figure 5.18
Chaucer, **printed by the Kelmscott Press, 1896 William Morris (1834–1896)**
Unhappy with the quality of printed books at the turn of the century, William Morris and the Arts and Crafts movement returned to the art of fine bookmaking for the material qualities of the printed page. Letterpress printing has tactile and visual qualities not found in more contemporary production technologies.

movement in the early part of the twentieth century was a reaction to the qualities of machine production of the Industrial Revolution. Morris's Kelmscott Press responded to the ubiquity of commercial lithography by returning to traditional letterpress printing as a more "authentic" practice (Figure 5.18). Type was set one character at a time, inked, and pressed in contact with paper. Functioning much like a medieval guild, artisans produced elegantly printed books and prints, intended to raise the aesthetic standards of middle-class homes.

Today's book design wrestles with the technology of the twenty-first century. E-books imitate the qualities and behaviors of traditional books. Pages still "turn" on an iPad; the Kindle uses e-ink to simulate the reflective qualities of printing on paper, rather than the backlit attributes of a computer screen.

As we spend more time on screen with typefaces that reveal their origins in high technology and seamless Photoshop images that show little evidence of human intervention, designers again show interest in form that appears to be handmade. The popularity of hand-drawn typographic and illustrative form humanizes a visual world shaped by machines. It speaks with a singular, personal voice rather than with anonymity. When the communication task calls for evidence of the author or designer, or when the irregularities of older technologies seem appropriate to the message, form that forgoes computer precision contributes to interpretation.

Figure 5.19
Obsession book cover, 2009
Isaac Tobin and Lauren Nassef
Tobin was dissatisfied with attempts to produce the cover to *Obsession* digitally. Instead, he returned to the original efforts by Nassef to pinprick the letterforms in paper. Materiality, in this case, is evidence of painstaking work by hand and consistent with the content of the book.

**Figure 5.20
Campaign for Something Raw, International Dance and Performance Festival, 2009–2015
Theater Frascati/
Flemish Arts Centre
De Brakke Grond
Concept and Design:
De Designpolitie
Photography:
Arjan Benning**
The design solution for promoting a dance and performance festival is decidedly material. Performers are literally taped with information. The direct physicality of this interpretation is appropriate for the title and content of the festival.

**Figure 5.21
A|X: Armani Exchange packaging and signage program for Giorgio Armani, 1992
Alexander Isley, Inc.
Ad Agency: Weiss, Whitten, Carroll, Stagliano
Creative Director: Alexander Isley
Designers: Alexander Knowlton, Tim Convery**
The package design for Armani Exchange uses simple craft materials, reinforcing the fashion company's use of natural fibers and accessible line of street chic clothing in the Armani brand. Boxes open like drawers in a dresser or closet.

Isaac Tobin, in his design for the book cover *Obsession*, tried to produce the effect of pinpricks on the computer (Figure 5.19). He said, "My first attempts were made on the computer, but just didn't work—the computer made the repetition meaningless" (Tobin, 2008). Tobin then created the typographic form in paper and photographed it for the finished effect. The slight irregularities are evidence of how the form was produced. De Designpolitie's solution to advertising a dance and performance festival also depended on the material qualities of the image. Oversized tape carrying the title of the festival, *Something Raw*, was applied directly to the bodies of performers (Figure 5.20).

In some cases, the materials used carry the message. Alex Isley's packaging for Armani Exchange uses earthy craft materials (cardboard and rope) to communicate informal style and the use of natural fibers. Known primarily as a high-fashion company, the A|X materials set the identity for this casual line of clothing (Figure 5.21). Similarly, the Graphic Thought Facility design of signage for a business school is the opposite of the slick materials and consistent typography we associate with corporate wayfinding systems. A collection of differently sized components uses raw wood, stencil letters, and metal troughs to "collage" identification signs for various rooms in the building, a reclaimed brewery in London (Figure 5.22).

Materiality, therefore, contributes to what things mean. Materials and processes signify things over and above the denotative content of the message. They speak to the origins of form and to their individual authorship.

Figure 5.22
Hult International Business School – Wayfinding
Wayfinding and Graphic Elements: © Graphic Thought Facility
Project Architects: Sergison Bates
Interior Design: Fiona Kennedy
Project Management: David Harris
Photography: Mike Bruce
This signage breaks with the convention of single-surface, silk-screened nameplates and a consistent typographic treatment. Numbers and letters on differently sized materials sit in metal troughs mounted on walls, functioning as sculpture in the environment. The stenciled letters and ad hoc quality of their combination feels appropriate to the school's location in a reclaimed brewery in London's Whitechapel.

SUBSTITUTION

Substitution is the act of replacing one thing with another. Substitution plays with the reader's expectations, upending the known for the unknown or unanticipated. Substitution extends the range of possible meanings, and the power of the substitution lies primarily in the gap between the meaning expected and the meaning delivered.

Substitutions can take many forms, but two in particular are relevant for designers. These are borrowed from written and spoken language but work equally well in visual communication. *Metonymy* is the replacement of the name of something with another thing with which it is associated; "Washington" is substituted for the Federal Government of the United States, for example. *Synecdoche* is a part substituting for a whole or a whole standing for a part; workers are often called "hands" and cars are called "wheels." The terms are figures of speech but are also useful in describing how images work.

As a visual strategy, substitution plays with audience expectations. Whether in text or image, a thoughtful or humorous substitution wields the power of both the original expected content, the substituted content, and the synthesis of the two. For that reason, it can have significance for the interpretation of meaning.

A *rebus* is a substitution of visual elements for words, sounds, and syllables. The rebus challenges us to build complex ideas from schematic but familiar parts. David Drummond's design for *The Crow's Vow* book cover substitutes an image for a word, but goes a step further and makes the image possessive (Figure 5.23). Designer Paul Rand added humor to the corporate environment with his poster for computer giant IBM (Figure 5.24). The work is consistent with the formal rules of Rand's graphic standards for the company's identity, making its humor all the more surprising.

Oliver Byrne's 1847 design of *The First Six Books of the Elements of Euclid in Which Coloured Diagrams and Symbols Are Used Instead of Letters for the Greater Ease of Learners* predates modern work yet is refreshingly simple in its accessible, visual explanation of geometry (Figure 5.25). In contrast to today's textbooks, which typically separate text and illustration, Byrne's design forces us to read the two channels of information simultaneously. In an 1880 application to the Royal Literary Fund, Byrne described the purpose of the substitution strategy as assisting "the mind in its researches after truth" and as increasing "the facilities of instruction." Byrne claimed people could master the mathematical concepts in one-third the time under other methods. In other words, his use of substitution was grounded in a theory about learning.

Figure 5.23
***The Crow's Vow* book cover, 2011**
Véhicule Press
David Drummond
Drummond's design for Susan Briscoe's book replaces a word with an image in a spare composition that heightens the substitution by making the image grammatically possessive.

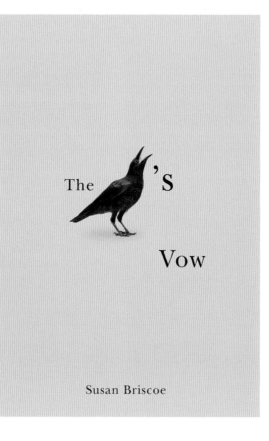

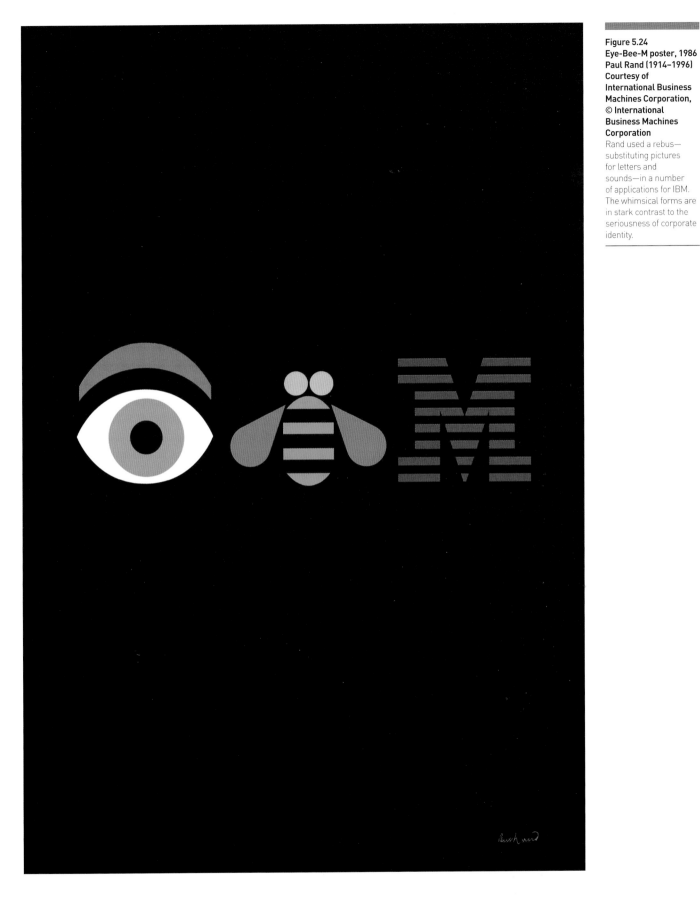

Figure 5.24
Eye-Bee-M poster, 1986
Paul Rand (1914–1996)
Courtesy of
International Business
Machines Corporation,
© International
Business Machines
Corporation
Rand used a rebus—
substituting pictures
for letters and
sounds—in a number
of applications for IBM.
The whimsical forms are
in stark contrast to the
seriousness of corporate
identity.

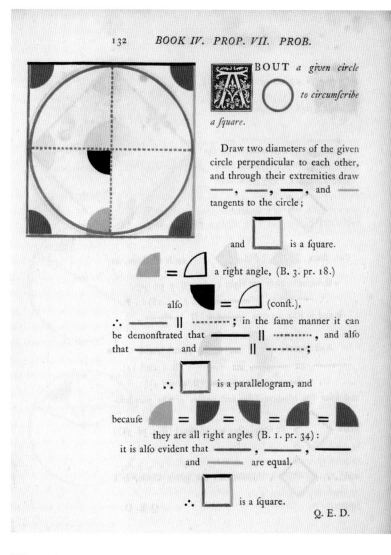

BOOK IV. PROP. VII. PROB.

Figure 5.25
The First Six Books of the Elements of Euclid,
1847
Oliver Byrne
(1810–1890)
Byrne's nineteenth-century design forces readers to read two channels of information simultaneously. Geometric forms substitute for words in explanations of mathematical concepts.

Similarly, the Walker Art Center's design of the graphic identity for the School of Visual Arts Design Criticism program reduces the name of the program to *D-Crit* and provides an inventory of objects that substitute for the hyphen. The objects describe the range of subject matter included in the program's critical cross hairs (Figure 5.26). The D-Crit identity is an alternative to the rigid corporate systems of the late twentieth century in which the designer anticipated every combination of elements and regulated their form through a detailed graphic standards manual. More recent systems function as "kits of parts" that readily accept new combinations within a general framework for maintaining visual continuity from one application to another.

Metonymy is a favorite substitution strategy of postmodern communication designers. Images are often substitutes for the complex issues of gender, social class, and other cultural concepts. Such substitutions expand the possible range of meanings beyond a simple one-to-one, denotative illustration and are consistent with the postmodern belief that plural meanings and cultural biases are inevitable. Meaning, in this case, is always open, never resolved.

We can think of numerous literary and visual examples where *synecdoche* functions: the crown for the kingdom; plastic for a credit card; a wedding ring for marriage. In the design of the Holocaust Museum, the task was to communicate the emotional significance of six million Jews killed under the Third Reich. Wherever possible, exhibition designers supported statistics, documents, and textual narratives with artifacts that framed history in human terms. One installation includes a glass bin containing 4,000 shoes, substituting for their owners who died in the Nazi killing centers during the Second World War (Figure 5.27). A small paragraph of text supports the installation, but it is clearly secondary to the shoes. And these are not just any shoes; they conformed to the feet of the men, women, and children who wore them and they bear the signs of extreme wear and duress. Visitors describe this as the most searing exhibit in the museum's galleries. It is notable for the designer's restraint: for allowing the objects to speak for the tragedy.

Figures of speech depend on cultural associations—networks of meaning that are built through experience. As such, they can resonate with us in ways that denotation alone cannot. They communicate with attitude and expressive character.

Figure 5.26
School of Visual Arts
D-Crit program identity,
2007
Design: Walker Art
Center Design Studio
The identity for the
Design Criticism
program at the School of
Visual Arts substitutes
images beneath the "X,"
much as the program
places designed objects
in the cross hairs for
criticism. Objects and
people may change in
each application, but the
typographic components
remain constant from
one use to the next.

Figure 5.27
United States Holocaust
Museum Exhibition,
1993
Ralph Applebaum
Associates
From the collections
of the State Museum
at Majdanek in Lublin,
Poland
The exhibit at the
Holocaust Museum is an
example of synecdoche.
The 4,000 shoes stand
for Jews who died in
the Nazi killing centers
during the Second
World War. While the
number 4,000 is large,
the emotional impact
of the worn shoes is
much more moving
than statistics and more
compelling than a single
pair of shoes would be.

METAPHOR

A metaphor describes something by saying it is like something else that is otherwise unrelated. It is an analogy that makes comprehensible something new or unknown by comparing it to something already understood.

Her uncle is a bleeding heart liberal. You'll eat crow. My instructor is all thumbs. We all use metaphors in speech and often without thinking. It is a colorful and efficient means of communicating complex characteristics or expressing qualities. While all languages appear to use metaphor, analogies are especially relevant to design. If designers only illustrate subject matter with literal representations of concepts, they forgo the opportunity to challenge viewers with more than the obvious; to engage us emotionally and reflectively at levels deeper than the surface meaning.

William Gordon, in his book *The Metaphorical Way of Learning and Knowing*, describes different types of metaphors. A *direct analogy* is a one-to-one relationship between two things. For example, *a door is like the cover of a book*, hinged on one side, open on the other. Direct analogies tend to rely on physical characteristics and statements of fact. A *compressed-conflict analogy* is the union of two seemingly opposite terms that describe the concept (Gordon, 1973). For example, a door is a *closed invitation* or a *movable wall*. Compressed-conflict analogies are often more poetic than direct analogies and invite contemplation. Rather than "making the strange familiar," they "make the familiar strange," allowing us to see the everyday in a new way (Gordon, 1973). Thinking about things in this way can lead to visual ideas that cause others to reflect.

Metaphors operate on a principle called *categorization*. We sort incoming sensory stimuli and life experiences into mental categories in which things that are grouped together are alike but different from the members of other groups. Because members of the category share something in common, seeing one of them can recall qualities that are shared by others. In this way, some members of the category can substitute for others in recalling the general concept. The Ford Mustang convertible, for example, can stand for "muscle cars," "fast driving," and "machismo," but it is less likely to represent "soccer moms." Such categories are often defined by cultural experiences and vary from group to group, so it is important to use metaphors that are likely to be within the realm of audience experience.

Linguist George Lakoff and philosopher Mark Johnson describe types of metaphors that are also categorical. *Orientational metaphors* arise from the fact that we occupy space. So when we say, "I'm feeling up today" what we are really saying is that happiness is an up-oriented concept (Lakoff & Johnson, 1980). When we say, "I am on top of things" what we really mean is that we are in a superior position that we associate with elevation. We refer to "stocks dropping," "prices going up," and "looking forward and looking back" into the future and past (Lakoff & Johnson, 1980). Because orientational metaphors make physical references, it is easy to see how they might influence compositional or illustrative strategies and the interpretation of meaning.

Ontological metaphors relate to our experiences with objects and substances. For example, we can refer to the mind as a machine when we say, "the wheels are turning," "I'm a little rusty," or "I'm running out of steam" (Lakoff & Johnson, 1980). *Personification* is when we describe a physical object as having humanlike behaviors or qualities. So when we say email is "eating up our time" or "inflation is the enemy," we assign human significance to things and concepts (Lakoff & Johnson, 1980). These metaphorical structures are part of our language and help designers generate meaningful strategies for presenting new information. Such metaphors are often starting points for brainstorming visual ideas (Figure 5.28).

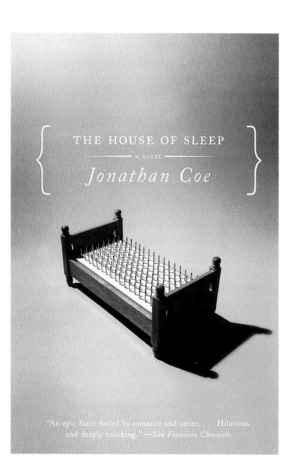

Figure 5.28
House of Sleep **book cover**
Designer: David J. High
Photographer:
Ralph C. del Pozzo
An ontological metaphor relates experiences with objects to something else. In High's design, a "bed of nails" serves as a metaphor for author Jonathan Coe's tale of demented scientists studying people with sleep disorders.

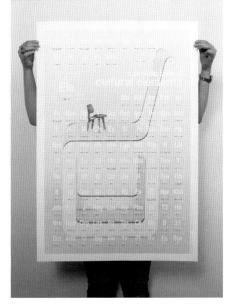

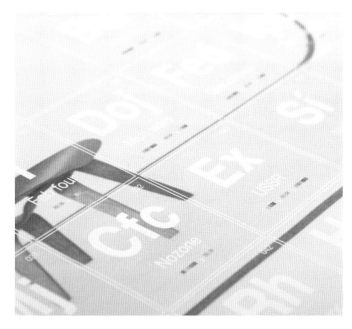

Figure 5.29
Strathmore elements of culture poster, 2001 Rigsby Hull
Rigsby Hull used Mendeleev's Periodic Table of the Elements as a metaphor for organizing "essential" cultural experiences such as design magazines, public radio, instant messaging, and jpegs.

Designers sometimes juxtapose a word and an image to set up a metaphorical comparison. The Rock of Gibraltar, a historic fortress on the western entrance to the Mediterranean Sea, represents Prudential Insurance. A charging bull represents the confidence of Merrill Lynch financial services and Kemper Investments uses a sheaf of wheat as the metaphor of a good harvest.

In Lana Rigsby's *Periodic Table of Cultural Elements*, for Strathmore's *Elements* paper, the structure of the scientific chart is used as a metaphor for classifying major cultural organizations, objects, and events, such as National Public Radio and the Fab Four (Figure 5.29). In the case of Art Chantry's poster, style serves as metaphor. Chantry uses the graphic qualities of vintage United States agriculture and national park posters as a metaphor for an event promoting the legalization of growing industrial hemp (Figure 5.30).

The use of metaphor, therefore, is a powerful way to bolster a message with meaningful associations, provided that the references are culturally relevant and appropriate. Not all cultures share the same network of associations, however. To a Chinese audience, a dragon might symbolize generosity and goodness, while a European audience might read the mythical creature as threatening or fearsome. Likewise, today's teenagers have cultural experiences that are quite different from their baby boomer grandparents. For this reason, the use of metaphor is complicated. There is no guarantee that a cleverly conceived metaphor will make sense to an audience that has no cultural frame of reference for the associations the designer is trying to make.

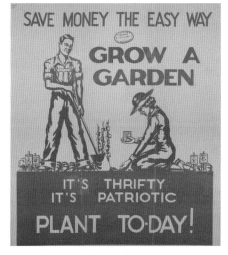

Figure 5.30
Hempfest poster, 1999 Jamie Sheehan and Art Chantry

Save Money the Easy Way. Grow A Garden. It's Thrifty. It's Patriotic. Plant Today!, **c. 1945 Louisiana Agricultural Extension Division Reproduced with permission by the LSU Agricultural Center In special collections at the USDA National Agricultural Library**

The choice of style in Sheehan and Chantry's Hempfest poster serves as a metaphor. The poster recalls US Department of Agriculture propaganda encouraging victory gardens during the Second World War.

APPROPRIATION

Appropriation is the act of borrowing something from another culture, context, period of history, or designer and repurposing it in a new context or application. Appropriated form carries the connotations of the source into a new setting, and thus, produces a different meaning from the one it held in its original context.

In 1917, when Marcel Duchamp submitted a urinal for exhibition at the American Society of Independent Artists exhibition in in New York City—and signed it *R. Mutt* and titled it *Fountain*—a new chapter in modern art began. Many cultural historians consider his use of a common, pre-made artifact as an artwork to be the founding act of appropriation as a strategy for art-making in the twentieth century. While probably not the first time an artist used pre-existing materials in his work, the challenges it posed to viewers' notions of originality and authorship turned this object into an infamous example of appropriation in modern art.

Appropriation of cultural form is not unique to the art world, however, and it is a frequent strategy in film, music, and visual communication design. Its power stems in part

from its shocking affront to traditional Western values for originality or individual authorship in creative work. This is not a universally shared concept, as artists in many cultures consider carefully copying existing works to be an important means of glorifying tradition and demonstrating mastery.

Designers in the 1980s and 1990s found meaning in the vernacular form of typefaces produced by commercial sign painters and others not formally trained in design. As a backlash to decades of elegantly refined typographic form, these designers rejected the notion that form could be a neutral visual carrier of verbal meaning. Critical theory of the late twentieth century suggested that no message is void of cultural perspective and found new possibilities for constructing meaning in the forms of popular culture

Figure 5.31
"Copycat" Swatch poster, 1984 (left)
Paula Scher

Swiss Tourism Poster, 1936 (right)
Herbert Matter (1907–1984)

A debate erupted within the design profession when Scher appropriated Matter's famous 1936 design to advertise the Swiss watch company, Swatch. Critics accused Scher of copying, but Scher argued that she considered her poster a parody of the earlier work.

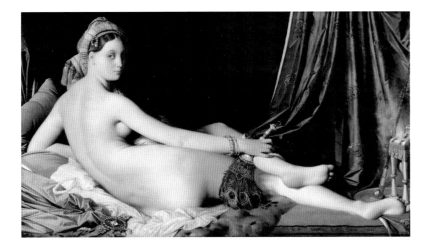

and the "low art" of advertising. When these references appear in a poster for an important college lecture, for example, there is a clash of signifiers; the appropriated vernacular form seems at odds with our expectations of a scholarly discussion. This ambiguity of meaning causes us to reflect.

Designer Paula Scher, with permission of the designer's estate and AIGA (the professional association for communication design), appropriated a famous 1934 Herbert Matter poster for Swiss tourism in her 1986 design of a poster for Swatch, the Swiss watch company that pioneered fashion-conscious, inexpensive watches (Figure 5.31). Critic Rick Poynor discussed Scher's appropriation as being neither parody nor *pastiche* (it is not just in the style of Matter), but a new edition of the same image (Poynor, 2003). In Scher's work, Poynor pointed out, the head is titled toward the wristwatches, but the image is otherwise a reassignment of the same meanings to a new objective, to sell watches (Poynor, 2003).

This poster inspired lengthy debate in the communication design community about the ethics of such appropriation. Design historian Phil Meggs said, "Should a designer sit down and find novelty in a historical style, they wouldn't set out to copy any exact piece. They would learn the *language* it spoke and use its vocabulary of forms and form relationships, reinventing and combining them in unexpected ways" (Meggs, 1998, p. 481). Scher considers the work "a visual joke, a parody of a famous poster by Herbert Matter" (Scher, 2002).

Do women have to be naked to get into U.S. museums?

Less than 3% of the artists in the Met. Museum are women, but 83% of the nudes are female.

Statistics from modern and contemporary galleries, Metropolitan Museum of Art, New York, 2004

GUERRILLA GIRLS CONSCIENCE OF THE ART WORLD
www.guerrillagirls.com

The Guerrilla Girls are an activist group that protests the suppression of women artists by the art establishment. The members of the group remain anonymous, appropriating the names of famous women artists of the past. In their protest graphics—which appear on billboards, in posters, and as full-page advertisements in newspapers—the Guerrilla Girls appropriate famous works of art. In Figure 5.32 the composition "borrows" the work of Jean-Auguste-Dominique Ingres, a nineteenth-century neoclassical painter from France.

Figure 5.32
Le Grande Odalisque,
1814 (above)
Jean-August-Dominique
Ingres

"Do Women Have to be
Naked to Get into U.S.
Museums?", 2011 (left)
© Guerrilla Girls

The Guerrilla Girls, an activist group protesting the patriarchy of the art world, retained their individual anonymity by adopting names of famous women artists of the past. In this work, they appropriated the work of a French neoclassical painter.

AMBIGUITY

Ambiguity is vagueness or uncertainty. It occurs when an image or text has multiple possible meanings that compete simultaneously for priority in the interpretation. When used with care, ambiguity slows down the interpretive process and causes us to reflect on our initial perceptions or content that we might otherwise ignore or take for granted.

Ambiguity requires an additional investment of audience effort in interpretation. It can be frustrating, confusing, captivating, or mysterious. It can challenge not only the meaning of the specific message, but also the way in which meaning-making works, thus posing larger questions about design and communication. Asking audiences to invest in this kind of processing time makes sense when interpreting something like cultural commentary, but we don't want ambiguity in the sign that directs us to the right exit on the highway or printed procedures for taking medicine. The designer, therefore, must make critical decisions about how much and when to slow down readers by using images and text that open interpretation to more than one meaning.

Ambiguity can occur in the processing of sensory information: is what we *think* we see, actually what we see? French filmmaker Jacques Tati created a humorous scene in his 1967 film, *Playtime*, a visual critique of modern architecture. Seeking an appointment with someone in a glass high-rise, a visitor sees the man with whom he hopes to meet reflected in the windows of the lobby in the adjacent building. It appears to the visitor that the man is in the other building, when in fact both are only a few feet apart in the same building. The filmmaker uses the visitor's confusion to comedic advantage, but the sensory ambiguity produced by ceiling-to-floor glass also serves as his commentary on the sterile, disconnected experiences that result in modern architecture.

Alex Isley's *Spy* magazine layout for an article titled, *The Canadians Among Us*, plays with spatial ambiguity in the treatment of typography (Figure 5.33). The headline exists simultaneously in front of and behind photographs. In this case, the ambiguity of spatial location is consistent with the content; Canadians are interspersed throughout American culture but in many ways are indistinguishable from natives of the United States.

Ambiguity also raises questions of interpretation through what appears to be conflicting information: does something really mean what we *think* it means? For example, in the fanciful nineteenth-century story of Lewis Carroll's *Alice in Wonderland* we recognize the innocence of Alice in her blue dress and white pinafore sitting next to a rabbit hole that takes her to an entirely strange world. We acknowledge the lunacy and circular logic of the Mad Hatter at the tea party. The story and images have been recirculated in countless ways throughout our culture. *The Annotated Alice* by Martin Gardner, however, applies twentieth-century insight and values to a critical analysis of the story. The book presents the story as written by Carroll and illustrated by John Tenniel in 1865, but uses Gardner's factual annotations in the adjacent margins to raise questions about the true meaning of the story. Was Lewis Carroll a little too interested in young girls, and in particular Alice Liddell, a 10-year-old family friend? Does the Mad Hatter's Tea Party reflect Carroll's publicly shared concerns that science will never know things for certain? Did we know that residents of Victorian England speculated on what might happen in a free fall to the center of the Earth? *The Annotated Alice*, therefore, is both a sweet children's tale and a cultural critique of the time in which it was written. The annotation or juxtaposition of conflicting information is often a design strategy used to destabilize the authority of one set of ideas by another.

Figure 5.33
Spy magazine, "Canadians Among Us," 1988
Art Director: Alexander Isley
Writers: Alexander Isley, Donna Abelson

Isley's layout for *Spy* creates ambiguous space, as words pass in front of and behind images at the same time. In this way, the design displaces the typical foreground/background relationships as a reflection of the topic of Canadians in America.

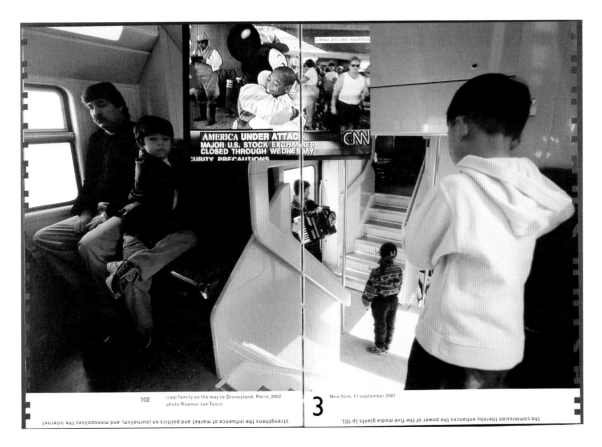

102   Iraqi family on the way to Disneyland. Paris. 2002
      photo Roemer van Toorn

3   New York, 11 september 2001

Figure 5.34
Iraqi Family on the
Way to Disneyland,
Paris 2001/New York
9.11.2001
Collage from Jan Van
Toorn's *Design's Delight*,
2006
Jan van Toorn,
Amsterdam

Van Toorn uses ambiguity
to engage the reader as a
"co-writer" of messages.
In this example, an Iraqi
family was on the way to
Disneyland, Paris when
terrorists flew planes
into the World Trade
Center and Pentagon in
the United States. This
juxtaposition of signifiers
keeps the reader
from reaching easy
conclusions about the
meaning of the image.

As the example of Alice illustrates, ambiguity is highly influenced by cultural context. Differences in our cultural experiences may lead us to miss the ambiguity in a message, if only because we don't perceive the full range of possible meanings. International students, for example, report that the jokes, idioms, and slang phrases in social communication are the most troublesome interpretations they are asked to make while studying abroad. They are ambiguous because they have both literal and metaphorical meanings that depend largely on cultural experience. In other cases, we may read too much meaning into something. It is cultural tradition in the Indonesian island of Bali, for example, for male dancers to play the roles of female characters. Because this is not the case in the United States and Europe, some of us may assign too much significance to a female character that is obviously male.

Postmodern work of the late twentieth century viewed the ambiguity of images as support for theories that readers construct meaning. Dutch designer Jan van Toorn discussed the properties of a *dialogic image*, which invites viewers to become the co-writers of a message with designers. The image in Figure 5.34 shows a father and his children riding a train in Europe. On the deck below is a musician, and overlaying the image is a scene from American television in which Mickey Mouse hugs a child above a news scroll stating, *America under attack—major US stock exchanges closed*. The caption to the spread explains that the man and the two boys are an Iraqi family on their way to Disneyland in Paris and that the television screen is from September 11, 2001, when terrorists flew commercial planes into the World Trade Center in New York and the Pentagon in Washington, DC. What initially appears to be an ambiguous combination of signs takes on political meaning when we view these elements in a dialog with each other—that is, we actively analyze the ironic juxtaposition of Disneyland, a family from the Middle East, and the American war on terror. Through ambiguity, the designer makes us work for this interpretation, thus investing us as co-authors of the message.

Ambiguity is rarely an end in itself and the history of late twentieth-century postmodernism taught designers that the public has precious little attention and processing time to work through communication that does not make its relevance known. Yet there are times when ambiguous form is useful in slowing down the process of interpretation for a gain in critical reflection.

COGNITIVE DISSONANCE

Cognitive dissonance is the conflict we feel when faced with contradictory ideas, emotions, or values at the same time. We have a natural preference for order, regularity, and predictability and we try to reconcile the meaning of elements that stand in opposition to each other.

Cognitive dissonance makes us uncomfortable and we often go to great lengths to resolve the apparent conflict of meanings. For example, we are likely to rationalize an uncharacteristically expensive purchase by saying we got a good deal or deserved a reward. We describe watching reality television as a "guilty pleasure," making it easier for us to reconcile a dissonant self-image as someone interested in stories of such little consequence.

Visual and verbal messages also result in cognitive dissonance. At some time in our lives, we probably encountered regulatory signs or instructions that left us wondering which of two conflicting procedures to follow. And the autocorrect function in cell phone text messaging often produces some very puzzling communication. In these cases, two plausible interpretations struggle for dominance in our minds. Both are reasonable explanations for part of what we see or read, but we engage in extra thought to resolve their presence in the same message.

Steff Geissbuhler creates cognitive dissonance by replacing "STOP" with the word "AIDS" in the typeface and colors we are used to seeing in road signs (Figure 5.35). We do a double take—did we see what we thought we saw? The strong graphic characteristics of the sign are familiar and make us think of the word "STOP." But again, we look twice because the text is inconsistent with our repeated experience with a hexagonal red sign. To resolve this dissonance, we mentally complete the message, "STOP AIDS."

Japanese designer Shigeo Fukuda used a similar strategy in his poster titled *Victory 1945* (Figure 5.36). We expect to see the bullet exploding out of the barrel of the gun, but instead it moves in the opposite direction. The designer forces us to reconcile the physical impossibility of this action as a message on the senselessness of war.

In Jamie Reid's iconic cover artwork for the Sex Pistols' single, *God Save the Queen*, the designer defaces a classic portrait of the Queen by replacing her eyes and mouth with typography torn from magazines (Figure 5.37). Release of the record coincided with Queen Elizabeth's Silver Jubilee celebration in June 1977. The phrase "God Save the Queen" is typically said or sung as the British national anthem with reverence for both the woman and the monarchy. The ransom-note treatment of the text changes the meaning of the phrase to something much more sinister, a demand by dangerous criminals who hold the royal hostage. The shocking juxtaposition is consistent with the punk rock band's reputation for provoking social outrage, public mayhem at their concerts, and violent encounters with fans.

DEPT OF TRAFFIC

SUMMARY

Theories of language and cognition tell us something about how we find significance in signs. Although audiences construct meaning—with all the intervening influences of our own experiences and surrounding context—designers still hold responsibility for framing messages and crafting form for our consideration. Because communication depends on connotations established by living in a social world, there is an enormous range of potential interpretations resulting from the selection of signs, their arrangement in space and time, and their history of use. Figures of speech—such as metaphor, metonymy, and synecdoche —leverage cultural understanding by applying something we already know to new circumstances. Likewise, the appropriation of form transfers meaning from one context to another. While legibility and readability are goals, we are wired to tolerate ambiguity and dissonance as trade-offs for deeper reflection.

Figure 5.36, top
Victory 1945
Shigeo Fukuda
(1932–2009)
Fukuda's poster produces cognitive dissonance by inverting the direction of the bullet. In doing so, he comments on the futility of war.

Figure 5.37
God Save the Queen **cover for the Sex Pistols, 1977**
Image: Jamie Reid
Courtesy of John Marchant Gallery
Copyright Sex Pistols Residuals
Reid's design for the irreverent punk band uses ransom-note typography for a phrase more typically sung in honor of the monarch.

Retaining and extending meaning

It is easy to think of design as supporting a one-time experience with an immediate interpretive result, and in some respect, that is what design does. But the intent of the designer—and certainly of the client—is rarely a quick, short-term impression. Thoughtful design asks us to reflect on experience in deeper ways and shapes how we view the world long after the encounter with the message is over. Good design is memorable as well as communicative and has consequences in culture that reach far beyond a single person.

Memory and categorization

Most clients have two goals for communication design: to reach audiences with a compelling message and to achieve some outcome of mutual benefit to themselves and their audiences. Simply noticing and deciphering a message has little value if it doesn't lead to thinking that supports future action. As interpreters of messages, we judge whether attending a concert, supporting a political candidate, or buying a product is in our best interest. Typically, time passes between encountering the message and following through with action. This delay means that communication must be memorable as well as compelling.

There are different kinds of memory. *Sensory memory* is very brief recall and can be acoustical or visual. Film, for example, creates the perception of continuous action through memory of twenty-four still images per second; we don't notice the breaks between frames, and we quickly replace the memory of one frame with the experience of the next.

Working memory is longer than sensory memory but still short in duration (about thirty seconds). We use working memory to manipulate or act on concepts and plans. It allows us to store verbal, visual, spatial, and acoustical information for short periods of time and during naturally occurring tasks, such as reading and listening. Working memory has its limits and research shows that most adults can retain no more than seven chunks of information in working memory at any one time (Miller, 1956). Grouping helps. We recognize and remember the names of three companies better than what appear to be nine random letters (CBS, IBM, and BBC rather than CBSIBMBBC). Advertisers and copywriters address this limited capacity for working memory when writing headlines or grouping units of information under larger concepts. And typographic arrangements can assist in chunking multiple units of information as groups or in reducing text to keywords that trigger larger ideas.

It is also thought that working memory forms relationships among elements. Imagine reading a chart that shows the relationships between the degree of difficulty in a task and the skills of someone performing the task. If the difficulty of the task is high and skills are low, people become anxious.

Low difficulty and high skills result in boredom. We can hold these relationships in working memory and think about actions that are consistent with the findings—for example, in determining difficulty at various levels in a computer game. But if the number of variables increases—for example, if we add the effect of monetary reward on performance as the Z axis of the chart—we have more trouble remembering the different relationships among the three variables: skill, task difficulty, and reward. This is important to think about when designing visualizations of complex data.

Cognitive load is the mental effort used by working memory. Figuring out what behavior the communication design requires of us—that is, orienting ourselves to proper use—is part of that load. The rest of the cognitive load is made up of the mental work it takes to deal with the content of the message (interpretation) and to put it into permanent storage (long-term memory). There are limits to our ability to deal with cognitive load. The goal of design is to limit the orientation effort so the remainder of our working memory can be devoted to processing the content of the message. If the form of the message is ambiguous in what it asks of us, then we spend more time in understanding how to approach form than in interpreting the content of the message.

Long-term memory is the storage of experience and information for recall over long periods of time (sometimes decades). Memories aren't stored as whole experiences but distributed in various parts of the brain. Explicit memory includes the *episodic* memory of events in time and can be recalled through other triggers—for example, the name of someone who was with you at the time of an event. *Semantic* memory is about facts. *Autobiographical* memory includes personal experiences. And *emotional* memory stores experiences that have strong affective content (fear, sorrow, or joy, for example) and that can produce physical responses when recalled.

Categorization is an unconscious mental process through which we identify stimuli in the environment and group them in long-term memory as members of a category, similar to others in that category but different from members of other categories (Augoustinos & Walker, 2006). A category may be something like "things that are scary" or "people who are wealthy" or "femininity." Researchers believe that categorization allows us to communicate through metaphor; some members of the category can substitute for others and still cause us to recall the larger idea that connects them. When we encounter a new stimulus, we compare it to similar concepts stored in memory and use the concept category to guide our interpretations. Some members are central to the category—that is, "best examples"—while others are toward the edges of the group and may be stored under other categories as well (Augoustinos & Walker, 2006). For example, a tulip may be a good example in the category of "flowers," while the status of a dandelion as a "flower" is debatable and may be a better example of "weed." A tulip may also be a member of the category of things associated with the Netherlands or spring. This matters to designers. Choosing an image to stand as a metaphor for a concept that is on the fringes of the category can easily deflect the interpretation to an unintended meaning (weeds rather than flowers, for example). In other cases, some images are so central to categories that they are clichés—for example, a light bulb for an "idea" or a handshake for "partnership." In choosing these images, designers not only recall the topical category, but also the concept of overuse. Cliché images have been robbed of the power of their original meanings.

Schemas are mental structures that organize categories and the relationships among them. They not only recall concepts but also suggest what we should think about them and how we should behave in response. Schemas arise from our experiences in a social world and can be organized by time (as *event schemas*); by location (as *place schemas*); or by roles (as acquired or ascribed *role schemas*).

For example, we have an *event schema* for what it means to check out a book from the library; experience teaches us to use a library search engine to narrow the options, identify relevant book titles by call numbers, and then visit the library stacks. We don't start a topical search by scanning an alphabetical listing of all titles in the library

collection or walking randomly among the stacks hoping to discover something relevant to our work. However, new technologies often introduce new procedures. The library at NC State University, for example, stores and retrieves books by robot, with no need to shelve them by call numbers because the robot always remembers where it last put each book. Physically walking among the shelves is no longer part of the event schema for checking out a book in this library—the robot does the walking. But to retain informative aspects of the original search schema, the design of the library's digital interface allows users to see what books (with clickable tables of contents) used to be left and right of the chosen book when they were shelved under the Library of Congress system (Figure 6.1). In other words, in the redesign of the technology for checking out a book it was important to retain essential aspects (browsing, for example) of the earlier event schema.

Place schemas include familiar settings such as a classroom, kitchen, or vegetable garden. When we recall the place, we are able to identify typical elements and the general spatial arrangement of the schema, as well as the activities likely to take place in the setting. Cultural experience strongly influences these schemas. In some Middle Eastern countries, for example, public space ends and private space begins at a high wall surrounding the home. Strangers must be invited to pass through the wall. Residents of the United States, on the other hand, define private space as beginning at the front door of the home or apartment.

Role schemas include those attributes we ascribe to people as a result of their personal characteristics (for example, gender or age) and others that are acquired through training or effort (for example, a profession or economic status). Stereotypes are a kind of role schema in which many characteristics are grouped in memory; any single visual trait can recall the entire grouping, including all the emotions and biases we associate with

Figure 6.1
James B. Hunt Library user search interface North Carolina State University
Software Developer: Kevin Beswick
Photography: Brent Brafford
The Hunt Library retrieves and shelves four million books entirely by robot. It maintains the event schema for a traditional library search, in which users physically browse shelves through a digital interface that shows the books to the right and left of the selection on the Library of Congress "shelf." The interface system shows the book covers and tables of contents.

the role (Augoustinos & Walker, 2006). A study with young children showed them a photograph of a male nurse and a female doctor. Asked later what they had seen, the children reversed the roles, describing the doctor as male and the nurse as female. Gender—erroneous in this case—was stored in long-term memory as part of the role schemas for medical professionals.

These schemas develop within social and cultural contexts and differ from individual to individual. However, careful study of human behavior and context often reveals recurring patterns in people with similar life experiences. For better or worse, the social practice of design contributes to the formation of schemas. The children in the previous example were not likely to have developed gender bias when describing medical professionals solely from their limited encounters with their own doctors and nurses. Representations of doctors and nurses in the media contributed to this schema. The social responsibility of design, therefore, is to promote complete and accurate representations that contribute to schema development and to undermine negative stereotypes when possible.

Research also shows that our reasons for looking influence how we process visual compositions, and therefore, what we remember. Studies of eye movement show we fixate—that is, spend the most time looking—on things that we think will be most informative to the interpretive task. If we look at a photograph of people and are told to remember ages, we fixate on faces (Spoehr & Lehmkuhle, 1982). But if the task is to remember their locations within the room, we scan rapidly from one person to the next (Spoehr & Lehmkuhle, 1982). This behavior argues for text working closely with images to ensure that verbal messages guide viewing. A headline or caption can tell us how to process the adjacent image.

Our ability to retain information has something to do with how we receive it. Research shows that visual memory is superior to verbal and auditory memory (Cohen, Horowitz, & Wolfe, 2009). Studies also show that repetition and the intervals of space between exposures to information influence our memory for certain messages. So communication strategies clearly gain retention value when designers consider the channel, format, and timing of audience encounters.

A *mnemonic* is a tool that aids memory. Advertising jingles and rhyming slogans, for example, encode information in a form that is easily retained. Many of us learned and recall the number of days in each month by reciting a simple rhyme ("thirty days hath September ..."). It is much more difficult to remember that June has thirty days without mentally going through the full performance of the rhyme. Stories often function mnemonically. Fables and myths represent schemas that deliver moral lessons. We may not recall all the details of Aesop's fable of *The Tortoise and the Hare*, but we do remember, "slow and steady wins the race." And it would be difficult to use images of the two animals in combination in communication without invoking the fable and its moral.

The concepts of categorization and memory guide design decisions about form. Designers need to understand the experiences that shape the associations people assign to different kinds of visual information and what makes design memorable. The implications for design are both psychological and cultural.

Extending the impact of form

The things we see and hear, therefore, sharpen and build memories that aid us in the interpretation of future messages. But they also shape the culture in which we live; messages add up and contribute to the worldview through which we interpret new communication. Skinny models in fashion magazines shape public perceptions of female beauty. Nasty housewives on reality TV and the branding of athletes create impressions of wealth and celebrity. These messages accumulate over time—accurately or inaccurately, they express our collective values and interests.

Communication design, therefore, is an act of social and cultural production. It carries the burden of both reflecting the culture as it is and shaping the culture of the future. Beyond the decision to promote particular products or ideas, designers must evaluate what their choices about visual messages do to *normalize* certain values and behaviors; to express certain meanings and beliefs in the ordinary experiences of everyday life.

We can look to history for evidence of the role communication design plays in setting the cultural agenda. American advertising of the 1950s illustrated what post-war life could be under greater economic security and the expansion of suburbia. These images had little to do with the actual qualities of the products being sold. Motor oil companies depicted people dining in style at the edges of a country club pool. Women in party dresses and high heels gushed over the leisure time they gained by owning a new washing machine or freezer. In the 1980s, Nike advertising sold fitness without even showing shoes. The goal of these ads was to describe a desirable future in which the consumption of goods was linked to an attractive lifestyle.

Today, cultural content circulates more rapidly than ever before in history. Technology ignores national boundaries and makes it possible for people to form communities of interest with their own values and ways of interacting. Designers have the responsibility to study culture for strongly held beliefs and practices and to anticipate the consequences of design in the afterlife of messages.

STEREOTYPES

A stereotype is a type of role schema, a mental structure that contains general expectations and knowledge about people and social roles. Stereotypes—whether accurate or not—form through past experiences and guide our attitudes and behavior in a social world. A number of traits are grouped in the mind and may be called forth by a single visual cue, such as skin color or dress.

The term *stereotype* is derived from eighteenth-century printing processes. Once a printer locked type and illustration plates in place in a layout, he made a duplicate impression of the arrangement in papier-mâché, plaster, or clay. From this, he cast a more durable lead copy that he used in the mass printing of things such as newspapers or broadsheets. Since it was impossible to make changes to this unified block of type, the term *stereotype* acquired the everyday meaning of an impression, attitude, or image that could not be changed. Over time, the term lost its association with printing and acquired its modern meaning.

Today we understand a stereotype to be a grouping of distinctive characteristics that are thought to typify a whole group of people or objects (women are nurturing, men are good at fixing things, dolls are for girls, and so forth). The characteristics need not be accurate and they are often exaggerated simplifications that overstate certain aspects of the group at the expense of actual diversity. Even when the assertions are positive—for example, people who wear glasses are smart—stereotypes gloss over meaningful differences for the sake of generalities. Throughout history, stereotypes have been inspired by ethnic or racial bigotry.

Because characteristics of stereotypes are grouped in the mind, it is very difficult to dislodge them; one visual characteristic can activate the entire group (Augoustinos & Walker, 2006). Our memories are often schema consistent; even when confronted with information or experiences that are inconsistent with the stereotype stored in memory, we remember it in ways that match our prior experiences or beliefs.

Stereotypes in our culture are often built and reinforced by the popular media, as well as by first-hand experience. The characteristics we associate with powerful women in the workplace, for example, have as much to do with portrayals in contemporary movies and tabloid news as with any real interactions we have in our daily lives. And stereotypes shift over time. Over recent history we have seen changes in the stereotypes advertising uses to promote products. In selling shoes, polished male athletes who represented wealth and physical perfection

gave way to scrappy, streetwise warriors who reached the top by sheer determination. And the ideal male in today's advertisements for products ranging from French fries to SUVs is a sensitive father as well as a breadwinner, a change from advertising of the 1950s and 1960s. None of these representations is likely to be 100 percent accurate for all people and most are overly simplistic in defining "type," but repetition in the media reinforces them as prevailing cultural views.

Despite this phenomenon, it is possible to undermine the power of stereotypes. The artist Kara Walker appropriates racial stereotypes to challenge viewers to think more critically about her images. Using silhouettes, Walker enacts historical dramas that mimic the visual language of racist stories and scenes (Figure 6.2). Their flatness and lack of detail focus our gaze on certain exaggerated characteristics of the caricatures, while Walker weaves complex visual narratives that make simple interpretation difficult.

Designers must be careful not to perpetuate schemas and stereotypes that have little basis in reality. For example, it is generally assumed that children favor simple illustration styles. Many books for children in primary grades employ this visual strategy. A research study compared children's preferences for a range of illustration styles (cartoons, representational drawings, expressionistic drawings, and photographs). When shown only pictures and asked what they would most like to read about in a book, there was no significant difference between children's preferences for cartoons and photographs (Myatt, 1979). And when adults first read the story to the children from various books before showing them the images, children selected the cartoon for the fanciful animal story and the photograph for a more realistic description of animals (Myatt, 1979). In both cases, representational and expressionistic drawings were ranked lower than the other two illustration styles (Myatt, 1979). What this study shows is that, generally, young children are as attracted to photographs as cartoons in their literature and that they make discriminating choices on the basis of content. Our stereotypical notion that children demand simplicity is not upheld by the study.

A 2014 article in *The Atlantic* argued that children's toy design is more divided by stereotyped gender roles than it was fifty years ago, "when discrimination and sexism were the norm" (Sweet, 2014). While girls' toys from the 1920s to the 1960s focused largely on domestic chores and raising children, boys' toys prepared them for work in industry—the Erector Set (a construction toy, which includes perforated metal beams, fasteners, pulleys, and gears for building structures and machines) was originally conceived as grounding for engineering careers. Gender-specific toys in general declined in the 1970s under the first wave of feminism, but re-emerged when laws changed allowing program-length advertising for toys on children's television and a newer version of feminism argued for a range of life options for girls (Sweet, 2014). Today, boys' toys are typified by color, heroes in fantasy stories, and skill-oriented activities, while girls' toys are passive and feature "princess" roles (Sweet, 2014). Stereotyping in toys, therefore, illustrates the relationship between changing values in culture and design.

Designers must ask important questions about the use of stereotypes. What depictions contribute to the formation of stereotypes? While the various civil rights movements of the late twentieth century (based on race, gender, sexual orientation, and ability) have increased our cultural sensitivity to many of the most outlandish stereotypes, our culture and media continue to perpetuate subtle, pernicious, and new ones. Designers must challenge themselves by asking whether their own use of form and text reinforces prevailing assumptions or undermines false realities in an effort to shift attitudes.

Figure 6.2
Gone: An Historical Romance of a Civil War as it Occurred b'tween the Dusky Thighs of One Young Negress and Her Heart, 1994
© Kara Walker, courtesy of Sikkema Jenkins & Co., New York Photography: Gene Pittman

Artist Walker explores race and gender in her work. Her cut-paper silhouette friezes are deceptive. The medium is associated nostalgically with nineteenth-century documentation of important events and people. Walker exploits this sentimental stereotype to illustrate abuses of slavery and racism.

ARCHETYPES

An archetype is a commonly recognized image, idea, or model upon which other things are based or copied. It is usually perceived to be an ideal and something to be emulated.

Archetypes are used throughout history in a variety of ways. The *hero*, for example, appears across literature, comic books, and stories children tell one another. Similarly, we can find *mother as nurturer* in countless nursery rhymes, myths, and movies.

Advertising uses archetypes to build new messages upon those already established in the culture. Advertising does not have the luxury of time with the audience; it must communicate its message within a thirty-second television commercial, a "drive-by" down the supermarket aisle, or the space between articles in a magazine. As a result, it depends on quick assessment of a new message that builds on existing cultural knowledge. Advertising is accessible and memorable precisely because it is consistent with something we already know or believe within the culture.

But over time, the values of the culture shift. We can see the clash of an archetype with modern history on the cover of the book, *Finding Betty Crocker* (Figure 6.3). Betty began as a character on "The Betty Crocker Cooking School on Air" sponsored by General Mills in the 1920s, and the fictional Betty later responded to letters from homemakers about cooking and nutrition (Marks, 2005). Despite the fact that a real Betty never existed, she was voted the second most popular woman in a 1945 poll by *Fortune Magazine* (Marks, 2005). There has been a total of eight different Betty Crocker portraits. With each transformation of Betty, the company modified the notion of the ideal homemaker. The archetype moves from a competent, nurturing mother figure to a professional home economist, managing family nutrition. The 1996 Betty Crocker was based on a computer compilation from seventy-five different women from the Spirit of Betty Crocker contest, which created a more multicultural woman.

We can find similar changes in attitudes toward race. Figure 6.4 shows an image of Aunt Jemima when the pancake mix was first introduced at the 1893 Chicago's World Fair, only thirty years after President Lincoln issued the Emancipation Proclamation freeing slaves. More than 100 years later and after the Civil Rights Movement, the image of a smiling, benevolent servant seemed inappropriate,

Figure 6.3
"Betty Crocker"
General Mills
The depiction of the fictional Betty Crocker on food packaging has changed a number of times since 1947 when Betty Crocker cake mixes were first introduced with the Ginger Cake Mix. Images of the stereotypical homemaker changed with American demographics.

but the company had more than a century invested in the archetypal idea of a friendly African-American "mammy" cooking breakfast and recast Aunt Jemima as an efficient homemaker. How the use of this archetype is read as a way of selling pancake mix depends on the cultural position of the audience.

Cigarette advertising was the target of the activist culture magazine, *Adbusters*. Joe Camel, an archetype for the Camel cigarette brand morphed over time from a realistic illustration ("I'd walk a mile [in the desert] for a Camel") to a stylish, macho cartoon figure. *Adbusters* showed the trademark character in bed hooked up to an IV and renamed "Joe Chemo" (Figure 6.5). The irony in this image depends first on recognizing the archetype; the brand and cigarettes don't appear. Had the camel not been firmly established in the culture, we wouldn't understand the critical commentary.

Archetypes, therefore, are deeply situated in culture and change only when the context demands an adjustment in the outward representation of the concept. They are distinguished from stereotypes by their longevity, social consensus about their meaning, and ability to take more than one visual form while retaining their defining qualities. They are culturally familiar and an efficient way to communicate deep-seated values.

Figure 6.4
Aunt Jemima Pancake Flour, 1915
Among the evidence in a trademark dispute was this image used to advertise Aunt Jemima pancake flour. The image shows the archetype of the nurturing slave who raised the children of white families and guaranteed that the household ran smoothly in the American South prior to the Civil War. Needless to say, the company found this image unjustifiable following the Civil Rights movement of the 1960s. Reluctant to abandon a successful brand, the company recast Jemima as a savvy professional.

Figure 6.5
Joe Chemo, 1996
Concept: Scott Plous
Illustration: Ron Turner
Adbusters
The Joe Chemo character spoofs the archetypes in tobacco advertising.

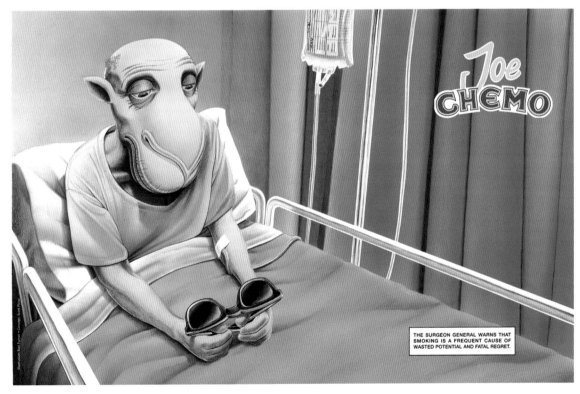

NARRATIVE

A narrative is a schematic sequencing of events, a story. Narratives may be read, seen, and/or heard. While some narratives—particularly in film and literature—deliberately play with the reorganization of time, most follow a structure characterized by a beginning, middle, and end.

Cognitive psychologist Jean Mandler describes knowledge, not as discontinuous facts, but as organized structures that exhibit specific patterns. *Serial knowledge* concerns items that are understood by their connection to one another (such as the letters of the alphabet or a chronology of historical events) and *schematic knowledge* is an understanding of parts-to-whole relationships (for example, that walls and ceilings are parts of a room, stanzas are parts of a poem, and verses are parts of a song) (Mandler, 1984). *Narrative knowing*, says Mandler, is being able to structure information by linking together various events to make a story. It is different from serial knowing because there is a contribution of the events to the whole or theme; it is more than a listing or chronology (Mandler, 1984). A story, therefore, has a beginning, middle, and end and its episodes move the narrative forward to completion.

Communication designers use narrative form for a number of reasons and in a number of ways. First, stories organize lots of information in a compact, memorable form. Parables and fables, for example, contain instructions for living moral lives but do so in a way that is more memorable than a sermon or a list of dos and don'ts. And stories bring things to life. We empathize with characters and understand the contributions of setting to our interpretation of things. For this reason, narrative is an effective strategy for organizing complex or confusing information: how to complete a difficult task; how to establish trust in one company over another; or how to understand the importance of an invention in history.

We also read narrative in images that make them memorable; we remember the story of the image, rather than an inventory of its parts. As discussed earlier, it is possible for a single image to be narrative when elements are connected through some transaction, as described by a vector or invisible line that joins them. A man passing through a room and looking at a ripe apple on a table establishes a vector by his gaze. We are able to imagine a story, an unfolding of possible actions because of the vector, and the apple is not just another object in the room. In the case of Eve Arnold's image in Figure 6.6, the *lack* of transaction between the two people in the foreground tells a story. They stare in opposite directions, their attention landing on things outside the picture frame. We tend to interpret introspection—people being lost in their thoughts—in images where the object of the gaze is beyond our view. More than setting or style of dress, therefore, the oppositional forces in the composition invoke the narrative and confirm the title of the image, *Divorce, Moscow*.

There is also a difference between simply showing objects and showing them in action. Imagine a layout with a stack of silhouetted images of farming tools from the nineteenth century. The museum-like display of objects evokes the category of tools. Their visual characteristics tell us something about the time in which they were made and used. And their presence as members of a group suggest that they are related in some way, with any single object less important than the category to which it belongs. An image that nests the objects within a story, shows them in use, and surrounds them with a context tells us something more than we can surmise from the inventory alone. We remember the scene, while we may not remember the objects alone.

A *scenario* is a script for action, a story that anticipates the unfolding of future events. As a concept, it dates from the Italian Renaissance when written notes pinned to the back of scenery describing the characters, plot, and actions told actors how to create an improvisational performance. Today, scenarios guide designers in solving problems. In constructing a scenario, designers tease out

the complexities of the situations in which communication will occur, such as the use of a website or the experience of a museum exhibition. Scenarios include a context; a communication system, object, and/or message; various stakeholders and their goals; activities through which stakeholders interact with the context, system, and each other; and time. These components comprise a story that drives a very specific challenge to the designer and ensures a user-centered understanding of the design problem.

Personas are descriptions of the stakeholders; they are characters in the story of the scenario that describe in detail the needs, wants, and behaviors of a variety of users. Typically a scenario will include several personas that either mirror real users or combine a variety of users in several composite personalities. Many designers describe

extreme users, believing the average user will be satisfied by a design solution that is acceptable to people with strong preferences. From scenarios and personas, designers determine the optimal character and configuration of elements and experiences in design. Stories drive the design process.

Narrative, therefore, provides a schematic structure that explains the presence of certain elements in a composition. We remember the elements because they play a role in an overall story. When used as a structure, narrative serves as a description of desired outcomes from design and informs designers' understanding of people, activities, and settings.

Figure 6.6
Divorce, Moscow
Eve Arnold
The lack of eye contact in this photograph tells a story.

MNEMONICS

A mnemonic is a memory device that aids in information retention. Acronyms, phrases, songs, and visuals can assist in transferring information to long-term memory.

"Red sky at night, sailors' delight. Red sky in morning, sailors take warning." "Spring forward, fall back." A simple phrase, lodged in the minds of millions, is a mnemonic device. It makes difficult or arbitrary information accessible and easy to remember. Mnemonic devices shift information into other forms whose structures are memorable; they frequently chunk information into fewer units and use techniques such as rhyming to call up the key words in the phrase.

We can store information visually and verbally, but some things are easier to remember in one form over another. We are more likely to remember the new people we met at a party from their faces than from a list of names. On the other hand, a list of ingredients for making cupcakes may be simpler to recall as a list. In general, information that is stored in both modes is easier to remember than information we experience in either visual or verbal form. For example, we may be more likely to recognize different breeds of dogs after seeing them in pictures than by reading their names, but our memory will be best when words and images are used together (something called *dual coding*).

At the same time, adding other sensory detail can help improve our memory. The AFLAC insurance company uses a sassy, quacking duck as its trademark and in advertising; the name of the company sounds like a duck (reinforced in its television commercials) so we store brand-related information through three channels (word, image, and sound), increasing the likelihood of recall. Similarly, the alliteration in *Dunkin Donuts* and *Krispy Kreme* are more memorable than *Entenmann's Bakery*. We remember how the name of the company sounds when spoken.

Abstract information is especially hard to remember. We must learn it through repetition and distinctiveness. The more unusual the form, the more likely we are to remember it. We recall the overall shape of a Volkswagen Beetle more easily than a BMW—try drawing those two cars from memory—because the Beetle has changed very little over time and its shape is not very car-like.

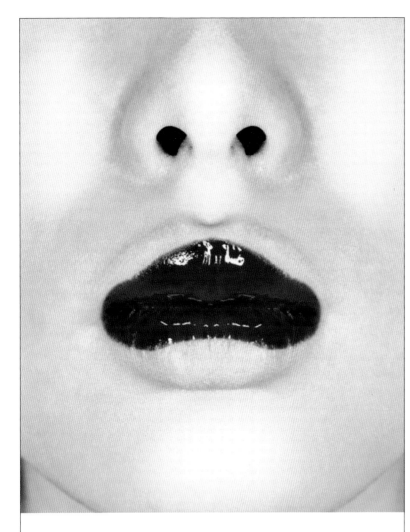

Beige with red leather. The New Beetle Limited Edition.

Figure 6.7
Advertising campaign, new VW Beetle, 2007
Winkler and Noah
Volkswagen has built brand recognition by consistently referring to the unique shape of the VW Beetle over decades of its production and advertising. The shape has become a mnemonic for the automobile.

Figure 6.8
CBS eye logo, 1951
William Golden
(1911–1959)
Golden's logo design for
CBS is so well recognized
in the United States that
text is unnecessary.

At various times in its history, Volkswagen used the shape of the car in its advertising and imprinted our memory with this iconic form by poking fun at the car's distinctive contour (Figure 6.7).

Likewise, logos and branding elements function mnemonically. Sixty-five years ago, creative director William Golden designed the CBS "eye" logo, referring both to the journalist (who watches the world) and to the viewer (who watches the television) (Figure 6.8). So linked is the logo with the television network, that it doesn't need the letters "CBS" for recognition. Not all branding is as successful. Imprinting the brand in the memory of consumers requires repeated and consistent exposure, as well as clear differentiation from other visual marks. When logos are too much alike, their effectiveness as mnemonics is compromised.

Charts and graphs improve our memory of abstract data, or at least the general trends represented by data. We recall the direction of a line graph, even if not the detailed statistics that underlie the visualization. We navigate roads in a car with some memory of the route on a map. And a timeline helps us remember the sequence of events in history. Visualization is critical when textual or numerical explanations are too complex to commit to memory.

In some cases, we remember something through a distinguishing feature, rather than as the depiction of the entire object. We may not be able to discern a maple tree from an oak tree, but we easily recognize differences in the shapes of their leaves.

These findings suggest that symbols, for example, need to be distinctive, accompanied by text as the public learns their affiliations, and part of a larger communication strategy that associates the mark with other positive messages and through several channels. It also suggests that affiliating the company or concept with an abstract mark may require greater redundancy than with iconic shapes that express objects or activities or with letters that trigger a familiar name.

It is possible, however, that the vivid and unique qualities of communication design may not be enough to do the job of design. While we may remember an advertisement by its jingle, storyline, or the visual qualities of its production, we may not connect the message to the company or product. This is more likely to occur with ads that depend on visceral emotions, gut-level feelings that bypass rational thought. We may remember the slow motion, close-up photography of washing tomatoes fresh from the garden, slicing mushrooms, and grating aged cheese, but not recall the name of the pizza company a few minutes after the thirty-second advertisement ends. So the design task is not just crafting a memorable experience but also one that connects the experience with the originator of the message.

CHUNKING

Chunking is the grouping of elements when performing a long-term memory task. It involves the organization of complex information into a smaller number of units that imposes some kind of order on the information.

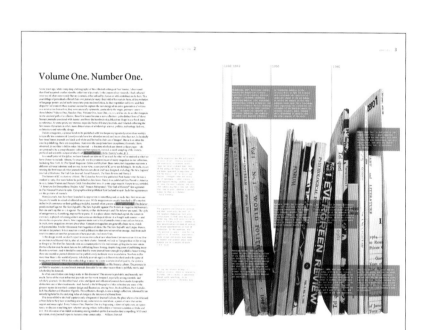

Presented with a ten-digit number, say 4875559376, and asked to recall it moments later, the task is not particularly easy. But break the number into smaller groupings—487-555-9376—as the telephone industry has done, and suddenly the number becomes more available for retrieval. To spell *Wednesday* correctly we break it up into more easily remembered parts—Wed-nes-day.

The term *chunking* comes from a study of how many units of information we can hold in short-term memory (seven, plus or minus two) (Miller, 1956). By chunking information into content-related groupings, we reduce the amount of time we spend figuring out the interpretive task; elements that are grouped must have something in common to warrant their physical proximity (Miller, 1956). Through typographic treatments, chunking tells us what to read first and the function of the grouping. A magazine sidebar has a different character from the main article and a quote appears different from a caption. Knowing this allows us to break down the reading task and to move information from working to long-term memory incrementally (Figure 6.9).

Figure 6.9
Below the Fold spreads
Winterhouse
Chunking introduces space between paragraphs or segregates different discussions by varying the visual qualities of typography among different kinds of information. Chunking gives the reader some idea of when to rest the eyes or to exit to other text or images.

In task-oriented communications—such as instructions for taking medications, recipes, or explanations of complex procedures—typographic chunking is critical in communicating a time-based sequence of steps. We focus on one step at a time, grasping the meaning of that step only and then moving on to the next with little need to retain the previous step in working memory. Space separates discrete actions and indicates stopping points in the process.

Studies by the American Association of Retired Persons (AARP) show that chunking is critical in printed and web text for people with aging eyes (AARP, 2004). While indentation of the first line of text typically signals the start of a new paragraph, adding a line space between paragraphs, setting type flush left, and using subheads increases legibility by clearly defining the start and stop among units of information. This chunking strategy allows older readers to find their place in the text after briefly exiting the information to rest their eyes or when their attention drifts. On the other hand, indentation of entire sections of text can set information apart as discrete discussions and as subsets of previous content.

Chunking also matters in our interpretation and memory of headlines and short amounts of text, such as raised quotes in a magazine article or regulatory information in signs. The general rule in these cases is to "break for sense." This phrase means designers should insert line breaks in multi-line text at the end of complete thoughts, rather than simply where space runs out (Figure 6.10). By breaking for sense, typography not only reads as it is spoken—with all the pauses and emphases of natural speech—but also defines coherent thoughts that are more memorable than random sequences of words based on line length.

EATS SHOOTS AND LEAVES

It was the best of times and the worst of times

EATS
SHOOTS
AND LEAVES

It was the best of times and the worst of times

Figure 6.10
Break for sense
Line breaks in headlines determine how they are read. In the example on the left (drawn from Lynn Truss's book on grammar), the meaning of the title depends on where breaks occur. On the right, breaks that don't correspond to pauses in speech slow down reading.

Images can be chunked as well. Imagine a collection of detailed pictures that explains a primary image or groupings of images by categories. For example, an ordered row of small images could show the sequence of positions in the use of the object in a larger picture. A large poster showing all breeds of dogs in the Westminster Dog Show might cluster the spaniels as separate from terriers and hounds. We are more likely to remember the different kinds of spaniels under the chunked layout than if the images of all dogs were simply arranged alphabetically with equal spacing among them. The spaniels enter our long-term memory as a group with similar characteristics rather than as individual species.

Chunking is not only important in printed communications but can also be critical in the design of other experiences such museum exhibitions. Most of us visit museums for entertainment, not for detailed scholarly work. Textual explanations that support objects need to be short and placed in the path through the exhibition where they are most useful, rather than in a single lengthy text as an introduction to a gallery. Such information can designate a content grouping of objects in an otherwise undifferentiated display within a gallery, providing broad categories for structuring our experience in memory. And museum visitors rarely follow a predictable path. While curators like to tell chronological narratives, there is no guarantee that visitors will respect their ordering of information. Therefore, chunking must account for variations in the reading sequence.

REDUNDANCY

Redundancy is the consistent and timed repetition of a message, often across multiple channels and formats, in order to build audience recognition. Advertising campaigns and branding depend on such repetition of related messages.

**Figure 6.11, below left
Mail Pouch Tobacco
advertising, 1890–1992**
Farmers in twentieth-century America were offered $1–$2 per year by the Bloch Brothers Tobacco Company to advertise on their barns. As the country became more mobile, the redundancy of ads on barns reinforced the company in the minds of motorists.

**Figure 6.12, below right
WORKac identity
Project Projects**
This identity system for WORKac uses theme and variation. Rather than a single logo for the company in all communications, somewhat redundant forms offer interesting variations that are still recognizable as originating from the same organization.

In the 1890s, before radio and television advertising, the Bloch Brothers Tobacco Company devised a novel means for promoting *Mail Pouch Tobacco*. They offered farmers $1–$2 per year to advertise their product on the sides of barns throughout several states in America, provided that the barns were visible to drivers along major roads (Figure 6.11). Using large, hand-painted lettering, this advertising campaign operated on the principle that redundancy and exposure would keep the company's product in people's minds. The consistency of the lettering, its scale, and slogan (*Treat Yourself to the Best*) provided continuity to a campaign that seared its message into the heads of travelers.

While not the first advertising campaign, these iconic barns represented a strategy that designers and advertisers have used for centuries; that the more often audiences experience a consistent message associated with a source, the more likely they are to remember it. The strategy is the basis of corporate identity and branding, which depend on maintaining recognizable representations of the company, expressed through graphic elements, characteristics of products and environments, and message content. The repetition of such messages may be across formats, media, and channels, reinforcing meaning in a slightly different but recognizable form each time.

Redundancy is more effective in some kinds of messages than others. Information that we process viscerally—that is, that bypasses the parts of our brains that control reasoning—is more likely to benefit from repetition. We can watch the same television commercial dozens of times during prime time viewing if it doesn't require us to process it on a rational level. More reflective advertising (a political campaign, for example) requires a different kind of processing and is annoying when repeated too many times in one evening. We resent devoting processing effort to the same message over and over again. This is evident in voter fatigue during political campaigns that can run for many months.

Some companies are successful in developing campaigns that vary widely in their content but present a consistent visual attitude toward the design of individual units. *Theme and variation* is a strategy common in music. A piece begins with a theme in the main melody and then introduces slight variations in the melody over time. Variations may use a different rhythm or harmony or elaborate the primary theme through additional notes. We often notice theme and variation in movie scores, where the emotion of the scene must change yet maintain continuity from scene to scene.

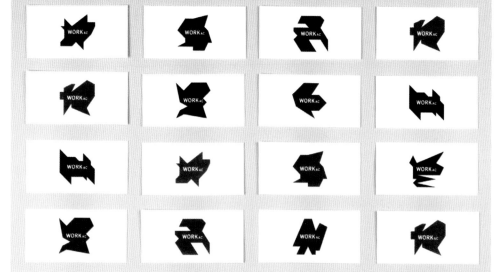

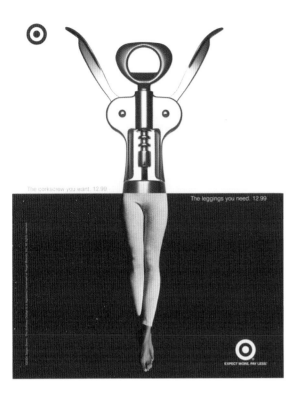

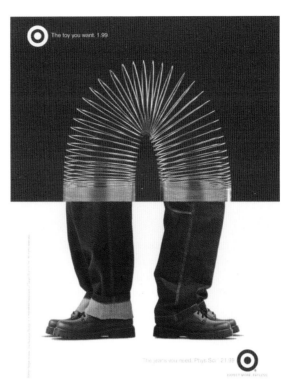

Figure 6.13
Target advertising, 2004
Ilan Rubio
Target uses its bullseye logo in most advertising, but a consistent visual approach over time is equally important in identifying the company. Because the company sells many items—some not visually notable in their own right—the company's approach has been to focus attention on the shapes of objects in combination. The television versions of these ads animate pairs of everyday objects that have no functional relationship but make playful visual connections. The redundancy of this shape-oriented strategy can be found across media and designers.

As in music, visual themes exhibit recurring structures that allow us to recognize them despite changes in other aspects of their form and separation in time (Figure 6.12). Typically, visual theme and variation is found in more than surface style in the rendering of elements. It involves deep structures and underlying attitudes toward the role of visual form, verbal language, sound, and motion that we find familiar in less obvious ways.

Target, an American discount store, sells a myriad of products and brands as well as their own. Although the company's television commercials often repeat the color red and the company's bullseye logo, we recognize a Target commercial before these elements even appear on screen. The redundancy across Target commercials depends on playful, inventive visual relationships among diverse products, not on stories, celebrities, or voice-overs describing the benefits of purchase. Many Target ads treat each item, regardless of its purpose, as a shape (Figure 6.13). This allows the company to represent a diversity of consumer products—which are often not visually remarkable on their own—while maintaining the underlying sense of design for which the company is known and that separates it from other big box stores. Through theme and variation, viewers detect a Target commercial without obvious reinforcement of its name or logo and under frequent changes in the advertised products.

The effectiveness of redundancy also depends on the timing between messages. If there is too much time between a "save the date" announcement for a conference and the actual registration window, for example, conference organizers have to work harder to produce attendance than had registration followed closely behind the first message. And the longer the time between messages, the more assertive the identity of the company or organization needs to be.

Redundancy across channels also matters in our retention of messages. If messages repeat content in word, image, and sound, we have multiple ways to enter information in long-term memory. Wayfinding signage systems often repeat both the textual directions and visual cues at regular, repeating intervals so that visitors don't have to retain too much information for too long a period. Similarly, the voice-guided instructions for driving by global positioning systems (GPS) typically announce an exit at the start of a journey segment, two miles before the exit, and then again at the exit, using redundancy to combat the driver's divided attention.

Given that information over-saturates our visual and auditory lives, redundancy is a design strategy that must be used with discretion and purpose. Too frequent repetition and we become annoyed or overwhelmed; too infrequent and we might not retain the information. But when used effectively, redundancy is a powerful tool to keep attention focused and to ease the cognitive load of a complex task.

GRAPHIC IDENTITY

A graphic identity is a coordinated visual system for the identification of a company or organization that generally consists of a logo or logotype, typefaces, color palette, and set of rules for their application in a variety of formats. A memorable and consistent graphic identity ensures that products and communications are associated with the company over time, in a variety of locations and media, and under different designers.

Graphic identities have a history in heraldry and trademarks. First developed in the twelfth century, heraldry distinguished fighting knights in the confusion of battle (Mollerup, 1997). Eventually, heraldry took on a diplomatic role under established rules for the design of coats of arms. Different kinds of lines divided shield shapes in different ways, each with particular meanings (Mollerup, 1997).

Stonemasons, furniture makers, printers, and other craftsmen developed trademarks to identify their work in the marketplace. In some cases, these marks designated a guild, rather than an individual. Watermarks designated paper quality and size; today we still equate watermarks with expensive paper stocks.

The ability to capture the essence of an organization in a few expressive and memorable elements is the basis of corporate identity. Companies and organizations use simple marks to establish their identities in the world of business. The designer describes the acceptable use of elements in a graphic style manual that includes specifications for print, broadcast, digital, and environmental applications. Many manuals include detailed measurements for the placement of elements (logos, typefaces, and colors) within various formats and examples of appropriate and inappropriate applications. Designers frequently "lock in" the relationship between a logo and the name of the company or organization so that primary identification remains consistent in all formats and at all scales. Graphic identity systems also guide the use of photography, illustration, and motion. Style manuals allow many designers to produce work for the same organization while speaking with one visual voice (Figure 6.14).

Figure 6.14
NIZUC Resort & Spa
graphic identity
Carbone and Smolan
Agency

Carbone and Smolan's identity for NIZUC's luxury resort and spa in Cancun, Mexico includes a range of products and online communications consistent in production values with the sophistication of the target audience. Not only does the identity include logos and typefaces, but also an attitude toward the art direction of photography and applications across a variety of media.

More recent graphic identities are less rules-based (Figure 6.15). Designers develop a "kit of parts" that defines the character of visual communications but adjusts to the requirements of different and new communication demands. The graphic identity for the Walker Art Center, for example, uses an original type family design by Matthew Carter and recurring visual patterns that change color and size in various applications (Figure 6.16). The elements have a strong visual character that allows designers to recombine them at will without sacrificing continuity.

Graphic identities often undergo periodic updates across the history of companies and organizations. Some changes reflect evolving consumer preferences for certain kinds of form. Procter & Gamble's 140-year-old logo was an engraved profile of the man in the moon and stars contained within a dark circle. Now known for making personal and household products (toothpaste, razors, soap, etc.), the company's logo reflected its original business as a candlemaker and the idea of serving customers throughout the phases of their day (Stampler, 2013). Preferences at the time of the original logo design favored pictorial images, but beginning in the 1980s, rumors circulated that the image was of the devil and that curls in the beard and hair were Satanic references to "666" (Stampler, 2013). While none of this was true, the company tired of defending the mark in lawsuits and news articles and hired Landor Associates to replace it in 2013. The new mark uses block letters within a blue circle but maintains the moon reference as a sliver of lighter blue within the rim of the circle. Not all stylistic changes have an impetus for change as dramatic as the case of P&G, but shifting tastes for graphic style and changes in a core business encourage companies to remain current, despite the investment of communication capital in their heritage.

Other revisions in the form of logos arise from expanded use of communication media. Colors or shapes that read well in print, for example, may vibrate on television and computer screens. Logos that are legible on stationery and the sides of vehicles may not be readable on mobile phones. And as the visual landscape becomes more cluttered and diverse, the need to separate the logo from other communication also becomes important.

The value of a graphic identity system, therefore, lies in maintaining consistency through repeated use of the organization's name and symbols. It extends recognition of the organization beyond its facilities and individual experiences with products or services. Today's graphic identity systems are part of larger branding efforts and play a critical role in reminding audiences of organizational values and history.

**Figure 6.15
Bob Industries
graphic identity
AdamsMorioka
Sean Adams**

Adams's design for Bob Industries, a Los Angeles company of entertainment producers and directors, includes a mark, typographic elements, and color palette. The contrasting elements of the logo form a comical face (with various expressions) and establish an appropriately playful theme of related but slightly different layouts across applications.

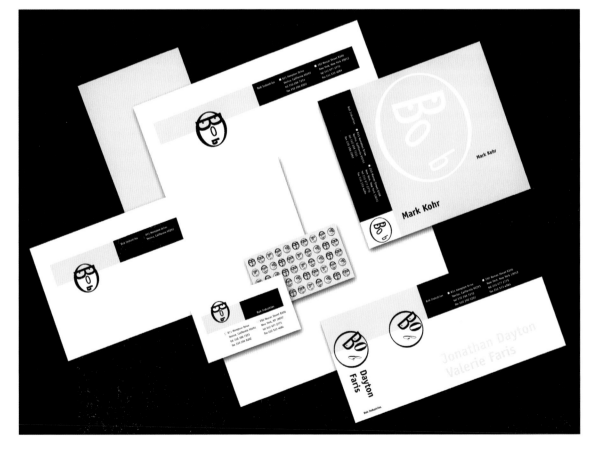

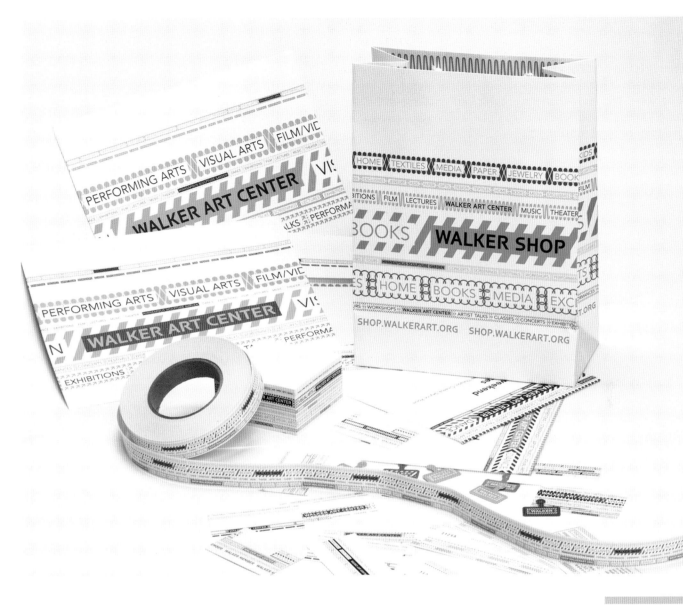

Figure 6.16
Walker Art Center
graphic identity
Typeface: Matthew
Carter and Walker Art
Center Design Studio
Design: Walker Art
Center Design Studio

The Walker Art Center
identity uses a "kit of
parts" approach that
combines the museum's
signature typeface with
a variety of patterns in a
family of colors. Unlike
the singular set of rules
that characterized late
modernist corporate
identities, contemporary
systems often unify
messages through more
flexible applications of
identity elements.

BRANDING

Branding is the practice of communicating the story of a company or organization through the coherent use of visual elements, messages, and services. It is more than the graphic look of communications and products and is an expression of company values and its relationship with audiences and consumers.

Brand strategist Alina Wheeler says, "As competition creates infinite choices, companies look for ways to connect emotionally with customers, become irreplaceable, and create lifelong relationships" (Wheeler, 2009, p. 2). Branding is expressed through touch points with stakeholders (employees and consumers) and becomes intrinsic to a company's culture (Wheeler, 2009). Touch points are moments of stakeholders' interactions with a company that are not strictly visual, but can range across all of the senses. The Ritz-Carlton chain of hotels has developed their own branded scents that they utilize both within their own bath products and across their hotel chain as an ambient fragrance. Similarly, the chimes that software companies use upon device start-up are a way of reinforcing a specific tone and sensibility each time an application or a device is turned on. Starting up an Apple computer sounds unlike opening a Windows PC.

The mistake many designers and business people make is to assume that a logo or identity system is *branding*. Branding is the communication of the position an organization holds among others and the values that contribute to the full range of experiences people have with the organization over time. A company can have a logo that communicates care for the environment but not be sustainable in its practices or products. An organization can depict itself as people-centered in brochure photography but make it difficult to reach a real person by telephone. An institution can circulate images of diversity but develop programming for a very narrow slice of the population. Branding, at its best, is an honest reflection of the organization and its values, expressed by its communications, products, services, and people.

Wheeler describes how a brand is authentic. It starts with the organization knowing "who we are" and communicating that identity through core messages (Wheeler, 2009). In some cases, branding is used to reposition a company that believes its current identity is inaccurate or no longer relevant, but such shifts are successful only if the new brand accompanies changes in the company's operations and reaches consensus among stakeholders. Targeted messages reinforce general perceptions and have a particular "look and feel" that is consistent with the overall character of the organization. A logo or logotype captures the brand culture in an economical form that stands for the larger communication effort, but it is rarely the place to begin with a brand strategy. Branding starts with an authentic story built by the stakeholders.

Brand architecture reflects the divisions or discrete activities of the company. It communicates the hierarchy or market position among components of the larger organization. Sub-brands frequently allow the company to diversify its activities or attract focused audiences for specific products and services. The GAP, for example, also owns Old Navy, Banana Republic, Intermix, and Athleta. Each of these companies seeks a different consumer and the styles of clothing and prices reflect those target audiences. For this reason, each company has a distinctive brand that makes no reference to the parent company. FedEx, on the other hand, has a number of sub-brands (FedEx Office, FedEx Freight, FedEx Trade Networks, and so forth). Designers built the brand architecture around the well-known corporate logotype with a change in color and secondary text varying by operation (Figure 6.17). They have recently updated their branding by using purple and orange for all segments and using only the text below the logo to identify the operating company.

Figure 6.17 FedEx Collective logo. ©2016 FedEx Corporation. All Rights Reserved.
The well-known FedEx logo appropriately captures an arrow in the negative space between the E and x.

FedEx brand architecture
Corporations often have more than one division and need to differentiate operations. The FedEx brand architecture uses color and names to designate divisions while maintaining a strong affiliation with the primary brand. They have recently updated their branding by using purple and orange for all segments and using only the text below the logo to identify the operating company.

Figure 6.18
MassMutual *Society of Grownups* **website, 2014**
Design and Development: IDEO
Branding includes the design of services. MassMutual is an insurance company that partnered with design firm IDEO to open up the conversation around money and addressing the inherent tension in balancing short-term needs and long-term goals for the millennial generation.

Figure 6.19
Teachers Know Best **website**
The Bill & Melinda Gates Foundation
Design and Development: IDEO and The Bill & Melinda Gates Foundation
Branding also involves tools and systems that establish relationships between an organization and its participants or customers. IDEO's design of the *Teachers Know Best* website for The Bill & Melinda Gates Foundation connects edtech entrepreneurs to the needs of students and teachers in K-12 classrooms.

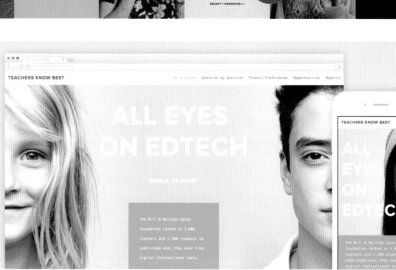

Branding influences the look and feel of the products a company makes but also the services it delivers. Today, increasing numbers of new businesses don't make anything; instead, they provide services that have to be designed. Zipcar, for example, is a business that offers on-demand personal transportation to people who don't want the responsibility of owning a car. Zappos doesn't make shoes but provides one-day delivery with a no-cost return policy if consumers are not happy with their purchase. Adobe no longer sells software packages and uses a subscription model in which users log into the cloud. These companies developed service ecologies that anticipate a variety of touch points between users and the company. The design of mobile applications for reserving a Zipcar, locating it in the city, and unlocking the car door determine how consumers feel about the company. Zipcar users, however, may never speak to a person throughout their entire transaction.

IDEO's branding for insurance company MassMutual's subsidiary, *Society of Grownups*, is designed to connect with young adults who need a place to talk and learn about money. The design of the website talks directly in the visual language of twenty-somethings, not in the language of insurance (Figure 6.18). IDEO's design of the *Teachers Know Best* website connects edtech entrepreneurs with the needs of students and teachers in K-12 classrooms (Figure 6.19). In this example, the primary intent of the branding effort is to establish connections and conversations, not to sell products. Both sites feel very different from the hard-sell strategies of product advertising, a reflection of the values of the organizations.

Branding, therefore, is the "face" a company or organization presents to the public. Good branding not only describes the qualities of relationships the company hopes to develop with people, but also reflects the true nature of all aspects of the company's operations.

SUMMARY

Philosopher John Dewey described an experience as defined by a quality, by an aesthetic relationship among activity, thought, and emotion. Good design is an aesthetic experience; its effects extend beyond the moment of interpretation and resonate in our memories long after we have processed the information. The human mind strives for order and meaning in sensory stimuli. Schemas and narratives organize experience in structures that can be recalled, carrying with them all the detail of more complex interpretations. Graphic identity and branding use recurring forms and stories to connect companies and organizations to big ideas and long-term emotional relationships with the public. Collectively, form builds the culture in which we live and defines our interpretive context.

Conclusion
Glossary
References
Credits and acknowledgments
Index

CONCLUSION

Designers often speak about "form and content," distinguishing the things they make from what they mean. The discussions in this book make the point that "form is content," that we cannot separate our sensory experience of form from the act of interpretation. The real task of communication design, therefore, is to match form to *context*, to the conditions under which form must perform. By definition, this design task includes narrowing the possibilities for how audiences are likely to interpret what they see and hear, while inventing new form that is useful, usable, and delightful.

Understanding interpretive behavior that is essentially human—that doesn't depend on having had experiences in particular places or times—is a first step. Some of our responses to visual phenomena developed biologically and cognitively in humankind as responses to the physical environment and are so deep in our DNA that designers can count on them as reactions to physiological perceptions that produce common interpretations of form. We don't *choose* to see an object in an open visual field as a figure on a background, or things that are alike as more related than things that are different. As the examples in this book illustrate, however, reaching conclusions about these phenomena in isolation can be misleading; particular combinations and circumstances produce different results. Interpretation of these phenomena is relational; it requires our judgment among competing stimuli. Visual messages are always seen in a context, so how audiences make these judgments matters to design.

Making meaning out of what we see and hear, however, is not all about biology. Culture intervenes in our interpretive processes. Our reading of form depends on past experiences, motives for interacting with information, and characteristic ways of processing what we see and hear, all of which are shaped by living in a social world. There is no guarantee that the interpretive judgments made by audiences will be the same as those made by the designer or that meaning will be the same, regardless of the circumstances in which the message is read or viewed. Therefore, designers must be students of culture, carefully assessing the role social experiences and environment play in interpretation.

Finally, the ultimate outcomes of visual communication are rarely short-term. They resonate throughout our lives and culture, expressing in concrete form the beliefs, values, and knowledge that influence what we think things mean in the future. This half-life of a message is the social responsibility of the design; an obligation to examine not only immediate effect but also long-term consequences of visual communication.

GLOSSARY

Abstraction—A process of distilling general qualities from specific, concrete examples; extracting the essence of something without concern for literal depiction or imitation.

Additive color—Produced when light is emitted from a light source, as from a projector.

Aesthetics—A set of principles concerned with the nature and appreciation of beauty, as well as a branch of philosophy that grapples with these notions.

Affordance—Action possibilities suggested by an object or environment. The affordances of a smartphone are the activities it enables such as texting, phoning, taking pictures, recording sound, and emailing.

Ambiguity—Vagueness or uncertainty that occurs when an image or text has multiple possible meanings that compete simultaneously for priority in the interpretation.

Annotation—A comment or explanation added to text, data, or images and that make a reference to something in the original.

Appropriation—The act of borrowing something from another culture, context, period of history, or designer and repurposing it in a new context, thus applying the connotations of the original source to the construction of a new meaning.

Archetypes—A commonly recognized image, idea, or model, upon which other things are based or copied. An archetype is usually perceived to be an ideal or something to be emulated.

Arts and Crafts movement—A movement in the decorative arts that first emerged in Great Britain at the turn of the twentieth century (1890–1910) as a reaction to the poor production quality and stylistic nostalgia of

products of the Industrial Revolution. The style was characterized by the honest use of materials for their intrinsic qualities, craftsmanship, and an interest in forms from nature.

Aspect ratio—The relationship of height to width.

Aspect shifting—A shift in the figure-ground relationship; a sudden perceptual change in which what was previously seen as the figure becomes the background.

Asymmetry—A lack of correspondence between elements on opposite sides of a plane.

Attention—The process of selectively focusing on one aspect of the sensory environment while ignoring other things that seem less important or less worthy of consideration. It is a means for concentrating the mind on a single object, element, or thought with the goal of narrowing the number of stimuli in a complex perceptual field.

Bauhaus—An art and design school that operated in three locations in Germany (Weimar, Dessau, and Berlin) from 1919–1933. The work of the school was known for rational functionality; simplified, modern forms; and innovation in the use of materials and processes of mass production.

Branding—The practice of communicating the story of a company or organization through the coherent use of visual elements, messages, and services; environments, products, messages, and services that express company values and the relationship with audiences and consumers.

Categorization—The sorting of incoming stimuli into mental categories in which the things that are grouped together are alike but different from members of other groups.

Channel—The route a message travels to its intended audience.

Character—Any letter of the alphabet, number, or punctuation included in the design of a typeface.

Chunking—The practice of breaking down a continuous text into smaller units to provide exit points in text or grouping elements into a smaller number of units of information to improve long-term memory.

Closure—The ability to see incomplete forms as a whole.

Co-creators—Users who create something jointly with designers.

Code—A grammar of form that is determined by cultural conventions. A tendency to read elements from left to right, top to bottom is a code established by the convention of reading order in English.

Cognitive dissonance—The conflict we feel when faced with contradictory ideas, emotions, or values at the same time.

Cognitive load—The mental effort used by working memory.

Color—The quality of an object perceived when wavelengths within the visible spectrum of light interact with receptors in the human eye.

Complexity—The quality of something with many parts that interact in multiple ways.

Composition—The arrangement of elements in visual space or time.

Compressed-conflict analogy—The union of two seemingly opposite terms that describe something metaphorically.

Concept map—The graphic visualization of relationships among elements or concepts to represent the organization of knowledge about something. Concept maps usually link nodes with lines.

Connotation—An idea or feeling that a representation invokes in addition to its literal meaning; a field of associations.

Constructivism—A 1917 Russian artistic movement focused on revolution and social reform. The movement focused on the material properties of objects and their position in space, as well as a relationship to industry. The Constructivists are credited with development of the photomontage, which combined images from a variety of sources into a single composition.

Constructivist theories—Late twentieth-century theories of interpretation that suggest that the reader (not the author or designer) constructs his/her own meaning and knowledge of the world under the influence of past experiences, motives, and ways of processing information. Further, meaning is seen as unstable, changing with context and each new encounter with information.

Context—The physical, psychological, social, cultural, technological, and economic circumstances that form the setting in which communication is interpreted.

Continuity—The perception of visual similarities across time and space.

Contrast—The state of being obviously unlike something else; the opposition or juxtaposition of different forms.

Convention—A customary way of doing something that is widely followed; a traditional form that is broadly accepted in its meaning.

Counterspace—The interior open space created by strokes in the design of a letterform.

Cultural experiences—Perceptions or feelings that result from exposure to the behaviors, beliefs, values, and symbols shared by a group of people.

Culture—A way of life by a group of people—represented by characteristic behaviors, beliefs, values, and symbols—passed from generation to generation. Not all cultures are defined by nationality or ethnicity—many are subgroups, such as hip-hop culture, which share lifestyles rather than origins of birth.

Denotation—The explicit dictionary definition of something, exclusive of the feelings and extended ideas that it suggests.

Depth of field—The distance between the nearest and farthest objects in a scene that appear acceptably sharp.

De Stijl—A Dutch movement from 1917–1931, typified by primary colors, geometric shapes, and vertical and horizontal lines. Proponents believed that reducing compositions to the most essential forms would establish the harmony missing from war-torn Europe.

Dialogic image—An image that invites the viewer to interact with it in order to resolve its ambiguous meaning.

Direct analogy—A one-to-one relationship between two things.

Direction—The line along which something appears to be moving with reference to a future point or region.

DIY—Do it yourself.

Double-page spread—Side-by-side pages in a publication. The left-hand page is called the verso and the right-hand page is called the recto.

Edge—The boundary between two things: object and environment or element and element.

Elements—The physical signs and symbols (for example, images, words, colors, and graphic devices such as lines and shapes) used to communicate the subject matter of a message

Embody—Express an idea or feeling in tangible form.

Emoticons and emojis—Emoticons are depictions of facial expressions made from punctuation and numbers, originally developed to overcome the expressive limitations of typing and text. Emojis are graphic symbols and smiley faces used in digital communication to indicate emotions, places, and things.

Event schema—A schema organized by time.

Feedback—Information given in response to an action or communication that serves as the basis for extending, ending, or improving communication performance.

Figure-ground—The ability to separate elements, based on contrast, into an object and a background.

Filter bubble—The result of an internet search in which the system guesses at what the searcher would like to see based on location and previous search history, thus separating the searcher from information that is inconsistent with his/her viewpoint.

Focus—The process of selectively concentrating on one aspect or central point of the visual environment while ignoring others.

Format—The material form, layout, or presentation of information within a medium. Brochures, websites, and posters are formats.

Framing—The construction of meaning through the designer's choices of what to include in the message and what to leave out.

Futurism—An early twentieth-century artistic and social movement (1909–1944) that originated in Italy and was characterized by fascination with the machine, speed, and undermining the syntax of typographic elements.

Gestalt—Developed by experimental psychologists in Germany at the beginning of the twentieth century, Gestalt refers to the perception of an organized whole that is more than the sum of its parts. Gestalt principles include similarity, proximity, figure-ground, and size constancy.

Graphic identity—A coordinated system for the identification of a company or organization that generally consists of a logo or logotype, typefaces, color palette, and set of rules for their application in a variety of formats.

Grid—A two-dimensional structure that divides a page or screen into columns and margins for the organization of typography and images.

Grouping—An orientation strategy that uses elements in formal proximity or with visual similarity to indicate a relationship among them that is different from their relationship with other elements.

Hierarchy—An arrangement or classification of things according to importance.

Hue—A named color in its purest state.

Human factors—A scientific profession that applies understanding of interactions among humans and elements of a system to design in order to optimize both human well-being and overall system performance.

Icon—A type of sign that physically represents the thing it stands for.

Index—A sign that points to something else or that refers to a cause and effect relationship between two things.

Industrial Revolution—A period dating from about 1760 to 1840, during which society transitioned to new technologies and manufacturing processes. The Industrial Revolution began in Great Britain, where the products of industrial innovation were first exhibited in the Great Exhibition of 1851.

Information anxiety—Richard Saul Wurman's description of the ever-widening gap between what we understand and what we know.

Information overload—Coined by Alvin Toffler, the term describes the glut of information reaching the senses in modern society.

Interaction—The back-and-forth relationship between two things. An action by one produces a response by the other.

International typographic style—Also known as "Swiss Design," the style developed in Switzerland in the 1950s, emphasizing readability and objectivity through the use of asymmetrical compositions, grids, sans serif typefaces, and photography.

Internet meme—A phrase, idea, or piece of media that spreads from person to person via the Web and may relate to specific subcultures.

Interpretation—The process of finding meaning in the things we see, hear, touch, smell, and taste.

Isotype—International System of Typographic Picture Education developed by Otto Neurath in the 1930s for the communication of statistical, scientific, and travel information.

Kitsch—A term used to describe objects thought to be in poor taste because they are garish, cheaply made, or nostalgic but appreciated in an ironic way or from a critical position on culture.

Layering—Laying one element over or under another in space.

Legibility—The quality of something that is visible also being discernible.

Linear perspective—A mathematical system for creating the illusion of space and distance on a flat surface. The system includes a horizon line, vanishing points, and orthogonal lines that converge as they recede in the distance.

Long-term memory—The storage of experience and information for recall over long periods of time.

Low art—A form from popular culture selected for its mass appeal.

Mapping—The activity of representing information spatially, in which the relationships among parts are expressed by proximity and location.

Materiality—The sensory qualities of an object that give it a particular character that is part of its meaning; the visual, spatial, tactile, auditory, kinesthetic, and temporal characteristics of form.

Medium—A mode or system of communication that extends human ability to exchange meaning. Film and drawing are media.

Metaphor—An analogy that describes something by saying it is like something else that is otherwise unrelated.

Metonymy—The replacement of an attribute or name of something for another thing with which it is associated.

Mnemonic—A tool that aids memory; an acronym, phrase, song, or visual that assists in transferring information to long-term memory.

Modernism—An overarching philosophy that arose from the transformation of Western culture in the late nineteenth and early twentieth centuries. Modernist movements in art and design shared a common interest in new approaches to depicting the world and responding to the effects of the Industrial Revolution. Modernists typically favored abstraction and the objectivity of geometry; rejected historical forms and styles; and sought representations that were thought to be universal rather than specific to a particular culture or time.

Motion—The action or process of changing place or position.

Narrative—A schematic sequencing of events; a story, typically with a beginning, middle, and end.

Narrative knowing—The ability to structure information by linking together various events to make a story.

Negative space/white space—The space around an element or between elements in a visual composition.

Objective—Not being influenced by feelings or opinions; the representation of fact.

Ontological metaphor—A metaphor in which an activity, feeling, or idea is represented as a person, object, substance, or something concrete.

Open source—Something for which the original source is made freely available for use, modification, and redistribution. Open source software is code that can be used by anyone without copyright infringement.

Orientation—The determination of the relative physical position or direction of something or someone within space.

Orientational metaphor—A metaphor that makes a physical reference to a location in space (up/down, in/out, front/back, etc.).

Pacing—The speed or rate at which something, such as a story or film, moves to completion.

Pantone Matching System (PMS)—A color system used by printers for mixing ink pigments.

Parody—An imitation of another style with intentional exaggeration and comic effect.

Pastiche—An imitation and celebration of another style.

Pattern—A recurring set of objects, elements, or events repeated at regular intervals.

Perception—The process of being aware of something through the senses.

Persona—A description of a stakeholder, often used with scenarios that describe the detailed needs, wants, and behavior of a user.

Personification—The description of a physical object as having human-like behaviors or qualities.

Phi phenomenon—The optical illusion of a series of still images as moving when viewed in quick succession.

Photomontage—The assembly of an image from various sources and points of view.

Place shema—A schema organized by location.

Point—A unit for measuring the size of type and the distance between lines of type. There are 72 points in an inch.

Point of view—The position from which something or someone is observed.

Postmodernism—A late twentieth-century movement that challenged modernist ideas of universal experience, objective reality, and social progress, believing that knowledge and experience are constructed, pluralistic, and always seen from someone's cultural position.

Pragmatics—Relationships among signs, their interpreters, and context; the effects of people, settings, and use on the interpretation of meaning.

Proportion—A constant relationship among parts of a whole, regardless of its size.

Proximity—The property of being close together.

Readability—The ability of text to invite reading.

Reading pattern—The behavior a reader exhibits when moving through text on a page or screen. Western languages have reading gravity; eye movement goes from left to right and top to bottom of the page.

Redundancy—The consistent and timed repetition of a message, often across multiple channels and in different formats, in order to build audience recognition.

Relational—The interdependency of the effect of one visual variable or quality on the presence of another.

Representation—The process of depicting something in a form other than the one in which it originated; for example, an idea as a drawing, five things as a number 5, and a feeling as a poem.

Role schema—A schema that describes people's ascribed roles (resulting from personal characteristics such as age or gender) and acquired roles (resulting from training or effort).

Rhythm—Movement, or the appearance of movement, through a patterned occurrence of weak and strong elements.

Saturation—The brightness or dullness of a color, sometimes called "intensity."

Scale—The proportional relationship between the size of something and the sizes of other things.

Scaling fallacy—Thinking that something that works at one size will work in the same way at another size.

Scenario—A script for action, a story that anticipates a future unfolding of events.

Schema—A mental structure that organizes categories of experience and the relationships among them. Schemas suggest what we should think about and how we should respond.

Schematic knowledge—Understanding of parts-to-whole relationships.

Semantics—The relationship between signs and what they stand for.

Semiotics—A science of signs developed at the turn of the twentieth century by Swiss linguist Ferdinand de Saussure and American philosophers Charles Sanders Peirce and Charles Morris.

Sensory experience—Perceptions or feelings that result from sight, touch, smell, sound, or taste.

Sensory memory—The very brief visual or acoustical recall for the sensory qualities of things.

Sequences—A collection of images or elements in a particular order suggested by some organizing principle such as numbers, time, gradation in size, or a story with a beginning, middle, and end.

Serial knowledge—A type of knowledge that is understood by the connection of one thing to another.

Series—A collection of images or elements that share something in common but that do not suggest a particular order.

Service ecology—A holistic system that includes communication, products, and services that work together to produce the qualitative experience someone has with a company or organization.

Sign—The smallest unit of meaning.

Signified—The person, thing, place, or idea for which a sign stands.

Signifier—The sound or image that represents a signified.

Size constancy—The mental ability to make sense of the approximate size and scale of objects, even when visual evidence suggests alternative interpretations.

Stakeholders—A person, group, or organization that can be affected by design decisions.

Stereotypes—A type of role schema in which a number of traits are grouped in the mind and called forth by a single visual cue.

Stimuli—A thing or event that produces a physical or mental reaction in someone or something.

Story—A sequential narrative organized by time so that it has a beginning, middle, and end.

Style—A distinctive form or way of presenting something that is characteristic of a time, place, or philosophy.

Substitution—The act of replacing one thing with another to extend the possible meanings.

Subtractive color—Produced when light is reflected off the surface of objects, as from a printed poster.

Symbol—An abstract sign whose meaning must be learned through association with what it stands for.

Symmetry—Correspondence in the size, shape, and arrangement of parts on opposite sides of a plane.

Synecdoche—A part substituting for a whole or a whole standing for a part.

Syntax—The relationship of one sign to others; the ordering of elements within a visual or verbal message.

Subjective—Open to individual interpretation and modification through bias.

System—A set of interacting and interdependent parts forming a complex whole.

Taste—An individual's pattern of preferences for certain qualities of form over others, influenced by social and cultural experiences.

Theme and variation—The repetition of a form or composition with slight variations to create interest.

Timeline—A way of organizing a graphic depiction or list of events chronologically.

Typeface—A single member of a type family.

Type family—Typeface variations in weight, posture, and proportion that share common characteristics. Helvetica Bold, Helvetica Italic, and Helvetica Condensed are members of the Helvetica type family.

Value—The lightness or darkness of a color. Tints (light) and shades (dark) are values.

Vernacular—The visual language used by ordinary people not trained in design, usually associated with particular parts of the country or types of work.

Wayfinding—All the ways in which we orient ourselves in space and navigate pathways from one place to another.

Working memory—A type of short-term memory used for holding, processing, and manipulating information.

X-height—The height of lowercase letters.

REFERENCES

AARP. (2014). *Designing Web Sites for Older Adults: A Review of Recent Research.* Retrieved on March 3, 2016 from: http://assets.aarp.org/www.aarp.org_/articles/research/oww/AARP-LitReview2004.pdf.

Alexander, C. (1964). *Notes on the Synthesis of Form.* Cambridge, MA: Harvard University Press.

American Psychological Association (2006). *Multitasking: Switching Costs.* Retrieved on September 1, 2016 from: http://www.apa.org/research/action/multitask.aspx.

Augoustinos, M. and Walker, I. (2006). *Social Cognition: An Integrated Introduction.* London: Sage Publications.

Barthes, R. (1977). "The Photographic Message." *Image, Music, Text.* Heath, S. trans. New York, NY: The Noonday Press.

Blauvelt, A. (2005). "Matthew Carter." Walker Art Center Magazine. April 1, 2005. Retrieved on August 1, 2016 from: http://www.walkerart.org/magazine/2005/matthew-carter.

Cartier-Bresson, H. (1999) *The Mind's Eye: Writings on Photography and Photographers.* New York, NY: Aperture Foundation.

Cohen, M., Horowitz, T., and Wolfe, J. (2009). "Auditory Recognition Memory is Inferior to Visual Recognition Memory." *Proceedings of the National Academy of Sciences of the United States of America.* Retrieved on September 17, 2016 from http://www.ncbi.nlm.nih.gov/pmc/articles/PMC2667065/.

Davis, M. (2012). *Graphic Design Theory.* London: Thames and Hudson Ltd.

De Certeau, M. (1984; 2002). *The Practice of Everyday Life.* Berkeley, CA: University of California Press.

Dewey, J. (1934, 1980). *Art as Experience.* New York, NY: Perigee Books, Berkley Publishing Group.

Entman, R. (1993). "Framing: Toward Clarification of a Fractured Paradigm." *Journal of Communication,* 43 (4): 51–58.

Ewen, S. (1988). *All Consuming Images: The Politics of Style in Contemporary Culture.* New York, NY: Basic Books.

Gerstner. K. (1964). *Designing Programmes.* Teufen, Switzerland: A. Niggli.

Gordon, W.J.J. (1973). *The Metaphorical Way of Learning and Knowing: Applying Synectics to Sensitivity and Learning Situations.* Cambridge, MA: Porpoise Books.

Gottfried, J. and Shearer, E. (2016). "News Use Across Social Media Platforms 2016." Pew Research Center. Retrieved on September 1, 2016 from: http://www.journalism.org/2016/05/26/news-use-across-social-media-platforms-2016/.

Koffka, K. (1935). *Principles of Gestalt Psychology.* London: Lund Humphries.

Kress, G. and Van Leeuwen, T. (2006). *Reading Images: The Grammar of Visual Design.* New York, NY: Routledge.

Lakoff, G. and Johnson, M. (1980). *Metaphors We Live By.* Chicago, IL: University of Chicago Press.

Lanham, R. (2006). *The Economics of Attention: Style and Substance in the Age of Information.* Chicago, IL: University of Chicago Press.

Lynch, K. (1960). *The Image of the City.* Cambridge, MA: MIT Press.

Mandler, J. (1984) *Stories, Scripts, and Scenes: Aspects of Schema Theory.* London: Routledge.

Marks, S. (2005). *Finding Betty Crocker: The Secret Life of America's First Lady of Food.* New York, NY: Simon and Schuster.

McLuhan, M. (1994). *Understanding Media: The Extensions of Man.* Cambridge, MA: MIT Press.

Meggs, P. (1998). *History of Graphic Design,* 4th edition. New York, NY: John Wiley & Sons, Inc.

Miller, G. A. (1956). "The Magical Number Seven, Plus or Minus Two: Some Limits on Our Capacity for Processing Information." *Psychological Review,* 63 (2): 81–97.

Mollerup, P. (1997). *Marks of Excellence: The History and Taxonomy of Trademarks.* New York, NY: Phaidon.

Myatt, B. (1979). "Picture Preferences of Children and Young Adults." *Educational Communication and Technology,* 27 (1): 45–53.

Nielsen, J. (2006). "F-Shaped Pattern for Reading Web Content." *Nielsen Norman Group.* Retrieved on December 28, 2015 from: https://www.nngroup.com/articles/f-shaped-pattern-reading-web-content/.

Nielsen.com. (2010). "US Teen Mobile Report Calling Yesterday, Texting Today, Using Apps Tomorrow." Retrieved on June 16, 2016 from: http://www.nielsen.com/us/en/insights/news/2010/u-s-teen-mobile-report-calling-yesterday-texting-today-using-apps-tomorrow.html.

Norman, D. (1993). *Things that Make Us Smart: Defending Human Attributes in the Age of the Machine.* New York, NY: Perseus Books.

Pariser, E. (2011). "Beware Online Filter Bubbles." TED Talk. Retrieved on November 30, 2016 from: https://www.ted.com/talks/eli_pariser_beware_online_filter_bubbles?language=en.

Pew Research Center. (2013). "Teens, Social Media, and Privacy." Retrieved on December 15, 2015 from: http://www.pewinternet.org/2013/05/21/teens-social-media-and-privacy/.

Poynor, R. (2003). *No More Rules: Graphic Design and Postmodernism.* New Haven, CT: Yale University Press.

Puhalla, D. (2005). "Color as Cognitive Artifact: A Means of Communication." Dissertation in NC State University library: accessible at http://catalog.lib.ncsu.edu/record/NCSU1758340.

Sanders, E. (2006). "Scaffolds for Building Everyday Creativity." *Designing Effective Communications: Creating Contexts for Clarity and Meaning*. Frascara, J. ed. New York, NY: Allworth Press.

Saussure, F. (2000). *Course in General Linguistics*, 10th edition. Peru, IL: Open Court Publishing.

Scher, P. (2002). *Make It Bigger*. Princeton, NJ: Princeton Architectural Press.

Spoehr, K. and Lehmkuhle, S. (1982). *Visual Information Processing*. San Francisco, CA: W.H. Freeman.

Stampler, L. (2013). "In Spite of Old, False Satanist Accusations, P&G Put a Moon Back in Its New Logo." *Business Insider*. May 21, 2013. Retrieved on December 14, 2016 from: http://www.businessinsider.com/pg-puts-moon-in-new-logo-despite-satanist-accusations-2013-5.

Sweet, E. (2014). "Toys are More Divided by Gender Now than they were 50 Years Ago." *The Atlantic*. December 9, 2014. Retrieved on June 1, 2016 from: http://www.theatlantic.com/business/archive/2014/12/toys-are-more-divided-by-gender-now-than-they-were-50-years-ago/383556/.

Terminal Design Inc. (2004). Clearview Hwy: Research and Design. Retrieved on August 1, 2016 from: http://www.clearviewhwy.com/.

Thorburn, D. and Jenkins, H. (2003). *Rethinking Media Change: The Aesthetics of Transition*. Cambridge, MA: MIT Press.

Tobin, I. (2008). Retrieved on May 15, 2016 from: http://faceoutbooks.com/filter/Isaac-Tobin/Obsession.

Toffler, Alvin. (1971). *Future Shock*. New York, NY: Bantam Books with permission of Random House.

Tschichold, J. (1928). Translation by McLean, R. (1995). *The New Typography*. Berkeley, CA: University of California Press.

Vecera, S., Vogel, E., and Woodman, G. (2002). "Lower Region: A New Cue for Figure-Ground Assignment." *Journal of Experimental Psychology*, 131 (2): 194–205.

Wertheimer, M. (1924; 1938). *Source Book of Gestalt Psychology*. Ellis, W. trans. New York, NY: Harcourt, Brace, and Co.

Wheeler, A. (2009). *Designing Brand Identity*. New York, NY: John Wiley & Sons, Inc.

Wurman, R.S. (1989). *Information Anxiety*. New York, NY: Doubleday.

Zeitchik, S. (2015). "Director of Adele's 'Hello' Video Explains its Look, Theme and, Oh Yes, the Flip Phone." *Los Angeles Times*, October 23, 2015. Retrieved on October 23, 2015 from: http://www.latimes.com/entertainment/movies/moviesnow/la-et-mn-adele-hello-video-song-flip-phone-20151023-story.html.

CREDITS AND ACKNOWLEDGMENTS

We must acknowledge the formative role that Chris Myers played in the conception and early versions of this work. His infectious wisdom and antic spirit inflects much of this work.

We are also deeply indebted to the exceptional research assistants Isabella Brandalise and Elena Habre.

Special thanks go to Senior Developmental Editor Lee Ripley, whose advice and attention to detail were invaluable. She was a persistent detective in tracking the obscure and a strong advocate for design in her recommendations.

Finally, we would like to recognize the many designers, design offices and institutions that generously contributed their remarkable work to this project.

2.2 TripleStrip typeface designs and photos, © Sibylle Hagmann. 2.3 Print Collector/Contributor/Getty Images/Hulton Archive. 2.4 Céline Condorelli, Support Structures, Sternberg Press, 2009/Design by James Langdon. 2.5 Courtesy of Georgia Museum of Art. 2.6 deniskomarov/iStock. 2.7 Designer: Baozhen Li; Designer/Creative Director: Rick Valenti. 2.8 © David Drummond. 2.9 Digital image, The Museum of Modern Art, New York/Scala, Florence. 2.10 Design: Allen Hori. 2.11 U.S. Demographics and Economy, Paula Scher MAPS 2015. 2.12 American Type Founders. 2.13 © Ernie Colon and Sid Jacobson.// 3.4 © Christian Richters. 3.6 ©Barnbrook. 3.7 Public Theater, Shakespeare in the Park, As You Like It, Season 2012; Design: Paula Scher. 3.8 CAA Design Poster; Katherine McCoy. 3.9 © Spin. 3.11 eli_asenova/iStock. 3.13 © Experimental Jetset. 3.14 ©2017 National Aquarium, Design: Tom Geismar, Chermayeff & Geismar & Haviv. 3.15 Illustration by Malika Favre. 3.16 Design by Matthew Carter. 3.17 Michael Bierut/Pentagram. 3.23 Design by Walker Art Center Design Studio/Scott Ponik. 3.24 © Heston Blumenthal, Art Direction and Design: Graphic Thought Facility, Photography: Angela Moore. 3.25 Designer: April Greiman. 3.26 © Dot One. 3.27 Neustockimages/iStock. 3.29 Private collection/Photo ©Christie's Images/Bridgeman Images, © DACS 2016. 3.30 © Doyle Partners. 3.31 © Bruce Mau Design. 3.32 Designer:

April Greiman. 3.33 The Graphic Design of Tony Arefin, curated by James Langdon, Ikon Gallery, Birmingham 2012, Photograph: Stuart Whipps. 3.36 Photograph: Josh Goldstein. 3.38 Geerati/iStock. 3.41 Designers: Brendan Callahan, Suzanna LaGasa, Ryan Gerald Nelson. 3.44 Olaser/iStock. 3.45 © Museum of the African Diaspora, 2004. 3.46 Courtesy of Abbott Miller, Pentagram Design. 3.47 2016 The Museum of Modern Art, New York. 3.48 Peter Steiner/Alamy Stock Photo. 3.49 Design: Paprika. 3.51 Design: Catalogtree. © Designer: Chip Kidd. 3.53 © cyan berlin. 3.55 Isabella Stewart Gardner Museum © Portraits by Brigitte Lacombe. 3.56 avdeev007/iStock. 3.58 Design: Barbara de Wilde; Photograph: George Eastman Collection. 3.60 © Jan Tschichold. 3.61 Yuri_Arcurs/iStock. 3.63 © Design: Armin Hofmann. 3.64 Designer: John Pobojewski; Creative consultation: Rick Valenti. 3.65 Design: ETC (Everything Type Company); SPIN Creative Director: Devin Pedzwater. 3.66 Website design by Matthew Peterson. 3.68 Design: Stockholm Design Lab (SDL). 3.69 Designer/Art Director/Typographer: Emma Morton; Creative Director: Phil Skegg; Creative Heads: Adam Rix, Simon Griffin; Photographer: Ben Wedderburn; Artworker: Jonathan Robertson; Design Studio: LOVE; Account Handler: Ali Johnson, Sarah Benson; Client: Silver Cross. 3.70 Designed by Thomas Yang, 100copies Bicycle Art, Singapore, 2012. 3.71 © Paul Garbett 2016. 3.72 Photograph © Ken Kohler. 3.73 Designed by Jon Sueda and Yasmin Khan; Edited by Jérome Saint-Loubert Bié. 3.74 AntonChechotkin/iStock. 3.75 Client: Pictoright; Concept and design: De Designpolitie, 2008 and ongoing. 3.76 © Harmen Liemburg. 3.77 Pentagram Partner & Designer: Eddie Opara, Associate Partner & Designer: Ken Deegan; Designer: Pedro Mendes. 3.79 Agency: F/Nazca Saatchi & Saatchi; Client: Leica Gallery, São Paulo; Creative Directors: Fabio Fernandes, Pedro Prado, Rodrigo Castellari; Art Director: Rodrigo Castellar; Copywriter Pedro Prado. 3.80 © Mark Havens. 3.82 Design direction: Katherine McCoy; Design team: Richard Kerr, Jane Kosstrin, Alice Hecht. 3.83 Touchstone Pictures/Columbia Pictures/1492 Pictures/Laurence Mark Productions, and Radiant Pictures; Designer: Matt Checkowski for Imaginary Forces. 3.84 © CASTERMAN S.A. //4.7 (left) parpann/iStock; (right) walencienne/iStock. 4.8 © Natascha Frensch 2011-2016. 4.9 © Marcos Weskamp 2004. 4.10 © Otto and Marie Neurath Isotype Collection, University of Reading. 4.11 © Graphic by Nigel Holmes. 4.12 © Rocket & Wink. 4.14 © 2017 Google. 4.15 Poulin + Morris Deborah Kushma/Deborah Kushma Photography. 4.16 Designer: Deborah Adler; Industrial Designer: Klaus Rosberg. 4.17 © TFL from the London Transport Museum Collection. 4.18 © Pentagram. 4.20 Design Director: Hugh Dubberly; Designer: Matt Leacock. 4.21 ©Erik Spiekermann. 4.22 Courtesy of Why Not Associates. 4.23 David Rumsey Map Collection, © DACS 2016. 4.26 Public Theater, Season Poster, Simpatico 1994; Designer: Paula Scher. 4.27 Michael Bierut/Pentagram. 4.28 Designer: Jakob Nielsen, April 17, 2006 (https://nngroup.com/articles/f-shaped-pattern-reading-web-content). 4.30 iStock; 4.32 Courtesy of Display, Graphic Design Collection; Design: Ladislav Sutnar. 4.33 © Adbusters.org. 4.34 © Cheapflights Media (USA) Designed in conjunction with NowSourcing. 4.35 Designed by Stripe/Jon Sueda and Gail Swanlund. 4.36 © Alexander Isley. 4.37 Creative Director: Lucille Tenazas; Designer: Kelly Tokerud Macy. 4.38 © Winterhouse. 4.39 Courtesy Cooper Hewitt,

Smithsonian Design Museum; Designer: Irma Boom. 4.41 Gift of the Photo League Lewis Hine Memorial Committee/George Eastman Museum. 4.42 Courtesy Austrian Technical Museum. 4.43 Design: Joel Katz Design Associates; © Center City District, Philadelphia. 4.44 © Graphic by Nigel Holmes. 4.45 © Alexander Isley. 4.46 © Rodchenko & Stepanova Archive, DACS RAO 2016. // 5.1 Design: Martin Venezky's Appetite Engineers. 5.2 Design by Art Chantry. 5.3 Design Director: Mike Scott; Digital Designer at Global Brand Strategy: Sierra Siemer; Design and Experience Firm: Siegel + Gale. 5.4 Courtesy U.S. Food & Drug Administration. 5.5 Design: Meeker & Associates, Inc. 5.7 Courtesy U.S. Department of Agriculture. 5.8 Courtesy Library of Congress, Washington, D. C. 5.9 Joe Rosenthal/AP Photo/Press Association Images. 5.10 J. Scott Applewhite/AP Photo/Press Associations Images. 5.11 © Henri Cartier-Bresson/Magnum Photos. 5.12 © Library of Congress, Washington, D.C. ↓loc.gov↑; Design: Sagi Haviv, Chermayeff & Geismar & Haviv. 5.13 Chase and the Chase Octagon logo are registered trademarks of JPMorgan Chase Bank, N.A.; Design: Tom Geismar, Chermayeff & Geismar & Haviv. 5.14 © Nicholas Felton. 5.15 © ERCO GmbH, Pictograms are subject to copyright. www.otl-aicher-piktogramme.de. 5.16 Courtesy U.S. Department of Transport. 5.18 Courtesy The British Library. 5.19 Design: Isaac Tobin and Lauren Nassef. 5.20 Client: Theater Frascati/Flemish Arts Centre de Brakke Grond; Concept and design: De Designpolitie; Photography: Arjan Benning, 2009-2015. 5.21 © Design: Alexander Isley. 5.22 © Graphic Thought Facility; 5.23 © David Drummond. 5.24 Courtesy of International Business Machines Corporation, © International Business Machines Corporation. 5.25 Courtesy Getty Research Institute/Archive.org. 5.26 Design by Walker Art Center Design Studio. 5.27 Photograph: Cynthia Johnson/The LIFE Images Collection/Getty Images; State Museum at Majanek. 5.28 Designer: David J. High; Photographer: Ralph C. del Pozzo. 5.29 © Rigsby Hull. 5.30 (left) Design by Jamie Sheehan and Art Chantry. (right) Reproduced with permission from the LSU Agricultural Center. 5.31 (left) © Paula Scher; (right) The Museum of Modern Art, New York/ Scala, Florence, © Herbert Matter. 5.32 (top) Heritage Images/Getty Images; (bottom) © Guerrilla Girls, 2011. 5.33 © Alexander Isley. 5.34 © Jan van Toorn, Amsterdam. 5.35 Design and illustration: Steff Geissbuhler. 5.36 © Shigeo Fukuda; Courtesy of Shizuko Fukuda and DNP Foundation for Cultural Promotion. 5.37 Image courtesy of John Marchant Gallery; © Sex Pistols Residuals. // 6.1 Courtesy James B. Hunt Library, North Carolina State University; Software developer: Kevin Beswick; Photographer: Brent Brafford. 6.2 © Kara Walker; Courtesy of Sikkema Jenkins & Co., New York; Photography: Gene Pittman. 6.3 © 2017 General Mills Inc. All Rights Reserved. 6.4 U.S. National Archives and Records Administration. 6.5 Concept: Scott Plous; Illustration: Ron Turner; Adbusters.org. 6.6 © Eve Arnold/Magnum Photos. 6.7 Design: Winkler & Noah; 6.8 © CBS Corporation. 6.9 © Winterhouse. 6.12 Design: Project Projects. 6.13 Design: Ilan Rubin. 6.14 Designed by the Carbone Smolan Agency for NIZUC Resort & Spa (Cancun, Mexico) 2007-2014. 6.15 Design: Sean Adams, AdamsMorioka. 6.16 Design by Matthew Carter and Walker Art Center Design Studio. 6.17 © 2016 FedEx Corporation, All Rights Reserved. 6.18 Design and development by IDEO. 6.19 Design and development by IDEO and The Bill & Melinda Gates Foundation.

INDEX

Locators in *italic* refer to figures; those in **bold** to glossary

Full chapter breakdowns are not given, please refer to contents pages 4–5